RISE UP!

RISE UP!

RISE UP!

Broadway and American Society from *Angels in America* to *Hamilton*

CHRIS JONES

methuen | drama

LONDON • NEW YORK • OXFORD • NEW DELHI • SYDNEY

METHUEN DRAMA
Bloomsbury Publishing Plc
50 Bedford Square, London, WC1B 3DP, UK
1385 Broadway, New York, NY 10018, USA

BLOOMSBURY, METHUEN DRAMA and the Methuen Drama logo are
trademarks of Bloomsbury Publishing Plc

First published in Great Britain 2019

Cover design: Louise Dugdale
Photograph: Broadway production of *Hamilton* © Joan Marcus

A catalogue record for this book is available from the British Library.

Library of Congress Cataloging-in-Publication Data
Names: Jones, Chris, 1963- author.
Title: Rise up!: Broadway and American society from Angels in America to
Hamilton / Chris Jones.
Description: London; New York: Methuen Drama, [2018] |
Includes bibliographical references and index.
Identifiers: LCCN 2018020365 | ISBN 9781350071933 (pb) | ISBN 9781350071957 (epdf) |
ISBN 9781350071957 (ePDF)
Subjects: LCSH: Theater–New York (State–New York–History–20th century. |
Theater–New York (State)–New York–History–21st century. |
Theater and society–United States–History–20th century. | Theater and society–United
States–History–21st century. | Broadway (New York, N.Y.)–History–20th century. |
Broadway (New York, N.Y.)–History–21st century.
Classification: LCC PN2277.N5 J66 2018 | DDC 792.09747/1–dc23
LC record available at https://lccn.loc.gov/2018020365

ISBN: PB: 978-1-350-07193-3
         ePDF: 978-1-350-07195-7
         eBook: 978-1-350-07194-0

Typeset by Integra Software Services Pvt. Ltd.
Printed and bound in Great Britain

To find out more about our authors and books visit www.bloomsbury.com
and sign up for our newsletters.

CONTENTS

Acknowledgments vii

2016: Prologue 1

1 1993: An Angel Lands 7

2 1994: The Emergent Power of the Solo Voice 23

3 1996: Fighting Urban Gentrification and Paying Rent 37

4 1997: The Lion King Roars and the Family Returns to Broadway 55

5 1999: A Short-Order Cook with a Long Path to Broadway 69

6 2001: Grief, Metamorphoses, and Transformation 81

7 2002: The Pull of Las Vegas and the Rise of the Meta 93

8 2002: Edward Albee, the Love of a Goat, and the Death of Off-Broadway 113

9 2007: A Recession Thwarted by an Ironic Blast from Chicago 125

10 2010: A Boulevard of Broken Dreams,
Awakened 135

11 2010: Bloody Bloody Wiki Wiki Self-Awareness 147

12 2011: Unlucky: Spider-Man and the Great
Broadway Overreach 163

13 2014: A Dream, No Longer Deferred 177

14 2016: Love Is Love Is Love Is Love Is Love Is Love
Is Love Is Love 189

Notes 216

Index 222

ACKNOWLEDGMENTS

Much of the reporting in this book came out of my work as longtime chief theater critic for the *Chicago Tribune*, which has been on-board for years with my bringing Broadway to our theater-loving readers. I deeply appreciate the paper's support of this book and would especially like to thank such current and former colleagues as Geoff Brown, Amy Carr, Bruce Dold, Doug George, Morgan Greene, Gerould Kern, Johnny Oleksinski, and Scott Powers. I'd also like to acknowledge my former colleagues at *Variety*, for whom I wrote about Broadway and the Road in the 1990s, especially Peter Bart, Greg Evans, Jeremy Gerard, Charles Isherwood, and David Rooney. Anna Brewer at Methuen Drama kept after me to write this book, Camilla Erskine kindly shepherded it through the writing process, and Dom O'Hanlon improved what is here, although the errors are all my own. My dear friends Jason Babinsky and Danielle Ippolito will recognize many of the ideas we discussed over the years at *Un, Deux, Trois*. Most of all I want to thank my patient and tolerant wife, Gillian Darlow, who not only read the manuscript but put up with my prowling Broadway at all hours of the day and night, and our two incomparable sons, Peter and Evan Jones, who are (almost) always willing to come with me to a show, even the ones far from Broadway.

ACKNOWLEDGMENTS

2016: PROLOGUE

As the cheers rang out for *Hamilton* on a warm November night in 2016, Brandon Victor Dixon clasped his hands, as if in prayer.

That previous August, Dixon, a two-time nominee for the Tony Awards who grew up in a suburb of Washington, DC, had taken over the role of Aaron Burr, the third vice president of the United States, from the actor Leslie Odom Jr. This was a great opportunity: Dixon was rising toward the peak of an already-formidable Broadway career. But this night, Dixon's mind was on the man who was about to become vice president of the United States: Michael Richard Pence. The vice president elect of eleven days' standing was in the theater, taking in the hottest show in town. Right there on West 46th Street. He'd even bought his own tickets. At the start of the show, there had been boos and cheers as he made his way to his seats with his family and his entourage.

Dixon had been appointed spokesperson for the cast after hurried whispers backstage. Word had come late that afternoon of Pence's attendance. Even though the show was over, Dixon was clearly nervous. His arms swayed as he thanked his audience for coming. His fellow performers stood behind him in a straight line, their arms locked. Some of their heads were bowed. Some looked straight out front.

"You know we had a-a-a-a guest in the audience this evening," Dixon said to the audience, most of whom had paid three-figure amounts for their tickets. He stuttered slightly as he gained momentum, staring intently to the right of the house at the Richard Rodgers Theatre.

Some in the audience laughed. More let out sounds of shock, perhaps wondering what was coming next.

Pence, seemingly sensing this might be a judicious time to leave, started to make the beginnings of an exit, under the boxes. But once Dixon started speaking, Pence stopped, stood still, and listened in the shadows.

"Vice President elect Pence, I see you walking out," Dixon said, his voice getting louder. "But I hope you will hear us just a few more moments."

Boos rang out: most in response to the early Pence exit, but maybe, in some quarters, also a few from those who felt it unfair to so confront a man, the Governor of Indiana no less, enjoying a rare night at a Broadway musical with his family. "There's nothing to boo here, ladies and gentlemen," Dixon said, going off script, his voice suddenly turning defensive, "we're all here sharing a story of love."

Love was surely in the room but it hardly was alone.

Lin-Manuel Miranda's *Hamilton* was the story of the birth pains of a new nation, bloodied by oppression and born in painful insurrection, and it was a new kind of historical musical, proudly anachronistic and as determined to define the present and the future as to reach for the past. This was a musical that had entered the zeitgeist like no other musical in history. Sure, *A Chorus Line* had made the cover of *Newsweek* in 1975, but the image was dominated by the legs of the actress Donna McKechnie and the text said "Broadway's New Kick." That was well within the penumbra of how musicals always had been covered in the media: sexualized, trivialized, marginalized. *Hamilton*, though, had been virtually workshopped at the White House, right in front of the first African American president of the United States.

Its author, Miranda, had enjoyed a mutually admiring friendship with President Barack Obama, who, some six weeks later, was to find himself penning a welcome letter to President Donald J. Trump, a real-estate investor and reality TV personality who was now the 45th president of the United States. Pence had just been elected as Trump's right-hand man; that night he was sitting in the orchestra seats at *Hamilton*.

For the progressives in the Broadway community, as for the majority of Americans who had voted for Hillary Rodham Clinton, the wounds still were raw that November night. They were less than two weeks old. In the days leading up to that night, many in the cast of *Hamilton* had found it hard to go ahead with their performances. They were depressed and fearful of what had befallen the country whose early years they were chronicling. It was as if everything that their show stood for had been rejected by the country at large.

Dixon was determined to say his piece. He pulled out a piece of paper—the *New York Times* would later report[1] that the words thereon had been co-written by Miranda, the show's director, Thomas Kail, and the show's lead producer, Jeffrey Seller—and he started to read. Dixon began by welcoming and thanking his quarry. Then he got to his point.

"We, sir, we are the diverse America who are alarmed and anxious that your new administration will not protect us, our planet, our children, our parents or defend us or uphold our inalienable rights, sir," he said, co-opting something of the hip-hop cadence of *Hamilton*. "But we truly hope that this show has inspired you to uphold our American values" (he emphasized the *our* in the phrase) "and to work on behalf of all of us. All of us."

Applause started to build. A few people cheered. Dixon began to point in the direction of Pence. The actor's voice filled with emotion.

"Again," he said, "we truly thank you for sharing this show, this wonderful American story told by a diverse group of men and women of different colors, creeds, and orientations."

The next day, Pence's new boss, Trump, was not amused.

"Our wonderful future V.P. Mike Pence was harassed last night at the theater by the cast of *Hamilton*, cameras blazing. This should not happen!" tweeted @realDonaldTrump, perhaps as yet unaware of the power and controversy occasioned by what would become his preferred presidential method of direct communication. Six minutes later, the president opined on the correct role of a Broadway show in American society. "The theater must always be a safe and special place," he tweeted, angering the majority of arts lovers who thought the theater must always be dangerous. "The cast of *Hamilton* was very rude last night to a good man, Mike Pence. Apologize!"

No apology was forthcoming. Dixon tweeted that "conversation is not harassment," the producers of *Hamilton* insisted the exchange had been respectful, and Pence even said he had enjoyed the show and had not been offended. On the TV show *The View*, Dixon, whose celebrity had been significantly increased by the incident, said that if people came to *Hamilton* to leave their politics behind, they had come to the wrong show. The studio audience applauded. *Hamilton*, Dixon said, was the kind of platform that *imbued* political and moral responsibility.

"We *had* to stand up," he said, his eyes flashing. "We had to look at him. He will remember us. He will *not* throw away our shot."

The studio audience applauded again. The appearance did not do the box office any harm. "Go see *Hamilton*," said Whoopi Goldberg, one of the show's panelists, as the studio audience cheered and Dixon grinned.

Even the longest memories on Broadway could not recall a comparable moment.

Finally, the American theater had landed right where generations of theater artists had wanted but failed to be—in the dead center of the political discourse. On the news. In the news. Of the news. A thorn in the side of the new occupant of the White House, even before he'd taken the oath of office.

And there were yet-deeper implications. That incident on Broadway on November 11 was, in many ways, the first major post-election clash between Trump and his supporters, and those who bitterly opposed his election. It would be prescient—one of the first public engagements, the first big Twitter clash of many, the first indication that those who had lost the election now were inclined to take their fight to the public square. The Women's March on Washington still was two months away. But it would draw millions of women.

Dixon's words, and the show's high-profile stand, would, just one night later, provoke a backlash at a performance of *Hamilton* in Chicago as a seemingly overserved Trump supporter, incensed by what he saw as the liberal politics of the show, started shouting back to the actors in the middle of the show.

"We won," the man, whose name was John Palmer, roared furiously from a balcony, at the top of his lungs. "We *won*." Palmer, it seemed, was not only inebriated but incensed that the artists before him were not falling into line. How dare they so politicize his night out!

An usher would lead him away, and eventually he would find himself in court, but not before he and his unscheduled exit had made the *Chicago Tribune*.[2]

All of this was transpiring at a Broadway musical. *Hamilton*, it would seem, was a whole lot more than "Broadway's new kick."

How could this have possibly come to pass? How did the theatre land right here? What had Broadway finally learned how to do?

We have to start back in 1993.

1
1993: AN ANGEL LANDS

As the audience at the Walter Kerr Theater on West 48th Street strained its necks upwards, there was a creaking and a groaning, a raining down of plaster dust, a great swell of triumphal music. Lights turned harsh and cold, then warm and golden, then green, then purple.[1] There was a sound designed to recall the sound of a meteor plummeting to Earth. And a fabulous angel, a creation with great, opalescent, gray-slate wings, crashed through the ceiling of the bedroom of a gay man.

A man betrayed by his lover, his politicians, and, above all else, his body. A man dying of AIDS. Like so many Americans living outside the doors of the theater.

"Greetings, prophet," said the arriviste Angel, four divine emanations manifest as one, the Continental Principality of America, a representative of religiosity of indeterminate denomination but invasive fervor.

"The great work begins," she said that warm spring of 1993, to all who would listen. "The Messenger has arrived."

She was heard. The American theatre would never be the same. "Not since Tennessee Williams," John Lahr would write in *The New Yorker*, "has a playwright announced his vision with such authority on the Broadway stage."[2]

Subtitled a "gay fantasia on national themes," this *Angels in America* was a blend of historicism and fiction, AIDS politics and personal redemption, the fantastic and the fabulous. Its complex, multilayered plot involved the agonizing death of the real-life figure Roy M. Cohn (a notoriously closeted, scorched-earth figure who was an advisor to Senator Joseph McCarthy, and a man who understood that being gay meant having no political clout); the struggles of a young, sardonic, fictional man with AIDS, Prior, and his chatty but self-absorbed lover, Louis; and the travails in New York of a wandering family of Mormons— Joe, Harper, and Hannah—each trying to reconcile the absolutes of faith with the messiness of their actual desires and lives.

The portentous angelic declaration notwithstanding, the owner of the bedroom, Prior, was not easily impressed with the pageant pastiche that had drenched him in sweat.

"God almighty," he said, "very Steven Spielberg,"[3] as audiences watched what later would be recognized as one of the most spectacular and revolutionary moments in the history of the American theatre, the centerpiece of a two-part magnum-opus play centered around the lives and collective consciousness of gay Americans, coming at the very moment that a plague was destroying the bodies of so many of them.

But in these final moments of "Millennium Approaches," the first part of this *Angels in America* penned by Anthony Robert Kushner, formerly of Lake Charles, Louisiana, now of New York City, Prior had summoned this angel to minister to his fevered dreams.

Fittingly, the angel that would transform Broadway had first come to Kushner in a dream.

The dream, Tony Kushner would recall years later,[4] had occurred in 1985, after the death of the first person that Kushner knew personally from AIDS. In the dream, Kushner had seen his dying friend (a dancer), and then a collapsed ceiling and an angel. The young writer had gone away in distress and written a poem, calling it, in the prophetically plural, "Angels in America." So there had been pain, then a poem, then a play.

The Kushner agony that seeded the play hardly was unique to anyone in the creative professions, which were being devastated by AIDS at that very moment; projects were being put on indeterminate hold, rehearsals were dissolving into tears, and Broadway show tunes were being heard at funeral after funeral. The agony, though, wrought change.

Unlike their European counterparts, many American playwrights of the mid-twentieth century had eschewed politics in favor of explorations of the schisms in the American family. If your intent was to get your play to Broadway, politics was not the way to go. Even as British writers like David Hare, Howard Brenton, and others were writing rapid exposés of the Margaret Thatcher years, American writers in the 1980s generally were dealing with family strife, intergenerational angst, or upper-middle-class ennui. These were the topics that had dominated post-war American drama.

Autobiography told through a nostalgic gauze reaped palpable rewards. Two blocks south of the Walter Kerr, Neil Simon's *Brighton Beach Memoirs* had opened in March 1983 and ran for 1,299 performances, not closing until May 1986. Lanford Wilson had thrived on Broadway with two early 1980s plays, *Fifth of July* and *Tally's Folly*, each part of a trilogy of dramas revolving around a family in Wilson's native Lebanon, Missouri.

As Simon's name dominated Broadway marquees, Kushner was passing time as a graduate student in the directing program at New York University. He'd met Oskar Eustis, who later would become artistic director of the New York Public Theater, but was then still the artistic director of the Eureka Theatre in San Francisco. In the spring of 1985, Eustis had happened to find himself in the audience at Theatre 22, a 28-seat theater on 22nd Street, for an earlier Kushner piece, *A Bright Room Called Day*, a rather dry play about the rise of fascism. Thrilled by what he'd seen and convinced that he'd witnessed the birth of a major new voice, Eustis called up Kushner and commissioned him to write a new play, stipulating in his commission that it be no longer than two hours.

In their grant application to the National Endowment of the Arts, Kushner and Eustis described a play with music featuring five gay men and an angel. Since there were three women in the resident acting company at the Eureka, that meant the play had to have female characters. As he worked on the grant application—$10,000 for the writer, $40,000 for the production—Kushner thought back to his poem, the one titled "Angels in America," and decided that he wanted to write a play about God, Roy Cohn,[5] and Mormons, there being, he would later say, only one real American angel, the one incorrectly identified by Joseph Smith as the Angel Moroni.

So if you had that title as your idea, Kushner's thinking went, you were obligated to pay a visit to Utah. Or, at least, to wonder what might happen if Utah came to New York.

* * *

Even as Kushner was working on *Angels in America*, the theatre was being devastated by AIDS. The closeted film star and heartthrob Rock Hudson was dying of the disease. He figures prominently in *And the Band Played On*,[6] the spectacular and definitive work of narrative journalism by Randy Shilts that told the history of AIDS primarily through a political and cultural lens. For Shilts, Hudson's death had been the moment when AIDS became an acronym familiar to everyone, a demarcation of America before the plague, and America thereafter. This was hardly the beginning of the crisis: Shilts reported that, even before the world learned of Hudson's diagnosis, some 12,000 Americans were already dead or dying of AIDS.[7]

Shilts had chosen his title carefully. Despite its cool, level-headed tone and well-sourced reportage, *And the Band Played On* attacked any number of constituencies for what Shilts found to be either willful inaction or sheer malevolence, especially during the early years of the crisis in the early 1980s. Shilts had plenty of blame to spread around: he went after politicians, both local and national, and had harsh words for the commercial interests who failed to act quickly to close the gay bathhouses that were helping the disease to spread. He generally praised the doctors and early research workers who tried to understand why all of these young men were dying, as he did many early gay activists, but he was sharply critical of the U.S. health establishment, not to mention the ego-driven battles over territory and jurisdiction that slowed progress at the Centers for Disease Control, the National

Institutes of Health, and its National Cancer Institute. "The bitter truth was that AIDS did not just happen to America," Shilts wrote.[8] "It was allowed to happen by an array of institutions, all of which failed to perform their appropriate tasks to safeguard the public health. This failure of the system leaves a legacy of unnecessary suffering that will haunt the Western world for decades to come."

One of Shilts's heroes was Larry Kramer, a Cassandra who just happened to be a playwright.

Kramer was not without controversy in the gay community. In a 1978 book called *Faggots*, he had argued that his fellow gay Americans had become so obsessed with sexual expression that they either lacked time or failed to understand the need to fight in the political arena (the book famously was removed from the shelves of the Oscar Wilde Memorial Bookstore, then Manhattan's only gay bookstore). This was an argument with which Kushner's Cohn character would not have disagreed and it set Kramer at odds with many in his community.

Once Kramer understood the implications of the sudden increase in deaths of younger gay men from a rare form of cancer called Kaposi's sarcoma, he raised his fists. He attacked the *New York Times* for what he saw as its shameful lack of press coverage, even as New Yorkers died. He excoriated public health officials for their fiefdoms and time wasting. He accused then-mayor Ed Koch of devastating inattention to young human life. He was part of one of the first major network news stories about AIDS, on the CBS Nightly News in 1982. By then, Kramer was being widely viewed as an alarmist, as writ large in a *cri de coeur* called "1,112 and Counting." Penned in 1983 for the *New York Native*, Kramer's article was a game changer when it came to awareness of AIDS within the gay community in New York, a group that included many who worked on Broadway.

And some who would not work there again.

The first sentence of "1,112 and Counting" read: "If this article doesn't scare the shit out of you, we're in real trouble." Kramer went on from there: "If this article doesn't rouse you to anger, fury, rage, and action, gay men may have no future on this earth. Our continued existence depends on just how angry you can get."[9]

By the summer of 1983, Kramer had channeled his rage into the beginnings of an autobiographical play. It would be titled *The Normal Heart*, which Kramer took from W. H. Auden's "September, 1939," a poem that ends with the line "We must love one another or die." *The Normal Heart* was to be a then-definitive dramatic exploration of the AIDS crisis and a thinly veiled allegory of Kramer's own travails between 1981 and 1984 at the Gay Men's Health Crisis in New York (he wrote himself into the play, in the guise of a character named Ned Weeks). Underappreciated at the time, *The Normal Heart* was an act of enormous political courage, a screed that demanded America wake up, while more of its young men still were alive. And unlike most every other play of that decade, *The Normal Heart* had been produced (at the New York Public Theater) within a year of the events depicted in the play taking place in reality. So this was a rare thing in the American theatre of that time: a reactive piece of docudrama, penned in the kitchen and produced while the burners still were hot.

And it was ecstatically reviewed. Such was the level of publicity surrounding the work that many city officials, including New York City mayor Ed Koch, were forced to respond publically to charges made in what was, in essence, an allegorical play.

Remarkably, Kramer had inserted the nonprofit theater right into the center of the public discourse. He had written one of the only plays of the latter half of the twentieth century that made news. By doing so, he leapt out of the theatre ghetto and demonstrated that theatre could and should be first, that it should go where Hollywood and the televisions networks feared to go. And if there was one topic they all were scared of, that topic was AIDS.

The Normal Heart was not the only play about AIDS to predate *Angels in America*. William Hoffman's *As Is*, a moving and intensely grief-stricken play about a group of New York friends living (and dying) with the disease, opened a month before *The Normal Heart*, even if

Kramer had begun his work first. And Kramer surely did not abandon the American playwright's love of the surrogate family, given that the men fighting therein were, in fact, a surrogate family in Kramer's telling, each being the only supporters many of them could trust.

But this remarkable play took a crucial step forward by focusing on politics over grief, the public square over the bedroom: Kramer saw his playwriting as an explicit extension of his activism and he thought that a well-publicized play at a high-profile theater might shame some recalcitrant city officials into action that could save lives. And, to a surprisingly large degree, he was right.

Moreover, The Normal Heart articulated Kramer's contention that AIDS had been an avoidable plague, a horrific manifestation of widespread homophobia. As Shilts noted,[10] the play argued that the gay-rights movement always should not just have been about sexual revolution (as it was so widely seen at the time) but about a revolution in human rights. The play's most sympathetic character, Dr. Emma Brookner, based on a pioneering and wheelchair-bound New York doctor called Linda Laubenstein, was speaking for Kramer when she said that "health is a political issue."

Hoffman's As Is opened on Broadway even before Kramer's play had made it to the Public Theater; it was an important and poignant play about human grief, but a work that built sympathy rather than expressing fury. As Is was nominated for a Tony Award, no small achievement for the era, although it ultimately, and unsurprisingly, lost to Simon's Biloxi Blues. For all its accommodations, the Broadway establishment still kept its eye on what was good for long-term business.

The Normal Heart did not make it to Broadway until 2011, when Joe Mantello (who, a decade after Kramer first sat down to write, had played Louis in Angels in America) helmed a deeply moving revival: it felt like a victory lap for, maybe even a vindication of, the author. Not that Kramer saw it that way, being of the conviction there was still too much unfinished business for any kind of celebration.

Indeed, on one warm night that spring, a 75-year-old Kramer could be seen outside the Golden Theatre, handing out old-school flyers in semi-anonymity as his audience filed out of the theater, brushing off compliments and still reminding anyone who would listen that America had slept while AIDS burned through a nation, and that people were still dying.

The flyers were headed "A Letter from Larry Kramer." In the first paragraph they said, "Please know that everything in *The Normal Heart* happened." Most people who got one did not know who had handed it to them. But a few people knew the messenger: A critic exiting from the show found himself staring at Kramer, and watching the brows that surrounded him furrow in wonderment and disbelief.

Kramer just went about his business. His unchanged business, there still being work left to do.

As Kramer's play was opening at the New York Public Theater, the man who would later run that institution, and help develop *Hamilton*, was discovering Kushner. As Kramer's play ran throughout 1985, and then into 1986, Kushner was at work on *Angels in America*, an act that involved the reconciliation of death and belief.

It did not come to him easily nor quickly.

After Eustis moved to the Mark Taper Forum in Los Angeles, plans for the show moved with him there: developmental work on "Millennium Approaches," the first part of *Angels*, finally intensified during 1989. By the spring of 1990, there was a workshop.

If Kramer had put himself in *The Normal Heart* as Ned Weeks, so Kushner put himself in *Angels in America* (mostly) as Louis, an over-intellectualizing New Yorker unable to stop kvetching and analyzing and self-justifying and talking, invariably out of sync with the actual needs of the situation.

Interestingly, both Kushner and Kramer painted critical portraits of themselves: Ned Weeks's inability to compromise generally puts people's backs up in *The Normal Heart*, while Louis fails the man he loves, Prior, by abandoning him in his hour of greatest need. It is an act for which the play does not forgive him. Perhaps there also is something of Kushner in Belize, the African American nurse who rivals Louis in his intellectual curiosity but who also has the moral clarity that the dribbling and driveling Prior lacks. Belize knows what's up, and when to shut up.

Angels in America actually opened at the Eureka in San Francisco, after that theater pointed out to Kushner's agent, Joyce Katay, that it had a contract giving it the right to the first production, even though the play's spiritual godfather, Eustis, was by now in Los Angeles. Kushner wrote "Perestroika" while "Millennium Approaches" was in rehearsal, taking a cabin on the Russian River and, he later reported, "writing 700 pages of 'Perestroika' in 10 days."[11]

All by hand.

"Perestroika" did not, of course, turn out to be anything like 700 pages in its final published version, which picked up from the angel's spectacular entrance at the end of "Millennium Approaches." But all of those pages and ideas meant that the rest of the creative process mostly was about culling what had already emerged from Kushner's brain. Although by far the biggest hit in the theater's history, that first production of *Angels in America* could not guarantee a long-term future for the Eureka Theatre, which already was mired in debt. The theater's future was marked by financial crises and the loss of its home in the rapidly gentrifying Mission District in San Francisco. On July 5, 2017, the Eureka would close down for good.

But the future of the play it premiered was entirely a different matter.

By 1992, the Royal National Theatre in London had produced "Millennium Approaches" and what turned out to be the first real, full production of "Perestroika" (the cast included Daniel Craig). The *New York Times* critic Frank Rich went to London to review Declan Donnellan's production, calling the play "a runaway sensation"[12] and dubbing Kushner "a messenger to be heard."

"As a piece of writing," Rich wrote, "the play is a searching and radical rethinking of the whole esthetic of American political drama in which far-flung hallucinations, explicit sexual encounters and camp humor are given as much weight as erudite ideological argument."[13]

Rich had written the most searching, influential, and prescient review of his career. He understood that Kushner was writing from an "uncompromising yet undoctrinaire" point of view. He got that *Angels* was completely unlike any other play that had come before: *Angels in America*, he wrote, "is the most extravagant and moving demonstration imaginable that even as the AIDS body count continues to rise, this tragedy has pushed some creative minds, many of them in the theater, to new and daring heights of imaginative expression."

After Rich's rave, many producers fought to get the Broadway rights. Creatively, Kushner gave the Broadway production of show to the director George C. Wolfe, thus abandoning Eustis, who had developed the work. Many thought Rich's review had precipitated the change, although Kushner said that the decision was made prior to Rich's appearance in London. Thus, with Wolfe in charge, "Millennium Approaches" opened at the Walter Kerr Theater on May 4, 1993. Its lead producer, Rocco Landesman of Jujamcyn Theaters, one of the three powerful commercial theater owners in New York City, would go on to head the National Endowment for the Arts under President Barack Obama.

"*Angels in America*," Rich wrote, of the Broadway production, "speaks so powerfully because something far larger and more urgent than the future of the theater is at stake. It really is history that Mr. Kushner intends to crack open. He sends his haunting messenger, a spindly, abandoned gay man with a heroic spirit and a ravaged body, deep into the audience's heart to ask just who we are and just what, as the plague continues and the millennium approaches, we intend this country to become."[14]

"Millennium Approaches" won the Tony Award for best play in 1993. "Perestroika" would snag the same honor one year later, although the second part would not make a profit, barely recouping its costs. Had the producers cared only about money, they would have been better off not producing "Perestroika" at all.

But *Angels in America* was about something a good deal more important.

Kushner—later often dubbed "Comrade Kushner" by the smart-but-waggish *New York Post* columnist Michael Riedel—was a secularist and a democratic socialist, his Jewish heritage notwithstanding. And in his young plays like *A Bright Room Called Day* (which Rich had hated), he had written very much from that point of view. Like any good socialist writer, he frequently would say that teaching history was an inherent part of the work of a political artist. Kushner, a scholar of theatre history, was enthralled with the work of Bertolt Brecht. He saw the Marxist critic Walter Benjamin—who referenced a backwards-flying angel of history—as a spiritual father of *Angels in America*. A creative dad right up there with Eustis.

But neither a secularist point of view nor Brechtian alienation, and surely not chilly Marxist historicism, armed you very well for the funerals of those who had seemed, just months or even weeks before, to have been so brimming with youthful life. The years when the AIDS crisis roared were, inevitably, a moment for centrist thinking. For, you might say, pondering God or even asking for forgiveness, just in case He happened to exist and forgiveness might prove to be necessary.

Who could traverse from funeral to funeral believing that death was final? Who could insist to a recently bereaved lover that was the case? Who could find full sustenance in cold, secular, democratic socialism? Did one not need a god to believe that death was not final? And if death was arriving with such frequency, without even remote regard for youth or deserving, was not a belief that death was final in direct opposition to the hope required for living? Especially in the midst of a plague?

Surely, to even allow for the possibility of immortal transformation, you logically had to make some attempt at a definition of a deity. And if you saw religion primarily as an opiate, or as a tool of the ruling classes, that was a tall order.

But did not one's tears, did not all these lost souls, at least demand you try?

It really was all as simple—and as complicated—as that.

Like so many self-reflective thinkers caught up in the AIDS crisis, Kushner found that any play paying attention to the moment had to allow for spiritual longing. It would be absurd to do otherwise.

Kushner's creative problem, though, was that he could not help himself from satirizing the extant religions, especially given their embrace of the illogical, their absurdly self-contradictory and campy mythologies, and, by no means least, their historical antipathy towards gays and lesbians. In Kushner's head, religions brought baggage. Intolerable (and intolerant) baggage. As the young Mormon woman Harper says in *Angels,* "In my church, we don't believe in homosexuals."

Or rationalists, she might have added.

But if the homosexual spiritual seeker wanted to travel without checked luggage, in what could he or she possibly believe? That was the dominant question.

Angels in America is many things to many different people, but what made it unique was its howl of pain for the inadequacies of religiosity, its raging for love, fidelity, and relief from a plague, a scream screamed without political compromise. This play was looking, in the concise words of one academic, for "the post-modern version of what it means to be a Christian or a Jew."[15] And it was trying to do so within the Broadway theatre, and, as such, it was a historic quest.

Kushner would later describe the work, accurately, as "a rejection — or at least a critique — of a completely rational response to the world as being sufficient."

"One has to make some place in one's epistemology for the irrational and the intuitive,"[16] he would say.

But what did that actually mean? How could Kushner avoid the charge that he and his loosey-goosey, sexuo-politicized angels were doing nothing more than grazing at a buffet of self-serving moral relativism and were thus unwilling to commit to the rules and responsibilities of life within a faith that either should be taken in its entirety, or not taken at all? That was the play's central existential problem.

In 1993, a case could be made that is was the central existential problem of America.

When *Angels* opened on Broadway, Bill Clinton already was in the White House, and the play's harsh words for Ronald Reagan and his administration, contemporaneous when Kramer had written *The Normal Heart*, were, by now, perceivable as references to the bad old days, soon to be swept away, it was thought, by enlightened Clintonian pluralism. That liberal pluralism would eventually give way to triangulation, and to a messy and inarguably abusive sexuality inside the White House itself, involving both the president and an intern named Monica Lewinsky. As *Angels* moved around the country, the fast-food-loving Clinton would often be charged himself with moral relativism, with expedience trumping deep theological questions. As a spiritual leader, Clinton would lose credibility, a deficit that would continue to haunt his wife Hillary's presidential campaign two decades later.

Of course, an unfettered sexual appetite was not what Kushner was seeking in *Angels in America*. He was well aware of the danger of his angel being, in essence, a more fabulous version of what he believed himself, of a vehicle for seeking out comfort without the attendant sacrifices.

"I've always called myself an agnostic," Kushner said, some years later, looking back on the play and the paradox at its very core.[17] "I mean that in the deepest sense that I can mean it, which is a genuine discomfort and an inability to say yes or no ... there's doubt, curiosity, instinct, and profound respect for the irrational with me."

So what did this play know, rationally speaking? Well, it surely knew what it did not like: fundamentalism, homophobia, conservatism, and, above all, hypocrisy. Unfaithful lovers were linked with the unfaithful government of the United States. Political ignorance signaled repression of self. In this play, religion and politics blended into the same thing.

"There are three important things in my life that are big themes in my work," Kushner would say.[18] "I'm a Jew so I have to engage with what that means, which has to have something to do with God. There are still people in the world who call themselves Jews who have survived centuries of oppression and torture and genocide and that has a lot to do with devotion and faith. I cannot dismiss that. Then I am a gay man, so I have to think a lot about sexuality. Yearning and desire are very central to all religious questions. Sexuality and spirituality have a very profound relationship. And then I am an American in a society that's fanatically devoted to materialism. We've transformed desire in this country from desire for connection, desire for God, human desires, to a fetishistic desire for things. I'm as corrupted in that sense as most Americans are."

Self-deprecating as it may be, that's hardly coherent religiosity, even if it's worth noting that most religions are tolerant of human confusion, maybe even explicitly encouraging thereof, being as we all are removed from the end times when everything will be made clear. Only then, after all, might we truly know God.

Put all that together and you arrive at the realization that *Angels in America* was, in the end, a work of singularly intense utopian dreaming, embracing both the spiritual and the political aspects of contemporary American life. And in 1993, what possible utopian imagining of a work of American theater would not include a cure for AIDS?

"We are where we have always been and probably always will be," Kushner would say.[19] But that wasn't even remotely true. In actuality, *Angels in America* had been a giant and thrilling leap forward, into, and out of the darkness. There never had been anything comparable on Broadway. And when a new National Theatre production of the play returned to Broadway in the spring of 2018, with Nathan Lane and Andrew Garfield in its lead roles, there still had not been anything to compare. Whatever anyone may have felt about that new production, the play seemed as vital as ever. More vital, really.

What did this magisterial play achieve? For one thing, and not unlike Kramer, Kushner brought *impatience* to the American theater, as well as fragility, both micro and macro, personal and existential, timeless and very much of the moment. He also brought a new level of ambition—bigger and smarter ideas, not to mention a long running time—and he taught the theatre that no level of magnum opus was inconceivable. He understood that audiences craved substance over situational laughs, that they would reward works that approached the act of living with complexity, and that when presented with a writer's own vulnerability, they would translate that human pain to situations of their own. Simply put, *Angels in America* was a watershed in American political theatre: a reminder that every radical since Brecht worth their salt had promoted change as a reaction, not just to political passions, but to human mortality.

Years later, as Kushner was finishing his screenplay to the 2012 Steven Spielberg film *Lincoln*, for which he would win an Academy Award, he'd say this:

> Death is not a nice process. There are emotional and physical burdens. Our huge capacity to connect makes our losing immensely difficult. But you can work on it by watching others. And it is a biological fact that the individual is fiction. The smallest reducible unit is two people, not one. What we really are is a network of relationships.[20]

In 1993, faced with death all around and having grown old beyond his years, he'd already known that to be true. Perhaps his greatest achievement was that he had defined Americans as more than one, the other being of the individual's choosing. He had penned a play that explored both the agony, and the necessity, that we all find a way to change. And he'd inserted theater back into the serious national conversation. Roy Cohn or no Roy Cohn, he'd made the point that Broadway could and must be about a lot more than snagging tickets to *Cats*. If only Broadway was able to understand its own potential.

Kushner had created the model. The messenger, you might say, had arrived.

Or—and with apologies to Prior's final lines in one of the most important American plays of its century—the Great Work had begun.

2

1994: THE EMERGENT POWER OF THE SOLO VOICE

On March 3, 1991, a group of Los Angeles police officers used brutal force to subdue a 35-year-old African American taxi-driver named Rodney G. King.

There had been a high-speed chase after two of the officers had noticed King speeding on the freeway. King, who had been drinking, had been worried that stopping could mean a conviction that could violate his parole (he'd already been convicted of robbery). So he kept driving. Fast. Eventually he found himself in a corner. The police, with their batons and Tasers, soon surrounded him. The police beating continued long after King was subdued.

What the officers did not immediately know was that their violence had been caught on videotape: this was a prescient moment in American society, which would in time become a place where most citizens carried a camera conveniently in their pockets, and where many African American citizens in particular would find good reason to hit the record button. But at the time, the presence of an externally produced visual record of a police action was a rarity. A man named George Holliday had taped the beating of King on a home video camera, working from his own well-positioned apartment.

Two days later, Holliday tried calling the headquarters of the local police department but got the sense that no one there was much interested in viewing his video. So he went instead to a television station, KTLA, which was very much interested and aired a portion of Holliday's explosive tape, which then ricocheted around the world.

Four of the police officers faced subsequent criminal charges for their actions, which wended their way through the court system. On April 29, 1992, three of the officers were acquitted of all charges, and the jury deadlocked on the fourth, voting 8–4 in favor of acquittal.

Within a matter of hours, the Los Angeles riots of 1992 had begun.

Billions of dollars in property damage occurred, with many businesses burned to the ground. Nearly 3,000 people were injured and more than 50 Angelinos were killed. It took both the police and the U.S. Armed Forces to restore order. On May 1, King issued an agonized, televised plea.

"Can we all get along?" he said, "Can we, can we, get along?"

* * *

In 1994, one person getting along without anyone else on a Broadway stage—while charging Broadway prices— was still a rarity.

Yet on the Broadway stage of the Cort Theatre, an African American writer and actress named Anna Deavere Smith could be seen standing alone, speaking with a thick Korean accent.

To many in her audience in the spring of 1994, it seemed that Smith had suddenly become both elderly and Korean, her facial expressions— indeed, her entire physicality—changing along with her voice.

"They destroy innocent people," Smith said, slowly, her face moving around the theater, staring intently, even accusatorily, at different audience members who met her gaze. "And I wonder if that is really justice for them to get their rights in that way?"

The "they" referenced the African American protestors who had been protesting after the police acquittals. The audience at *Twilight: Los Angeles* was listening to the words of a real-life person named Young-Soon Han, a shopkeeper whose liquor store had been burned to the ground in the riots. Han was, she had told Deavere Smith in an extensive interview, "swallowing the bitterness." And her former interlocutor now was interpreting her words on Broadway, capturing, it seemed, her every syllable, her every hesitation, her every mutter, as the actress translated this shopkeeer's thoughts from the Korean.

Twilight: Los Angeles, which had been commissioned by, and was first seen at, the Mark Taper Forum in Los Angeles and was directed on Broadway by George C. Wolfe, was the 43-year-old Smith's first Broadway show, although hardly her first major work. Indeed, *Twilight: Los Angeles* was a sequel of sorts to *Fires in the Mirror*, a 1991 Smith piece inspired by a different set of riots, those in the Crown Heights neighborhood of Brooklyn, New York, sparked after an African American had been killed in an automobile accident involving the motorcade of a Rabbi. *Fires in the Mirror*—which had raised Smith's profile and reputation—had its premiere at the New York Shakespeare Festival in 1992. It then moved around the country, and even had a stint at the Royal Court Theatre in London, but never went to Broadway. The scholar Cornel West described *Fires in the Mirror* as "the most significant artistic exploration of Black-Jewish relations of our time,"[1] mostly, he said, because Smith had served up the faces and ideas of ordinary people, and treated everyone with fairness.

Deavere Smith clasped her hands together. She was still inhabiting Young-Soon Han.

"I wish that I could live together with black people," she said. "But after the riot, it's too much difference. The fire is still there. Igniting fire, igniting fire is still there. It can burst out any time."

* * *

For most of Broadway's history, the phenomenon of the solo show usually had required a name far more famous than that of Anna Deavere Smith.

Ideally, the famous name would be attached to famous material from a famous character.

The defining Broadway solo show of the second half of the twentieth century had been the work of Hal Holbrook, the actor best known for playing the cigar-chomping literary raconteur Mark Twain. Holbrook's piece, *Mark Twain Tonight*, which he would go to perform all the way until a self-imposed retirement in 2017, had its origins on college campuses in the 1950s, where Holbrook first essayed the shock-haired and garrulous Twain, the master of the bon mot, the folksy anecdote, the abiding truism. Twain, of course, was especially famous for his attacks on the "Grand Old Asylum" (Congress) and "the inmates" (Congressmen).

By 1966 (and then again in 1977 and 2005) Holbrook as Twain could be seen on Broadway. The show was a one-man tour de force: Holbrook so appeared to inhabit the avuncular Twain persona that the lines between the two seemed to blur before your eyes. The whole point of the night was that you'd see Twain, not Holbrook. Obviously, the piece could not have been more different from *Twilight* ... but it nonetheless offered up a model for the solo voice, that model being one of total immersion in a persona. The experience was made all the more intense by the eradication of the necessity to share the stage.

Since Holbrook made you feel like you are in the presence of Twain, the hopeful thinking and marketing went, you wouldn't miss other actors. So complete would be the illusion, you'd still feel like you were getting good value for those Broadway ticket prices. The notion certainly put more pressure on the individual actor, but then Holbrook specialized in only one man. In some ways, this was an updating of the way things were on Broadway a century earlier, when actors would become synonymous with one particular character, whom they would play again and again. One actor, Joseph Jefferson, was so known for his performance as Rip Van Winkle that audiences would refuse to accept him in the guise of anyone else. These shows were all sold on a kind of deep-dive theory: the star was not expressing some political truth, but embodying one external character so completely that anyone would be lucky to share the experience.

About a decade after Holbrook's Main Stem bow, the actress Julie Harris appeared in William Luce's *The Belle of Amherst*, a 1976 show about another literary figure, in this case Emily Dickinson (Luce, a lover of the form, would go to write *Lillian*, a solo piece about the playwright and activist Lillian Hellman, for Zoe Caldwell in 1986).

But a greater influence on Anna Deavere Smith, surely, was a solo artist named Lily Tomlin. Tomlin was famous for quirky, solo comedy. And when she appeared on Broadway in 1977, she was billed as the first woman ever to appear alone on a Broadway stage. That might not have been fair to Luce and certainly not to Harris, but it was true that Tomlin was the first woman working solo on Broadway to actually use her own material.

Appearing Nightly featured Tomlin's most famous character, a hilariously dictatorial telephone operator named Ernestine. But unlike Holbrook or Harris, Tomlin did not restrict to herself to one persona.

By 1977, Tomlin already was a star. Her career had begun in her native Detroit in the early 1960s and, thereafter, Tomlin had become part of the New York improvisational community, hanging out with the likes of Richard Pryor on the Lower East Side. Since then she'd also become known for *Laugh-In* on TV, her appearance in Robert Altman's *Nashville* had netted her an Academy Award nomination, and vinyl recordings of her live performances were exceptionally popular. Tomlin was very much a character-based comedian; in interviews of the time, she tended to talk about how she would always let her characters take her wherever they wanted her to go. She was not especially ideological. Her specialty was a dead-on accurate portrayal of a familiar human foible. In that she was not unlike Holbrook.

That was also true of Gilda Radner, the headliner of the 1979 Broadway revue *Gilda Radner—Live From New York.*

Although not a solo show, this musical and comedic entertainment was centered around Radner, who had been one of the original cast members of *Saturday Night Live!* in an era when the NBC censor was more active. Only on Broadway could Radner sing a ditty, written by the late Saturday Night Live! writer Michael O'Donaghue, entitled "Let's Talk Dirty to the Animals." But if this Broadway piece basically was an R-rated version of a late-night sketch show, Radner still was a hugely influential force in American comedy, and on succeeding generations of women in comedy. Just a decade later, Radner would be dead at just 42 from ovarian cancer. But in 1979, she was at the peak of her fame and creativity. Her voice rang out loud and clear, and made a difference.

By the 1984–85 season, still a full decade before *Twilight: Los Angeles,* the director Mike Nichols had brought a showcase for a rising young African American comedian to the Lyceum Theatre. Her name was Whoopi Goldberg.

In her eponymous show, Goldberg essayed six different characters, all of whom she seemed to inhabit entirely. Goldberg was bolder and edgier than Tomlin and she did not hesitate to interpret characters of a different race or gender from herself. *Whoopi Goldberg* included, for example, both her take on a male African American drug addict and on a white 12-year-old, a so-called Valley Girl from California. There was a good amount of provocative social commentary in a piece that pushed the Broadway preconceptions of the era further than most shows would have dared, and, given that both Goldberg and Smith were extroverted African American progressives essaying a variety of serious characters of great diversity, Goldberg's influence on the rise of the solo voice is self-evident.

But at the time, *Whoopi Goldberg* still was billed, sold, and performed very much as theatricalized stand-up comedy, not as a work of political engagement or performance art or social commentary.

Even within the show itself, Goldberg repeatedly told her audience that none of her characters should make them nervous.

There was good reason for such caution; solo shows were still a tough sell. All the way back to Twain, the rap against them had always been that they would not be able to sustain the interest and attention of a broad audience. You can sense that worry lingering in Frank Rich's otherwise laudatory review of *Whoopi Goldberg*.

"What is in question," Rich wrote in his opening-night review in the *New York Times*,[2] "is whether she yet has the range of material and talent to sustain a night of theater. Don't be surprised if you leave the Lyceum feeling more enthusiastic about Whoopi Goldberg, the personality, than 'Whoopi Goldberg,' the show."

Rich never said that about Spalding Gray. It would have been impossible. Gray, the personality, and Gray, the show, were one and the same.

And Gray, too, in his quirky, WASPy way, paved the way on Broadway for Smith.

* * *

Gray, who first appeared alone on Broadway in 1991 in a piece called *Monster in a Box*, was a very singular monologist whose talent, range of material, and inherently bizarre personality was not even remotely open to question.

Gray's early work was mostly performed in Soho at the Wooster Group's The Performing Garage, where Gray collaborated with Elizabeth LeCompte and first created his eponymous character, Spalding. As his work matured over the years that followed, Gray's shows became more and more like voyages inside the performer's twisted psyche; the viewer would assume the role of voyeur as Gray recounted what felt like a series of impossibly intimate details from his impossibly complicated personal life, a life that underwent drastic changes over his years of performing, even if Gray's obsessions remained remarkably consistent. In an early solo piece at The Performing Garage in 1979, *Sex and Death to the Age 14*, Gray discussed his adolescent sexual encounters, and also his experience of encountering death for the first time, both of which would become constant themes in his later work.

Presented by the Wooster Group at The Performing Garage, *Booze, Cars and College Girls* was another chapter in the ongoing story of Gray's adolescence. *India and After* was a strange piece, infused with random association. It drew from a trip Gray took to India in 1976 with The Performance Group. Over time, Gray morphed from a downtown New York figure to a touring storyteller with a national reputation.

In terms of a broader sense of fame, Gray's breakthrough monologue was *Swimming to Cambodia*, a piece from the mid-1980s that would later be filmed by the director Jonathan Demme. Immersive and often disturbing, highly critical of the American bombing of Cambodia, it was based on Gray's experience working as an actor in the Roland Joffe movie *The Killing Fields.*

"This is the classic piece, my watershed," Gray would say later.[3] "The narratives went from the personal and the erotic to the psychotic; they demonstrate how you cannot explore psychoanalysis without looking at civilization as a whole."

That's not the easiest quote to unpack, but it made sense in Gray's universe: his monologues started out as personally esoteric, broadened over time to embrace macro issues of global conflict through the language of the individual therapist, and then narrowed again as Gray grew older and found what his fans all thought (wrongly, it would later seem) was a measure of personal happiness.

The show that made it to the Lincoln Center's Broadway venue, *Monster in a Box*, was a monologue about Gray's attempts to finish a novel called *Impossible Vacation*, his *8 ½*, and, therein, he described all of the life events that intruded.

In fact, *Monster in a Box* felt a lot like Gray was explaining the beginnings of his own nervous breakdown. Gray called the piece a work about "the dizziness that comes from not being able to deal with too much possibility."[4]

He was, he said, paraphrasing Kierkegaard. He also said he had almost not survived the doing of the piece.[5] Obviously, Gray was not the first person to draw from his own life. For Broadway, though, this kind of highly intense intrusion of personal psychology into scripted material was very far from the usual thing.

Gray would later return to the Vivian Beaumont Theater with works like *Gray's Anatomy* (1993), a monologue about approaching what Gray in the piece called "The Bermuda Triangle of Health," when he contracted a sight-threatening ailment in his left eye. *It's a Slippery Slope* (1996) dealt with how Gray's father and Gray's therapist both died in the space of a week, the same week that Gray left his wife of 14 years, Renee Shrinasky, after he found out that his much younger girlfriend, Kathie Russo, had become pregnant (Russo would become Gray's second wife). At one post-Broadway performance of the monologue in Chicago, Gray's audience actually booed when he spoke the line, "There's never just another son, but there's always another woman over there."

Gray just went on talking.

Morning, Noon and Night (1999) was a much happier piece. This would be the most optimistic of all his monologues, as it followed a day in the life of the integrated family he would later build with Russo and their children.

"It's a family album that takes place on Oct. 8, 1997," Gray said of that piece,[6] looking back, "although I have condensed many days into one day. It's an average day in our life; I take the audience through that arc. It begins with the sun going up and ends with my son kicking me as I go to sleep. It's like a Grecian urn frozen in time. I can't imagine doing a series of family monologues. It could cost them a lot of money in therapy. This one feels like the end, but then they all do."

The end would come much too quickly for a man who long had struggled with depression.

In 2001, Gray was the victim of a serious car accident while on holiday in Ireland with his family. They were hit by a black van, head-on. Gray suffered a fractured skull and a broken hip. Discussing what had happened with an admiring journalist the following spring,[7] Gray alternated between discussing the painful details and pointing out that, given what had happened on September 11, 2001, he felt like he had no right to sing the blues.

On January 10, 2004, Gray went missing from his home in Manhattan. He'd just seen the movie *Big Fish*. He left behind his wallet, keys, wife, and children. Where there had been years of talk, years of soliloquizing on every conceivable personal demon, every possible ailment of body or mind, every act of personal self-destruction, there now merely was a void of silence. It was truly bizarre. His absence seemed especially sinister due to the lack of any first-person narration, any confessional, from the man who had basically invented the form.

It was both ironic and, for his admirers, deeply disturbing. It was not inconceivable that Gray was in crisis—but it *was* inconceivable that the crisis would not have become a monologue, or that Gray would have absented himself and risked someone else taking over his own personal narrative.

For some longtime fans of Gray, there always had been the nagging feeling that he had willed the traumas of his life to make great theatre, albeit perhaps in his subconscious. In the days of his disappearance, that feeling became a kind of grand delusion, a hope that the inventor of a particular kind of reality theatre, a whole different solo experience, would never want to waste such great material. There was the hope that he was sitting somewhere, working on a new monologue.

On March 2, 2004, the monologist John Leguizamo, another one-person Broadway artist in debt to how Gray awakened Broadway to the solo voice, dedicated a comedy show in Chicago to his hero, who by then had been missing for six weeks.

On March 9 of that year, Gray's dead body was pulled from Manhattan's East River, into which he apparently had jumped from the Staten Island Ferry.

Gray's influence on the rise of the solo voice for mainstream audiences is difficult to overstate. Kushner and Kramer might have written themselves into their own plays, but Gray had invented a genre by fusing together personal revelation and complex philosophical ideas. He had mastered spontaneity, seeming to make every monologue unique, with a shelf life of only one performance and a delivery system for one hearer only. At all of his shows, it felt like you were the only one in the theater.

Gray had suggested his own epitaph in 1977: "An American Original, Troubled, Inner-Directed and Cannot Type."

In the devastating aftermath of his death for his friends, family, and fans, that felt right.

And most terribly wrong.

* * *

Of course, when Smith walked out on the stage of the Cort that night in 1994 to perform *Fires in the Mirror*, nobody knew of Gray's later trajectory. At that juncture, the solo voice he had helped develop was there for the taking. Not only was Smith able to build on Goldberg's and Tomlin's character studies, but she could fuse what they had done with Gray's obsession with biography, philosophy, and psycho-analysis.

All that was true—but Smith also was very much her own thing.

She was working under the direction of Emily Mann, who had written her own Broadway docudrama, *Execution of Justice*. Highly influential in its own right, *Execution of Justice,* a piece about the murder of the San Francisco supervisor Harvey Milk, had played Broadway in 1986; its cast had included the future movie star Wesley Snipes.

Mann was the right director. But Smith was the first to use the Broadway solo voice as a way to explore America's disastrous inability to deal with its own racial mistrust, all flowing, as it did, from its original sin of slavery. In so doing, she was a crucial link in the personalization and politicization of Broadway that would culminate in *Hamilton*, still years ahead.

Smith was not reliant on any playwright; her material was her own, the result of more than 175 interested parties around the Los Angeles riots, conducted over a period of more than eight months and chosen from a variety of contacts (interestingly enough, Tomlin introduced Smith to one of her interviewees). Smith had been in court when the charges against the police officers were dismissed—she'd even posed as a Brazilian journalist in order to slip into a post-trial press conference, following the verdicts.[8]

Her title came, in part, from an interview with a man named Twilight, who had worked on building a truce between the Crips and the Bloods, two of Los Angeles' most deadly gangs. In the piece, he is a central figure, and perhaps the character for whom Smith has the most obvious preference.

Smith did not disappear into her characters; on the contrary, her own persona was omnipresent. Yet whereas Gray had been so consumed by his own neuroses that he could not function as an honest broker of anything or anyone external to his own self, Smith gave voice to ordinary Americans, positioned as they were on all sides of some of the nation's most incendiary debates.

Like the one in Los Angeles.

Like all of Smith's work, *Twilight: Los Angeles* had its origins in a series of performance pieces called *On the Road, a Search for American Character*, which Smith had started back in the early 1980s.[9] She wanted, she said, to find that American character through the ways people speak. "The act of speech is a physical act," Smith wrote.[10] "It is powerful enough that it can create, with the rest of the body, a kind of cooperative dance."

That might sound like actor-training jargon, but it was a key to Smith's contribution to Broadway's turn toward the substantial.

In essence, Smith would go out and interview people involved in the racial conflicts that afflicted large American cities over time, and then persuade her subjects to cooperate by first convincing them that she was an honest broker of their point of view, and then by offering them in return a chance to see themselves performed.

Smith's work was, in some ways, the opposite of the usual way of doing things in solo shows on Broadway. Smith would not strive to inhabit characters in the bravura style of Holbrook, Tomlin, Radner, or Goldberg through close observation and impersonation of archetypes, but would strive to *be* inhabited by the characters' own words. A cooperative dance, you might say. Or a paradoxical de-emphasis of self.

In an article in *American Theatre* magazine in 1993, the writer Richard Stayton referred to the piece as "an urban Rashomon that provokes discussion without media interference."[11] Stayton accurately homed in on what made Smith such an innovator—her chameleon-like quality and her open embrace of the other than herself.

Smith's work did not begin as social commentary but as this kind of experimentation. Over time, she helped Broadway understand a more sophisticated vocabulary of the self and the other, and thus Smith extended out the notions of character study that had made up the work of Tomlin or Goldberg into the realm of social ideas. You might say she had learned how to combine Tomlin, Goldberg, and Gray.

But she was not interested in the personal crises or neuroses, but in broader questions of equity and identity: the matter of who has the right to tell whose story. You might think of it as a bridge from character into idea.

American idea. And American identity.

"In America," Smith wrote,[12] "identity is always being negotiated. To what extent do people who come to America have to give up something about their own identity to conform to an idea of what America is?"

That consideration of the perspective of another, of the need to walk in someone else's shoes, was pivotal to Smith's work. "Acting," she told an audience in 1998,[13] "places a physical and linguistic emphasis on the possibility of transformation."

Her point was that if actors could transform themselves to play a role, could that not be a metaphor for our inherent ability to reach out across the great racial divides?

"Our ways of talking," Smith said,[14] "tell us more about difference than the words we use."

Smith's work—Gray's too—had helped Broadway performers find *agency*. And she had used the solo form to suggest that the theatre had a vital role to play in American democracy.

There would be more of these controversies involving the police and the communities they served. In 2014, a man named Eric Garner died after being placed in a stranglehold by a police officer in Staten Island, New York City. His legacy included the phrase, "I Can't Breathe," which he repeated eleven times. In 2017, an 18-year-old man named Michael Brown was shot 12 times by a police officer in Ferguson, Missouri, igniting serious unrest, especially when the arresting officer was not indicted. In these and other violent acts that cut across racial lines, it would remain true that Americans often had strikingly different views of the same events, and they were defiantly unpersuaded by the views of those in opposition. That was exactly the point Smith had been making in 1993. But then only a small percentage of Americans went to the theater.

In 1993, Smith had said that she wanted to "decentralize the race discussion"[15] by opening up that discussion to more voices, and by zeroing in on the power of language. That is exactly what she did, and in doing so, she was ahead of her time.

Her influence was not limited to Broadway—on the contrary, Smith was one of the first to push for the collapse of the traditional boundaries between play and performer, and helped propel the success of the likes of Mike Daisey, Taylor Mac, Young Jean Lee, and, eventually, Lin-Manuel Miranda.

The rise of the solo voice was by no means entirely a Broadway phenomenon, but it was still a phenomenon that changed Broadway for good.

By 1996, a dancer called Savion Glover had arrived on Broadway in a show called *Bring in 'Da Noise, Bring in 'Da Funk.* This was no solo turn—it came with an entire company. But there was no question that its star, Glover, was a different kind of dancer, one who drew from his own internal voice, one whose feet could tap out a history of African American dance, a story of both appropriation and defiant self-expression. The show's director, George C. Wolfe, had found this dancing voice when he worked on *Jelly's Last Jam* in 1992, right before Wolfe would direct *Angels in America*. He might have been a dancer, but Glover was also a solo voice like none other who had come before; he changed forever what dancers would be allowed to do on Broadway.

By the time Glover had become a star, the rise of the original voice had become unstoppable. If only Gray had lived to see what he had helped put in motion.

3

1996: FIGHTING URBAN GENTRIFICATION AND PAYING RENT

It was April, but it was Christmas Eve.

It was cold out. It was beginning to snow. And people were dying.

On the stage of the Nederlander Theatre on West 41st Street, a scrappy Broadway theater rescued from dereliction on a block just south of Times Square that had hitherto resisted gentrification, the actor Anthony Rapp was playing a young filmmaker named Mark, sharing a loft in the East Village with his pal Roger, a songwriter, played by Adam Pascal. The two friends were starring in their own version of *La Boheme*.

Mark and Roger were too preoccupied with their own dramatic lives to know it, but their Manhattan version of La Vie Boheme, as lived in modestly priced digs in Alphabet City, was breathing its last gasp. Gentrification would soon take hold of every last inch of the island of Manhattan. Not that Mark and Roger knew what was coming.

Their world was one of landlords and home movies, searches for the perfect song, and worries about the fate of a vulnerable addict named Mimi and their HIV-positive friend, Angel. The Millennium was coming, and the apparent inability of America to adapt to the post-industrial economy had instilled fear in many. There was a possibility of transformation. But to Mark and Roger, children of the 1980s who had spit in the face of Nancy Reagan and refused to just say no, members of the first generation of Americans who had never known a world without the specter of AIDS and the first to worry that digital machines were killing what was left of human communication, this strange America felt more like a mysterious Twilight Zone.

"There is no future," they sang, "there is no past. I live this moment as my last."

Ironically, they'd become complicit in their own demise.

* * *

About a month before Jonathan Larson's *Rent* had opened at the Nederlander, the *New York Times* headline had screamed out from the Arts & Leisure section: "The Birth of a Theatrical Comet."

"It bust on the scene seemingly out of nowhere," the breathless piece about *Rent* began,[1] "this pulsing musical with the beat and cadences of the East Village."

Now it was questionable whether or not the East Village could really have been said to have its own beats and cadences, but there was no question that the rent there now was going up. Way up.

Especially since the New York City mayor Rudolph Giuliani, a fan of the notoriously racist and much-discredited "Broken Windows" theory of criminology, and his hard-driving commissioner of police, Bill Bratton, had been cleaning up the East Village, along with the rest of the island of Manhattan.

The mid-1990s saw the birth of a dramatic transformation in American society: the refusal of a new generation, the one known by the letter X, to follow their parents to the suburbs, and the reinvention of America's cities as coffeehouse-fueled, soon-to-be-digitized theme parks for the highly educated and the affluent. As technology was posed to reinvent the American landscape, a generation of consumers began to prize convenience, especially when combined with the seemingly artisan. More and more, the quotidian goods prized by an older generation were passed over by their children.

Gen Xers no longer wanted to be what they owned.

They wanted authentic experiences, not bulky household possessions, and they were willing to pay for them. They wanted emotional engagement in all things and at all times. They sure didn't want to be stuck in some nine-to-five suburban office-park, but they also didn't want to be stuck at home, either. They craved "third spaces," spots where you could work, network, *and* chill out, and entities like Starbucks soon would ride that desire to explosive growth and profits.

Chefs in Brooklyn or Chicago became the hottest celebrities; boutique was in; individuality, or at least the illusion thereof, took on a whole new meaning; and community building was starting to move online.

And Americans who had not been well served by the mainstream power structure were now demanding a new place at a more multicultural and omnisexual table; they were making their own communities within the very cities that had so scared their parents, whose savvier peers set about the business of trying to make money by making these cities safer for all these new urban professionals, and more receptive to all the money that they had to spend. There was plenty of irony to go around.

The gig economy was beginning to kick into gear, right here at the knife-edge of the Millennium.

Of course, most of the people who declared themselves to be against urban gentrification—especially the artists—promptly set about causing the very phenomenon they claimed to disdain. What could they do? They could not uneducate themselves nor throw away their humanities degrees in the same trash can as their parents' financial support, support fueled by a level of defined-benefit pensions that no subsequent generation ever would see again. They could not be expected to rot in the suburbs like their parents. So in one rough-hewn neighborhood after another, an artist would open a gallery, or a barista would import an espresso machine, or a real-estate developer would expose the high-beamed wood ceilings of an industrial loft and everything would change for good. Or for bad. It all depended on your point of view.

As *Rent* opened, Bratton and Giuliani had just parted ways: the ethics of the police commissioner's $350,000 book deal had reportedly provoked some mayoral skepticism, although it was widely assumed that the matter had a lot to do with Bratton getting more credit than the mayor for the reduction in crime in Manhattan during the early 1990s, and the inability of two giant egos peacefully to co-exist.

Still. By the spring of 1996, Giuliani and Bratton had waged relentless war on the drunks, the panhandlers, the graffiti artists, and the squeegee men, using a database called CompStat to target crime hot spots, a method that would be widely copied in other urban areas. They'd also gone after unlicensed nightclubs in Midtown by reviving the so-called New York City Cabaret Law, a regulation that banned dancing and that dated back to the era of Prohibition. That January, Bratton had appeared on the cover of *Time* magazine.[2] He could be seen there in a gumshoe raincoat—the skyline of Manhattan shimmering in the background. The headline reads, "Finally we're winning the war against crime. Here's why."

Bratton's methods would come to be seen as problematic in many ways, with their impact causing a serious spike in the number of African American men who found themselves thrown into prison, but the number of violent crimes in New York City also came down drastically under his watch. American cities would become safer, in fact as well as perception. White flight would begin to operate in reverse. And gentrification would explode in full and active force all over Manhattan.

And so with their occupants feeling newly safe being out and about on 41st Street, a no-go zone for nervous suburbanites just a few years before, limousines started pulling up to the Nederlander Theatre, anxious to see Rapp, Pascal, Daphne Rubin-Vega, and, hardly least, Idina Menzel making her Broadway debut as the performance artist Maureen Johnson. Taye Diggs, who would later marry a very famous Menzel, was on hand playing the small role of a mercurial landlord, Benjamin Coffin III, the encapsulation of the very behavior that *Rent* abhorred.

The creator of all these characters, Jonathan Larson, already was dead. His demise on the very brink of life-changing fame and fortune would prove to be one of the most devastating losses in Broadway history.

Larson, who was tall, broad-shouldered, and had black curly hair, had started this musical some seven years previously, borrowing ideas and sources but basically drawing from his own experience living in not-quite SoHo, waiting tables at the Moondance Diner, and trying to get a producer to back his shows. Like Mark, he'd made demo tape after demo tape to give to potential backers of his work. But he'd not had much luck.

Everything changed when a young playwright of Larson's recent acquaintance, Billy Aronson, a man from the Yale School of Drama whom Larson had known from working at Playwrights Horizons, suggested a contemporary musical based on Puccini's *La Boheme*.

As the two men sat on the roof-deck of Larson's walk-up apartment, Aronson argued to Larson that there were rich parallels to be explored between the Parisian Bohemians of the Left Bank and the arty denizens of the East Village. Larson immediately saw the logic of that idea, and he well knew that Broadway had not yet come up with a show that would appeal to a generation weaned on MTV. This, he figured, for he did not want for ambition, could be that show.

Larson lived on the West Side of Manhattan, not the East Village, where he sometimes was scared to go. But Larson was, you might say, among the last generation of artists who could truly have been said to be living *la vie boheme* on the actual island of Manhattan—he really did have a bath tub in his kitchen and a leaky roof, and he was across the street from a garbage-treatment plant. In the event of visitors to 508 Greenwich, Larson was obliged to throw the keys down to the street, a custom he would re-create in the musical he was about to write.

This was even as Giuliani and Bratton were sweeping away the hustlers, the panhandlers, the turnstile jumpers, and, especially, the addicts.

La Vie Boheme was a lifestyle Larson had chosen: He'd grown up in the decidedly non-bohemian environs of White Plains, New York.

The family home had been Tudor-style. Larson had developed an early affinity for Broadway musicals, heading into New York at a young age to see the likes of *Sweeney Todd*. He ended up in the theater program at Adelphi University on Long Island, where he became the star student. But he still hated being stuck in suburbia.

When Larson had moved into New York, his father, Allan, had been struck by how his son had, in essence, deliberately chosen a neighborhood similar to the one his grandfather, a Russian Jew, had worked so hard to escape.

Rent, then, had begun as a collaboration between Larson and Aronson, although the two parted ways during its gestation, with Larson telling Aronson he wanted to go it alone and promising his friend a check if the show happened to become a hit. By way of explanation, Aronson told the *New York Times* that the two had discovered they had different styles: "Mine was more an ironic, comic approach," Aronson said, "his was direct and gutsy."[3]

It had also become clear that Larson was the bigger talent. But his collaborative history, his affinity for input and teamwork, would create some trouble ahead. The following November, the dramaturg for *Rent*, a woman named Lynn M. Thomson, would twice file suit against Larson's estate (run by his father), claiming "authorship-in-collaboration" of at least a quarter of the final script of the musical. The evidence certainly suggested that Thomson had pored through countless drafts and notes, wrestling *Rent* into shape after its creator had died. She wanted both what she saw as adequate credit for the show's final form, and her share of worldwide royalties, estimated to have the potential of reaching $250 million.

In 1998, it was announced that the parties had settled; the terms were not disclosed. Thomson, it was revealed in the court proceedings, initially had received a flat fee of just $2,000 for her work on *Rent*.

The dispute with Larson—which raised the much broader question of where the role of the dramaturg ends and that of the author begins—would anticipate a similar dispute that occurred with *Hamilton*. Therein, members of the original Off-Broadway cast were successful in gaining a small royalty percentage of future grosses, after arguing that they had contributed lines and ideas to the final version of the show, following rehearsal exploration. But that still was years away. As with *Rent*, the issue was complicated and a consequence of a work unexpectedly reaping massive financial and popular success.

But as Larson struggled with the process of writing a musical, now without the help of Aronson, he could not have imagined anything of what actually came to pass.

Like the characters he would forge in *Rent*, Larson long had been living around the threat of AIDS, a disease with a heavy footprint in his neighborhood with its big population of gay men. He told his friends he wanted to write a show in celebration of those who had died young, people he had known, never of course imagining that he would himself die young.

Taking one of the most famous bicycle rides in Broadway history, Larson had first dropped off the materials for *Rent* in 1993 at the New York Theatre Workshop, which he'd decided would be a fine place to do the show. There had been a reading—attended by some producers—but the show had still been a mess, especially its second act. Larson, feeling intense self-created pressure, had then gone back to work on the piece. Meanwhile, the artistic director of that theater, James C. Nicola, had hired a man named Michael Greif to direct— and, of necessity, to shape—the piece. In 1996, the New York Theatre Workshop scheduled an Off-Broadway production.

But on the morning of the first preview performance Off-Broadway, Larson died at the age of 35, a victim of an aortic dissection, long misdiagnosed as influenza or stress.

Returning home late at night, Larson's roommate, Brian Carmody, had found him dead on the kitchen floor. Larson had apparently collapsed while trying to make some tea. He had just completed an interview with the *New York Times*. He likely had some sense that his life was on the cusp of enormous change, but he still could not possibly have anticipated what soon would happen with his *Rent*.

The very young cast of the show were so shocked by Larson's death that the first preview became, in essence, the most emotional of table readings: songs from the show were sung, and it seemed to those present that it was as if Larson had composed the score for his own funeral. How else could you explain one line in the song that formed the emotional core of the show, "Seasons of Love?" "Five hundred twenty-five thousand six hundred minutes," Larson had written, presumably after pecking away on his calculator. "How do you figure a last year on earth?"

How indeed, when that last year would turn out to belong to one of your own?

Certainly, it was clear to everyone that the American theatre now would be denied the future fruits of the talent of a young composer of singular gifts. *Rent* was both a beginning and, self-evidently, a final bow.

But Larson's parents were determined that their son's work should find the largest possible audience. So with the help of Greif and those rave reviews, they pushed onwards to the Nederlander. Producers circled the show: but Kevin McCollum, who then was 34, and Jeffrey Seller, who was 31, had the inside track, having paid part of the costs at the New York Theatre Workshop. Seller would go on to produce *Hamilton*.

Death infused *Rent* from the musical's very conception. But then so did advice for life.

Larson's score was about living in, and for, the moment: "There's only us," he wrote. "There's only this. Forget regret. Or life is yours to miss."

In 2016, when *Hamilton* won eleven Tony Awards, the ceremony would be held on an evening that followed hard on the worst mass shooting in American history. In response, the cast would sing a much-loved anthem from *Rent*, "No Day But Today." Lin-Manuel Miranda would write a speech consciously evoking the most famous song in *Rent*, a collective statement of solidarity called "Seasons of Love," a song so abidingly powerful as to be taken and owned by succeeding generations of show choirs and musical ensembles.

That night, as on all others, those involved in *Hamilton* well knew that, for a generation of young theatergoers, Larson's music had been a suit of armor against the ravages of the ongoing AIDS crisis, and the widespread fear of exactly what was promised by the impending Millennium.

Within weeks of its Broadway opening, *Rent* had achieved what almost no Broadway show—save for *A Chorus Line*—had previously managed: a cover package in *Newsweek*.[4]

The writer of the lead article, the late Jack Kroll, homed in on one particular scene in the musical as emblematic of its identity as the talisman of 1990s culture: the scene where Roger and Mimi, out together at a club, each discover that the other is HIV positive, after both their reminder beepers for an AZT dose go off at the same time.

"Clinch. Love duet," Kroll wrote, reminding his mainstream American readers that Puccini's Mimi had been racked by a different plague in a different time, tuberculosis. You could argue that Kroll's reaction was offensive—or even that the scene in the musical was open to a similar charge of emotional manipulation. Or you could argue that using the dose of a prescription drug designed to combat the onset of a fatal disease as a sensual act of bonding was a radical act of affirmation. Either way, no American musical had ever contained such a scene.

That first paragraph in the cover story of a newsweekly with massive power and circulation also was a reminder of how the reaction to AIDS had changed in the years since *Angels in America* and certainly since Larry Kramer's *The Normal Heart*. The HIV Positive had, it seemed, achieved a certain level of street credibility, a level of bohemian chic. And it mostly was because of *Rent*.

Larson's death, of course, had made the *Rent* story even more striking, emotional, and media-friendly. So much so, in fact, that some of his friends worried that the man they loved would be subsumed in history by the musical of his own creation. But a look at the press coverage of the time reveals a reaction not dissimilar to the one enjoyed by *Hamilton* two decades later.

Rightly or wrongly, *Rent* was perceived as an explosion of youthful talent, an entrée for the young audiences that Broadway was still finding elusive (at least at the prices it preferred to charge) and, all in all, a game changer.

As John Guare noted in a savvy article in *Vogue*,[5] the American musical in the Reagan-Bush era had taken what the playwright called "a somnolent detour" to the London of dancing felines and crashing chandeliers. *Rent* was so different that it made some of the other new musicals in that season look either quaint (hello, *State Fair*), or utterly ridiculous.

One such poorly timed show was *Big*, a new family-oriented musical based on the hit 1988 Tom Hanks film about a 13-year-old boy who wakes up in the body of a 30-year-old man, and a flop that, as *Rent* built its own mythology, often was given the role of Old Broadway, representing that which *Rent* and all it stood for was sweeping away.

Big, which featured a book by John Weidman and a pop Broadway score by Richard Maltby and David Shire, had the misfortune to schedule its opening one day before *Rent* arrived on Broadway. *Big* had cost $10.3 million, an enormous sum for a Broadway musical at the time, and came replete with a massive set that included a re-creation of the Port Authority bus terminal and what appeared to be a life-sized rollercoaster.[6] But it struggled to recapture the emotional vulnerability and big heart that fans of the film had adored; the actors seemed lost in the massive production.

Big also had negotiated a sponsorship agreement with the upscale toy emporium FAO Schwartz, the location of one of the most famous scenes in the source film. The much-criticized agreement led *Big* to feature scenes set in a grand re-creation of the toy store itself—an uncomfortable merging of art and commerce that could not have contrasted more sharply with the exciting, anti-establishment Bohemians who were prowling around in *Rent*, just a few blocks away.

At one point in the fraught Detroit tryout of *Big*, which did not go smoothly, a character was heard to declaim, of FAO Schwartz, "Is this some kind of store or what?" The toy store had paid more than $1 million for that privilege. And it looked like product placement.

Whereas *Rent* celebrated the East Village, *Big* seemed to belong to the suburbs. Where *Rent* was diverse in both casting and narrative, *Big* was a fantasy story centered on a straight white male. In short, fairly or not, *Big* came off as overproduced, old-fashioned, and out of touch in every way with where everything now was going. It was dismissed by most critics. And the show lost a fortune.

In the 1990s, an expansion-minded FAO Schwartz had opened 40 stores, fueled in no small measure by the publicity from *Big* (the movie, not the musical). By 2015, those stores all had closed. Even the famous flagship toy store on Fifth Avenue had finally disappeared, a victim of cutthroat competition from online retailing. *Big* the musical soon disappeared from most memories.

But *Rent*, it seemed to be clear, belonged in the rarified company of *Hair* and *A Chorus Line*, as one of the shows that dared to take a massive leap and changed Broadway forever.

"In an age when almost every show is predigested and presold by the media long before the public can decide for itself," the critic Frank Rich had written,[7] devoting his *New York Times* Op-Ed column to the show, following the Off-Broadway production, "the truly spontaneous pop-culture phenomenon is almost extinct." He continued: "But not quite. Two weeks ago, at a 150-seat theater in the East Village, a rock opera called 'Rent,' written and performed by unknowns, came out of nowhere to earn the most ecstatic raves of any American musical in the two decades since 'A Chorus Line.' And now the world is rushing to catch up."

No doubt the world was also doing other things—but this still was very much what Broadway's power brokers felt about *Rent.*

Kroll, meanwhile, rightly noted that *Hair, A Chorus Line*, and *Rent* all had featured "marginal Americans—1960s flower-children, the blue-collar gypsy dancers of Broadway, and now in *Rent*, the young people who follow a dream of art in a cold time for spirit and body."[8] All of that was defensible, and became very much part of the potent

Rent mythology, assuming you overlooked the inconvenient truth that Larson had, in reality, chosen his existence on the margins, and that, by dint of that choice, it thus wasn't really a life on the margins at all.

That did not matter. Stephen Sondheim was already among his biggest fans—years later, the guru of the Broadway musical would extend similar advice and a blessing to Lin-Manuel Miranda—but in the *Rent* gestation period, Sondheim was ready to go to bat for Larson whenever he could.

Larson had struggled for years, but he still could not have claimed to be living on the economic or the cultural margins. People had been playing him attention from very early in career. His potential was known; in reality, his biggest enemies were his own doubts and fears.

That said, *Rent* was one of the first Broadway musicals, and the first megahit, to feature a diverse cast and a plethora of openly gay characters. The smarter producers who had lost out on the bidding war immediately realized that here was the rare show that truly could change the demographic of who went to a Broadway show. A lot of shows in development were about to look very old-fashioned.

It is easy now to forget the level of hype that greeted the *Rent* opening: the 21 TV crews at the Nederlander from all over the globe; the A-listers like Steven Spielberg, Al Pacino, Tom Cruise, and Nicole Kidman all clamoring for tickets; the $1 million payment by David Geffen in return for the chance to make the original cast recording; Jody Whatley's (and Whitney Houston's) stated desire to record one of the show's hit songs; and the furious bidding rights (bids expected at more than $3.75 million!) for a movie that would not actually get made until 2005, and then would open with mixed-to-weak reviews.

Backstage, celebrities like Mel Gibson and Jodie Foster would sign what *US Magazine* described as a "kind of Broadway Wailing Wall."[9] Emotions were running that high.

Through all of that, Seller and McCollum shrewdly positioned themselves as the antiproducer producers, the young mavericks, the suits without a suit, the scrappy entrepreneurs who were not interested in limos and who did not have names that would guarantee them a table at Joe Allen. They claimed not to be motivated by profit but by a shared desire to challenge the mainstream, to reinvent it from the inside. They had a brilliant strategy and it was at least partly true. For now.

Seller and McCollum talked to any reporter who would listen about the seats in the first two rows, all priced at $20 and reserved for day-of-performance buyers, thus guaranteeing a daily line of interested young people at the box office. Throughout that summer, lines of people seeking one of those 34 available seats in the front would start forming as early as 6 a.m., with some *Rent* groupies showing up in the line as often as three times per week. Relationships developed in the line that would snake all day down 41st Street, a living, breathing, unpaid act of branding.

In the performances, the lucky $20 people—usually younger, noisier, and dressed very differently from those in the rows behind— would stand out. They'd scream the loudest of anyone, and they'd remind the people behind them that this was a cool experience.

But the top price for *Rent* was still a hefty $67.50. Seller and McCollum were still Broadway producers who wanted to make money; this was still Broadway. It was not the East Village.

The similarities between the contemporaneous impacts of *Rent* and *Hamilton* are obvious. But the full extent of the causal relationship between these two shows ranges far more deeply.

In a telling interview with Kroll, Greif, the director of *Rent*, revealed something when he said, describing his influence on the piece: "I was anxious to neutralize Jonathan's emotionalism and bring in some irony."

Greif did not stop there.

"Jonathan was such a wet guy emotionally," Greif said to Kroll. "He was exuberant, childish in all the good and bad ways. He had this enormous capacity for joy. He'd write a song and say, 'I love it,' and I'd say, 'Guess what? I don't.'"[10]

Read between the lines and you intuit that it was Greif, whom few would describe as emotionally wet, who provided the cool discipline and structure that gave the show the edge and attitude that made it famous. To attract young people (and people who still defined themselves as young people) with money, the characters had to be just a little terrifying. Not unlike the pre-Giuliani East Village. And they had to be just elusive and exotic enough to be worth that $67.50 per ticket. They could not just be emotional wells.

Meanwhile, it was Larson's emotional "wetness," another way of referring to Larson's romanticism, that, in a revolutionary musical, actually made *Rent* more mainstream than was immediately obvious to anyone reading the masses of press coverage. The songs—and the score of *Rent* is stacked with love songs—almost burst with melody and sentiment: "I'll Cover You," "Without You," "Seasons of Love."

Rich saw this right from the start: "For all the talk about how *Rent* speaks for the cyber-AIDS-Doc-Martens Generation X of Alphabet City," he wrote,[11] rightly, "Mr. Larson's songs are bigger than their milieu."

Precisely. You could construe the word "bigger" in many different ways, of course. But Rich quoted Sondheim describing the *Rent* score as "generous music," by which the great and paternalistic composer really meant that Larson had merged his own musical voice with the time-tested traditions of the Broadway composition (including, of course, Sondheim's own work; Larson liked to mimic his idol's lyrical precision). Sondheim saw that Larson wasn't repudiating. On the contrary, he was building. Taking something to the next level and offering it to a new audience.

"Generous music," of course, also would be an apt description of Miranda's score for *Hamilton*.

Generous music took care of those listening: even those far outside of the demographic of the composer. Once the audience was inside the Nederlander Theater, their experience was as traditional as it was revolutionary, a seeming paradox that Miranda also learned from Larson. *Rent* was excitingly billed as a rock opera; the truth was that relatively little of its score truly qualified as rock music, just as *Hamilton* hardly would confine itself to hip-hop. Once you were inside the theater, both shows would be a lot more accessible than you had realized. You would be able to congratulate yourself on the progressive nature of your own eclectic tastes. And you'd feel safe.

Kroll had it right when he pointed out that Larson had figured out a contemporary take on sentimentality or, to put that another way, Larson had managed to make sentimentality cool again. "Every generation has to invent its version of Paris in the twenties," Guare would write.[12] "And Larson does for his what Fitzgerald and Hemingway did for theirs."

"*Rent* dares you to feel sentimental,"[13] Kroll wrote, "showing how sentimentality can be turned into an exultant sweetness without which life is such a grim mechanism."

Still, it is easy to forget that no one previously had written a Broadway musical centered on what Rich described as "the multicultural, the multisexual, the homeless, the sick," all voices that would be given, and demand for themselves, much more prominence in the decades that followed. Larson hadn't so much sentimentalized these dispossessed Americans as given them voice—or, more accurately, a cascade of beautiful melodies wherein they could express their hopes and dreams, their seasons of love.

As John Sullivan would note in *American Theatre* magazine the summer after the opening of *Rent*, Larson had indeed been concerned with gentrification, but he expanded the notion of such to include "commercial encroachment into what we may refer to as our Bohemia of the mind—the private domain in which personal character and style are defined."[14]

To put all that another way, Larson had written something radical without doing what most Broadway radicals before him had felt obliged to do: to rip apart the traditional.

And he'd understood another timeless facet of the American musical: its inescapable relationship with optimism.

When Mimi came back to life, her fever broken and her recovery assured, *Rent* offered hope for anyone watching the demise of someone they loved—from AIDS, most certainly, but not exclusively.

Rent was a politically assertive show but its preferred weapons of change were of the heart. And thus it fit its form—not just aesthetically but from a business point of view. The heart always has sold the most tickets.

At the time, *Rent* was seen by the more discriminating observers as a great force of American unification—an ensemble piece that advocated for a pluralistic America at a nervous, pre-Millennial time of fear and division, most times being seen contemporaneously as times of fear and division. At one point in the show's gestation and rewriting process at the nonprofit New York Theatre Workshop, which really did most of the work for the commercial production that later would reap the rewards intensifying a new model, Larson had been pressured to say what the show was about in a single sentence.

He had written: "*Rent* is about a community celebrating life in the face of death and AIDS at the turn of the century."[15]

His characters had wanted to define themselves, terrified that some commercial entity would otherwise do the job for them. They all were a version of Larson himself. The actors who played them would have influential lives.

In 2018, Rapp (who had been one of only two gay actors in the original cast) would, with careful but forthright words, accuse the actor Kevin Spacey of molesting him when Rapp was 14 years old (in 1986), a full decade before *Rent*. The accusations, which became global news and were typically reported with a reminder of Rapp's subsequent role in *Rent,* would become a crucial part of the momentum of the so-called #MeToo movement.

"Larson's ability to infuse lyrical, wide-eyed optimism into the darker realities of contemporary life—homelessness, AIDS, dog-eat-dog capitalism,"[16] wrote John Istel in an especially clear-eyed and critical piece in *American Theatre* in the summer of 1996, "is exactly what helped move the musical uptown."

Exactly. And there is no shame in sentimentality. Not when you are writing a commercial musical. *Rent* could not compete with *Angels in America* when it came to sociohistorical context, not with *The*

Normal Heart when it came to raw rage. But it sold many more tickets than either of those two productions. And Larson definitely saw with a clear artistic eye the coming encroachment of technology on our lives, how our electronic devices soon would alienate us, one human being, Bohemian or otherwise, from another.

In 2017, Jeffrey Seller found himself being asked to contextualize *Hamilton* in terms of other revolutionary shows. How did it compare to *Rent*?

"Most shows have a negligible impact on American culture," the now-older producer said. "*Rent* did have an impact on American culture. It affected the everyday lives of people. *Rent* saved young people from suicide. It helped young people come out of the closet. But the appeal of *Rent* was for young people. People over 40 just didn't understand why they didn't just pay the rent. As people got older they enjoyed it less. But *Hamilton* has an appeal as powerful for the 70-year-old as for the 13-year-old and we have never seen that before."[17]

He was right. But that was all yet to come.

4

1997: THE LION KING ROARS AND THE FAMILY RETURNS TO BROADWAY

Leonardo DiCaprio put his fingers to his lips. "Shhh," he said, "give me your hand. Close your eyes. Step up."

By the time Kate Winslet had opened them, she was at the bow of a ship sailed by James Cameron at a cost of $200 million, at the time the largest amount of money ever spent on a single motion picture. "I'm flying," she said, as the camera panned around Cameron's costly facsimile of R.M.S. *Titanic*, a metaphoric flourish for an ecstatic moment. Strings, an Irish flute, and the high notes of Celine Dion all combined for a scene that would be viewed as among the most spectacularly romantic of all time.

Cameron's investors had spent their money well. With its story of love across the divides of class and wealth, *Titanic* would become the first movie ever to gross $1 billion, eventually pulling in close to double that across the world.

1997 was a year of intense emotional spectacle. In July, Gianni Versace had been shot dead by a killer named Andrew Cunanan. The following month, Americans had looked across the Atlantic at a nation in mourning, following the death of Diana, Princess of Wales, caused by a horrific car crash in Paris; it was to be a crisis for the British monarchy, whose steely stoicism in the face of a crisis did not do enough to nourish a grieving populace nor the media that fueled the intensity of a nation's tears. Diana's funeral had been watched by 2 billion people, including, it seemed, a hefty portion of the population of the United States.

But the year also brought moments of multicultural reconciliation: Bill Clinton, starting his second term, declared himself to be president of all the American people; later that spring he would issue an apology to the unknowing victims of the morally bankrupt Tuskegee Syphilis Experiment. And in June, Bloomsbury Publishing would release in London a fantastical adventure by an unknown writer called *Harry Potter and the Philosopher's Stone*. Although Americans would not catch on until at least the following year, this would be the beginning of a series that would revolutionize the relationship of books and families, and set in motion an international cultural phenomenon that not only would gross billions of dollars through a series of titanically successful films, but would unify the mostly young fans of its hero all across the globe. In the late 1990s, there were those who understood the magic meaning of life and there were the poor Muggles. No sooner had a page of a Harry Potter book been turned, than a spectacular movie would begin to play in the reader's mind.

In the midst of the great renaissance of culture for the whole family, there was *The Lion King*. A project of a nascent arm of the Walt Disney Company called Disney Theatricals, *The Lion King* would be acknowledged as one of the greatest musicals of all time, a family show with a level of spectacle still capable of stunning adults and children more than 20 years after its initial opening.

The Lion King would still be roaring over Times Square in 2018, routinely grossing in excess of $2 million per week, even suggesting to some minds that it would never actually need to close. Disney Theatricals had hit pay dirt—it had forged a blockbuster hit at the box office that was also a critical success, a seriously arty work with enough invention and indie cred to satisfy the most discriminating urbanite, but also a show with more than its share of romantic ballads in a cultural moment that seemed obsessed with them: "Can You

Feel the Love Tonight?" easily could have been featured in *Titanic*. In essence, it was another version of "My Heart Will Go On."

Like *Rent, The Lion King* was ahead of the curve when it came to a rapidly diversifying America: the cast of the show was multiethnic and multinational. The show was both set in Africa and featured a number of real Africans. The ensemble was predominantly cast with African Americans, many of whom seemed to assume the form and grace of the very earth itself. Here, in fact, was the first Broadway megamusical to at once feel like it was global, environmental, and kid-friendly. It was expected merely to be an adaptation of a highly successful animated film featuring songs by Elton John, but it would become a genuine cultural phenomenon.

In fact, it would become the first Broadway musical to gross $1 billion, just like *Titanic*.

And it was all down to a woman named Julie Taymor.

The woman who would further transform the Broadway musical had grown up near Boston, studied in Paris and at Oberlin College in Ohio, and, during her early twenties, worked extensively in Bali, Indonesia. When she returned to the United States in 1978, Taymor developed an enviable reputation among the cultural cognoscenti for her work with masks and puppets. She specialized in intense, avant-garde works with titles like *The Transposed Heads, Juan Darien*, and *Haggadah*. As her career developed, she became known for directing opera, initially in Japan, and then made some forays into the world of art films.

In 1991, Taymor was designated an early MacArthur Foundation "genius." By the time she was in her mid-forties, Taymor already had been the subject of a laudatory and spectacularly illustrated book-length study co-authored by Eileen Blumenthal and Taymor herself.

It was called *Julie Taymor, Playing with Fire*. As Taymor's star rose, there would be several editions.

Blumenthal focused in on Taymor as a fertilizer, an assimilator (but not in any pejorative sense), a connector of myriad performance cultures, a conceiver of huge ideas never afraid of either national or cultural borders, a theater artist as far removed from the conventions of Broadway as it was possible for any theater artist to be. By page seven, Blumenthal already had described Taymor as a genius.

"Taymor's work," Blumenthal wrote,[1] "is not so much eclectic as it is cross-bred. She draws on an enormous pool of forms, genres, traditions. She grasps the center of each form, how it works in its home context, and how it might resonate somewhere else. She conceives new theatrical organisms, combining trails from the most disparate of sources to bring original hybrids to life."

In the academic language of the 1990s—an era before the tricky matters of cultural appropriation came to the fore, before the moment when the race of the artist came to matter as much as the artist's work—Taymor was lauded as a "genetic engineer," a "cross-breeder," an "omnivorous" polyglot with a distinct visual language entirely of her own, rooted in puppets, masks, and a profound understanding of both human representation and human psychology.

Perfect, it turned out, for the needs of Disney, which wanted to stake a claim to Broadway before any other movie studio beat them to the mark.

Disney Theatricals had been founded in 1993 after the studio had sat by and watched a series of Cameron Mackintosh–produced blockbusters of European origin—*Cats, Les Miserables, Phantom of the Opera, Miss Saigon*—return the kind of profits that previously had been associated only with major motion pictures. The unit's first project, it was decided, would be a live version of the animated movie *Beauty and the Beast*.

When *Beauty and the Beast* had been released as a film in 1991, it was immediately obvious that it had a Broadway-quality score, penned by Alan Menken and Howard Ashman (Ashman, alas, had died during the making of the film). The movie—based, of course, on the familiar fairy tale—had contained eight musical numbers. It was part of the so-called renaissance of Disney's animated franchise: a successful era that had begun with *The Little Mermaid* (which had won two Academy Awards), continued with *The Rescuers Down Under*, and then moved on to *Beauty and the Beast*, which had been the first-ever animated film to be nominated for the best picture category of the Academy Awards (it lost out to *The Silence of the Lambs*). *Aladdin* (1992) and *The Lion King* (1994) would follow. *The Lion King*, a monster success as a movie with a worldwide gross of $766 million, would become one of the highest-grossing films of all time.

The incredible popularity of the film was often forgotten in discussions of the live show that followed: the movie, which had a staggering amount of title awareness among its target audience, offered an incomparable launching pad for the musical that shared its name. That was in no small part why its success proved so challenging to replicate.

Those Broadway-like scores had been a crucial part of the renaissance. Disney had discovered Ashman and Menken after the two had worked on a satirical Off-Broadway show called *Little Shop of Horrors*, which was co-produced by David Geffen and British producer Cameron Mackintosh, whose production of *Cats* would make its Broadway premiere later that year uptown at the Winter Garden Theater. At the time when the Disney call came, Ashman was depressed about his prospects on Broadway: his musical *Smile*, penned with the composer Marvin Hamlisch, had been a disaster. Ashman persuaded Menken to travel with him out west to work on *The Little Mermaid*. As Menken would later recount,[2] Ashman would come up with the idea of turning Ursula, the antagonist of the story, into a classic Disney villain; he would render the crab, Sebastian, as Trinidadian; and the two composers would essentially rewrite a song from *Little Shop of Horrors*, "Somewhere That's Green," and retitle it for broader appeal. It became "Part of Your World."

They used most of the same techniques for *Beauty and the Beast*. In essence, this meant treating the animated film as if it were a stage musical.

Alas, Ashman died from AIDS on March 14, 1991, putting an end to one of most extraordinary collaborations in the entire history of the Broadway musical. When Ashman died, the first screening of the recently completed *Little Mermaid* was just four days away. It was a demise that strangely echoed what soon would happen with Jonathan Larson, just a few years later.

Menken had not known about his partner's illness until 1990—Oscar night, in fact, for *The Little Mermaid.*

"He just said, 'When we get back to New York we have to have a talk,'" Menken would recall years later. "That was what he said. I did not want to have a talk. … It was like my brain had a protective device. All these symptoms had been happening. I knew that. It was a terrible time. But I still didn't know it. Or want to know it."[3]

When *Beauty and the Beast* was made into a stage musical, Menken would include a song for his dear friend and partner in what most people would consider the three greatest animated musicals of all time. In *Beauty and the Beast*, there is song called "Home." It was based on a song Menken had composed for Ashman, "My Old Friend."

In Disney lore, the studio's interest in Broadway was sparked by a Frank Rich end-of-year column in the *New York Times*, wherein the powerful critic, writing under the subheading "The Hit That Got Away," said that "the best Broadway musical score of 1991 was that written by Alan Menken and Howard Ashman for the Disney animated musical *Beauty and the Beast*."[4]

Michael Eisner, who then was running Disney, read that column and, in essence, ordered up a Broadway musical. Disney certainly had experience in live entertainment at its theme parks and in its licensed ice-shows, but it had not ventured into the realm of full-blown Broadway musicals, not least because the perception long had been that potential returns were limited. But Mackintosh's successes had changed that perception. It had become clear to Disney that there were millions of dollars to be made on Broadway

Obviously, the path of least resistance—and maybe the best idea—would be to basically stick the animated movie on a stage, adding in a few real humans for live musical performance, but very much retaining the fanciful, animated aesthetic and the lush, romantic sensibility of the original animated film. That would appear to have followed the Rich-Eisner prescription and that was pretty much what happened—to much popular success, even if critical reviews largely were negative.

Disney would tap Robert Lee Roth, a young director who had worked on shows in its theme parks. The production he directed would play for 5,461 performances and become the tenth-longest-running show in Broadway history.

Roth's production of *Beauty and the Beast*—replete with broad characterizations of such figures as the comic villain Gaston—would feature a variety of tricks, featuring Chip, the talking cup from the film who'd be given his own on-stage tray. Lumiere, a servant, would sprout candles from his fingers. And the production would become famous for its *Fantasia*-like centerpiece re-creating the signature "Be My Guest" number from the film. On stage, ensemble members would essay the roles of dancing cutlery.

Meanwhile, audience members would coo at bookish Belle and her emotionally tortured but thoroughly desirable Beast, whose transformation into a handsome prince would be a spinning coup de théâtre, although entirely in the pallet of the original animation.

Disney would be amply rewarded. But the producers at Disney Theatricals, now led by Thomas Schumacher, also had the sense that they could not just do the same thing again.

The next musical on their docket was *The Lion King*, an even bigger hit on film than *Beauty and the Beast*, and a piece that, given its setting in the African jungle and its cast of animated wild animals, presented a far more formidable set of challenges when it came to theatrical adaptation. Rich hadn't been talking *The Lion King* when it came to making a stage musical: at first glance, *The Lion King* looked like inherently untheatrical material. There were hundreds of animals in the movie, for one thing, not to mention an elephant graveyard and a wildebeest stampede.

Schumacher had first become aware of Taymor after her production of a 1985 piece called *Liberty's Taken*, a musical-theatre piece with a score by Elliot Goldenthal (who would become both a collaborator and a life partner) that Taymor had co-written (with David Sueshof) and that had been first produced at the Castle Hill Festival in Ipswich, Mass.

Drawing on both history and a picaresque novel, the work wanted to explore American identity, and, most specifically the convergence of fact and legend. Staged outdoors, the piece not only used unusual instrumentation but it featured a lot of Taymor's puppets—shadow puppets, rod puppets, hand puppets, and puppets on strings. There were also a lot of masks. The fearlessly eclectic piece, then, mixed forms, perspectives, and, crucially when it came to *The Lion King*, did so on an epic scale.

The show had been a big hit. Schumacher, who at that point was associate artistic director of the Los Angeles Olympic Festival, asked Taymor if she would bring the production to Los Angeles. But once she sent the details of the work to California, Schumacher decided it was too complicated to pull off.[5] He came to regret that choice. So after Schumacher rejoined his old colleague Peter Schneider and went to work for Disney Theatricals, and Taymor's name had been suggested by Stuart Oken, one of the early employees at Disney Theatricals, Schumacher approached Taymor again.

Taymor—who was always far more a populist than her early résumé would have implied—was excited to meet with Disney, especially since Schumacher told her that she should consider herself freed from the look and feel of the source movie. Disney had already decided that it wanted to produce a reprise of *Beauty and the Beast*, as in putting an animated movie on the stage—Disney wanted something from Taymor that would look and feel entirely original.

And that is what Disney got.

Taymor's first impulses had involved nontraditional venues—a massive spectacle, perhaps in an arena or maybe under a tent in the fashion of the Cirque du Soleil, a scrappy Canadian company that had been making huge inroads into massive, spectacle-based live entertainment. But Taymor was working for Disney—a phrase that rightly implies brand-driven focus, but also turned out to be a crucial force of creative discipline for so famously eclectic an artist. Eisner wanted a Broadway musical, period, staged in a legitimate Broadway house.

That was the gig. Period.

Taymor was given the freedom to develop her own story—to a point. This was a high-profile property and Disney was playing close attention to what was transpiring. Early in those conversations with the executives at Disney, Taymor floated the idea of setting Act 2 of *The Lion King* in Las Vegas, which at the time was exploding with new fantastical hotels, many of which were aimed at families. The Disney executives replied that the assignment required that Simba and his pals stay in Africa. The movie would have to retain that much of the movie. There were limits.

But Taymor had many excellent theatrical ideas, the most notable among them being the focus on the coming-of-age story at the center of *The Lion King*, the maturation of Simba, who in Taymor's head clearly became an amalgam of Hamlet and King Henry IV: he would have to earn his homecoming to Pride Rock before he could take up his rightful place at the top of the food chain. Two of the creatives from the film—the co-director Roger Allers and the co-writer Irene Mecchi—became involved.

The movie had five songs by Elton John and Tim Rice: "Circle of Life," "I Just Can't Wait to Be King," "Be Prepared," "Hakuna Matata," and, most famously, "Can You Feel the Love Tonight?" Not only was that number insufficient for a stage musical, but they clearly were Disney pop songs, and the work of two white, middle-aged British guys to boot. Taymor brought in the South African composer-performer Lebo M, known for his African choral music. There was even an existing album, *Rhythm of the Pridelands,* that Lebo M had recorded with Hans Zimmer and Marc Mancina. Much of the content of that album formed the basis of these crucial additions to the score—and since they required African instrumentation to be performed, they allowed Taymor to add African percussionists, kora and ethnic flute players to her wish list.

Taymor wanted to keep some of the lyrics in the original Zulu, so that meant importing performers from South Africa. And since her vision was for a visibly theatrical sense of the show's environment—

one in which the audience would be aware of the mechanics of the illusion even as they hopefully would be entranced by the illusion itself—Taymor decided to position these extra musicians in the theater's boxes, overlooking the stage and the dancers working to the choreography of Garth Fagan.

Why did *The Lion King* work so spectacularly well?

There were many reasons for its stunning success, not the least of which was the combination of the Disney producers, with their eye firmly on the wants and needs of the audience, the key to both longevity and profitability, with the creative fluidity of the mid-career Taymor.

In other words, Taymor had both liberty and guidance—the kind that is more easily granted by producers who had never known Broadway failure, which would inevitably follow for Disney Theatricals, who would later find out that it was hard when audiences expected every production to be comparable to *The Lion King*.

Unlike a financially strapped nonprofit, Disney also had the time and resources to fully develop *The Lion King* through both workshops and a full-blown tryout process, allowing Taymor the chance to try and refine her own ideas.

The show came with one particularly important and radical idea. Unlike almost every other Broadway musical, *The Lion King* reserved its greatest and most thrilling spectacle for its opening number— when a plethora of puppet recreations of African animals would parade down the aisles of the theater, delighting young children and thus their parents. This overt theatricality right at the opening—this sense of an environment being built before your eyes—allowed the audience, mollified that their money had not been spent in vain, to relax. And just as importantly, especially in the early days of the show, it sent out a signal that the movie should be banished from everyone's mind.

In essence, Taymor had used a theatrical language born in Asia to graft South African music and ecologically oriented iconography on to Elton John ballads and the kinds of cute two-dimensional characters you shoot for at a carnival game. It was of its moment and it was brilliant.

In the movie theater, you watched what already had been made. But *The Lion King* was to be a glorious piece of theatre, a world you saw built in real time, right before your children's eyes.

And it would be a very tough world to perform eight times a week: actors' backs would struggle with both the weight of the costumes and the requisite posture for anyone manipulating its puppets. When *Forbidden Broadway*, the satirical Off-Broadway show, decided to write a spoof sequence of the show, its maestro, Gerard Allesandrino, came up with "Can You Feel the Pain Tonight."

Disney also felt its share of pain during the out-of-town tryout in Minneapolis, where *The Lion King* opened on July 31, 1997. There were a variety of problems: the puppet elephant, known as Bertha, would not fit through the doors of the theater and the technical rehearsals proved to be so complicated that the first time the show was run from start to finish turned out to be before a paying, preview audience. But the response from the audience was euphoric, as was the case throughout the show's history.

The New York opening at the New Amsterdam Theatre on West 42nd Street (one block north of the Nederlander Theatre, the home of *Rent*) followed hard—bizarrely so, by today's standards—on the Minneapolis closing. John and Rice were there, as were Julie Andrews and Rosie O'Donnell. It's not atypical for an opening-night audience to burst into cheers—but what made *The Lion King* so unusual was that those cheers began at the end of an opening number that, in its depiction of animal life, managed to be as emotionally moving as it was thrilling. No show before or since had ever created so successful an opening number.

"The most emotional point in *The Lion King* is the rising of the sun, the sound of the voice, and the visibility of the people in the puppets,"[6] Taymor wrote. "And what that is—having experienced it all over the world from that first day in Minneapolis, when we all broke into tears because we couldn't believe the response of the audience—is DNA. It's in our DNA. It goes way back to the very first moment that someone took an inanimate object and made it come alive, a human being making the shadow of a rabbit on the wall with his hands. Grown men, bankers who don't even want to go to *The Lion King*, end up crying in the first five minutes, and there's no story yet—there's not even any English."

The reviews were ecstatic—the more discriminating critics having figured out that Taymor had managed to transcend two very different branches of the performing arts, avant-garde artistry and popular entertainment. It would take until *Hamilton* for such an achievement to be replicated.

* * *

At the end of her book-length description of the creative history of *The Lion King*, Taymor wrote, of Schumacher, Schneider, and Eisner: "I thank them for believing in my vision and backing it wholeheartedly."[7] She would not write that way about her experiences working on *Spider-Man: Turn Off the Dark*.

It is hard to overstate how much *The Lion King* transformed the extant Broadway notions of what was meant by family entertainment, and what was understood to be children's theatre.

To a far greater extent than with *Beauty and the Beast*, Disney always was careful to market *The Lion King* to adults, although it well knew that the family audience was its core. By so doing, it made the cost of the tickets appear more justifiable, as well as expanding the Broadway demographic. And the show had such visual appeal that, time and time again over the years, parents would be thrilled and empowered to discover that their young child was, in fact, capable of sitting through a full-length show, and surely could do so again. Maybe when they had children of their own.

Critics would look out over the years and swear they were watching families having their best night together ever.

The show thus became a must-see for anyone who appreciated artistry. In interviews, Taymor would frequently say some version of "it is not all about the spectacle."[8] Of course, it was all about the spectacle in many ways, but that is not to say that Taymor was entirely wrong. The emotional engagement was intense. It truly was about far more than the spectacle.

Disney Theatricals shrewdly had co-opted for Broadway the worlds of avant-garde, international performance festivals, opera, dance, and global spectacle. Americans had more disposable income and they were becoming more and more interested in spending that money not on stuff but on the kind of experience that could not be experienced anywhere else. So it went with *The Lion King.*

Looking back from years later, it is hard to imagine that the show would have survived without its use of African content and artists, its brilliant colliding of the rhythms and archetypes of a continent with accessible pop music. Had it not, it would have been accused of appropriation. And it would have seemed to belong to another, very different, era.

The Lion King also benefitted from another happy accident of timing: it arrived before widespread digitization in theatrical design, meaning that it had no visible digital technology to grow outmoded before an audience's eyes. It always felt hand-made, live, and thoroughly theatrical, and thus it functioned as an antidote to parents' growing alienation from their phone-addicted kids. And as that feeling of familial alienation grew over time, the show's appeal only intensified.

If *Rent* had featured "generous music," in Sondheim's phrase, *The Lion King* offered up generous spectacle. For everyone. And in service of the American family.

It was a visual extravaganza upon which even the most notorious aesthetic snob could not heap credible scorn, even though the smallest child would have no difficulty understanding what they were seeing. It was populist but avant-garde; epic but human; grand but intimate; hugely complex but seemingly as simple as pie. It utilized one of the most potent and universal of human stories: overcoming the loss of a parent and the subsequent assumption of adulthood with a symbolic nod from the one deceased. Audiences never tired of that theme, of course, because no one wearies of the hope that the people we've loved and lost are still there to take care of us, even if we cannot easily discern their form.

As Schumacher clearly saw, the show's emergent narrative was straight from the mythological theories of Joseph Campbell and connected to a plethora of primal myths. "These are fundamental elements of the human experience," he wrote in 2017,[9] "betrayal, redemption, acknowledgment and acceptance."

And this remarkable musical had all of the same criteria that would lead to *Hamilton*: invention, optimism, a forward-looking aesthetic, and a perception that there was something totally unique. It rewarded repeat viewings, being as the prime asset of the show was its theatricality. It had one heck of a wow factor. It had the best opening line in the history of the musical: "Nants ingonyama bagithi Baba!" as chanted by a baboon named Rafiki. And, helpfully for Disney, you did not need to know a lot of English to follow the plot.

Most important of all, *The Lion King* bathed its audience in comfort and hope. Like *Angels in America* and *Rent*, it insisted that the dead still can love, and that it is possible to walk yourself back from the brink and burst into renewed life.

The Lion King would run for more than twenty years on Broadway with no end in sight. It would play in 77 North American cities, and counting. There would be 23 international productions in 19 countries and nine languages. It would earn more than $7 billion at the box-office worldwide, and counting, a total that exceeds that of all of the *Star Wars* movies put together. And it would prove to be the high point of the creative lives of almost everyone involved, such a hit being almost impossible to replicate.

And it would function as a pinnacle—both financial and aesthetic—for every Broadway show that would follow.

5

1999: A SHORT-ORDER COOK WITH A LONG PATH TO BROADWAY

On a frigid December night in downtown Pittsburgh in 1999, the playwright August Wilson, a high school dropout and a former short-order cook in Minneapolis, was standing on a sidewalk, pacing up and down, and taking deep drags on a cigarette.

Wilson's latest play, *King Hedley II*, was about to open at the new Pittsburgh Public Theater in the playwright's home town. Wilson looked nervous but he had a friendly smile, reminding an out-of-town critic that he was about to see a work in progress.

King Hedley II would turn out to be a stunning piece of writing, under-appreciated in its moment. It would be a poetic howl of anguish at the horrors wrought on African American communities in the 1980s by guns, crime, economic blight, and urban neglect. *King Hedley II* would feel that night like the most passionate and surely the saddest work ever to come from the Bard of Pittsburgh. Here was an incomparably emotional indictment of America's abandonment of its crisis-strewn cities and their mostly African American populations. The play was set during the Reagan era, before most urban gentrification and renewal. But it was not as if all those urban problems had been solved by 1999. American cities—including Pittsburgh—still were awash with guns.

The whole play was set in the same rough-hewn backyard and there were just six characters on the stage, but *King Hedley II* hit that with almost unbearable force, especially here, just a few miles away from the neighborhood in which it was set.

The play's immensely likeable protagonist was a petty criminal poisoned by his own anger, envy, and financial devastation. The monarchial modifier was intended by Wilson to be bitterly ironic: this King Hedley ruled nothing beyond his own backyard. His kingdom mostly consisted of stolen refrigerators. But King Hedley talked like a gangster and, of course, he carried a gun. Everybody he knew, it seemed to him, carried a gun.

Not that solving problems with a gun was anything new in this nation, of course.

In 1804, in Weehawken, New Jersey, a verdant patch turned killing field just across the river from New York City, two of the brightest minds in the young United States had fought each other in a duel, a culmination of years of embittered competition. Alexander Hamilton and Aaron Burr both had carried Wogdon & Barton dueling pistols, famous for their concealed hair-triggers. After both men had provoked each other and implied that the duel was intended to end in their opponent's death, Burr mortally wounded Hamilton.

Hamilton was carried away from the site, got to see his wife just one more time, died the next day, and was buried in the churchyard at the corner of Wall Street and Broadway.

The pistols Hamilton and Burr used that day were made by London gunsmiths: they came from the very country from which Hamilton and Burr had spent their younger lives winning their independence. There was irony in Hamilton's death coming from a bullet fired from a British weapon, but wielded by a fellow American. It was death by friendly fire, but death just the same.

That would turn out to be a major theme of *King Hedley II*, indeed of all of this playwright's work. Here, Wilson was railing against how lethal firearms had crept (or, more accurately, been pushed by whites) inside the vulnerable and impoverished black communities living in America's cities. He had structured the play so that it felt partly like a Greek tragedy and partly like a western. *King Hedley II* ended with the most pathetic and self-destructive of shoot-outs, driven by the impulsive use of a gun, a scenario that would play out time and time again in American history over the years that followed. At the end of the play, the title character would be shot in the throat by his own mother, Ruby.

It was an accident. She had been aiming at another man.

Such were the ways guns ripped apart American families. The audience that night in Pittsburgh could not have anticipated the horrific shootings that would come to Sandy Hook or Margery Stoneman Douglas, but they did know about Columbine. That April, just a few months prior to the Pittsburgh opening of *King Hedley II*, two students named Eric Harris and Dylan Klebold had shot to death 12 students and one teacher in a high school in Jefferson County, Colorado. Thereafter, thoughts and prayers went out to the bereaved families and there were lamentations that troubled teenagers had such ready access to guns.

But nothing was done. Guns still were allowed to rip apart families, as, in America, they always had.

Some years after *King Hedley II* explored how guns thudded down through successive generations of Americans, fans of *Hamilton* would be told in song that Alexander Hamilton died on the same site where his teenage son, Phillip, also died, also at the hands of a gun, just three years before. Philip was trying to be like his father. One wasteful death had begat another, *Hamilton* would make clear. And this was precisely Wilson's point in *King Hedley II*, a play that ends with two successive generations of a family consumed by agony.

Pain is a constant in *King Hedley II*, a work that contained one of the most famous monologues its playwright would ever write. Written for a character named Tonya, pregnant with the title character's child and in despair over gun violence and the dearth of economic opportunity in the inner city, the speech would rail against gun culture and its ability to swallow and destroy the young.

"I ain't raising no kid to have somebody shoot him," Tonya would cry from the Public's stage, later that evening, demanding to be heard. "To have his friends shoot him. To have the police shoot him. Why I want to bring another life into this world that don't respect life? I don't want to raise no more babies when you got to fight to keep them alive."

The Pittsburgh Public was not the last stop for *King Hedley II* before Broadway—although the opening already was scheduled for the Virginia Theatre in the following spring. Before arriving in New York, *King Hedley II* still had to play the Goodman Theatre in Chicago, and then the Kennedy Center in Washington, DC. The cast and the guts of the production would remain the same each time, but the play would change a little with each new incarnation.

Wilson had figured out a whole new way to get plays to Broadway.

Over the previous decade, he'd built, in essence, a personal circuit of regional theaters that all were willing to stage successive episodes of his grand endeavor: a play reflecting the African American experience in each and every decade of the twentieth century. It would become known as the August Wilson Century Cycle and it would have a profound effect not only on the future diversity of the Great White Way but on the broader American culture. Broadway would become part of this unique achievement.

All but one of Wilson's cycle plays—*Ma Rainey's Black Bottom*, a story of exploitation and racial inequity in the music business of Chicago—would be set among the working-class denizens of the Hill District in Pittsburgh, where Wilson had been raised. He was the child of a remote white father (a German immigrant and a baker) and an African American mother. Close to his mother but frequently at odds with his violent-tempered father, Wilson grew up at 1727 Bedford Avenue and dropped out of school at the age of 15, having been wrongly accused of cheating. Thereafter, he'd educated himself in the local Carnegie Library.

Later on, Wilson joined the army. And by the 1970s, he was living in Minneapolis. It was there that Wilson started to write plays, beginning, after some experiments, with *Jitney*, a dramatization of the lives of six unregulated cab drivers in Pittsburgh. Wilson knew all about the city's jitney cabs, offering rides to a neighborhood that the official white cabdrivers were reluctant to serve. He had listened to the conversation of the drivers. He had laughed at their jokes and sensed their frustrations.

Unschooled in the way of the theater business but determined to learn dramatic structure, Wilson had penned *Jitney* in a fast-food restaurant in St. Paul. It would become the model for the plays that followed in one especially crucial way. "This was the first time,"[1] Wilson said of the play, when he was working on it again, many years later, "that I allowed my characters to talk and just say what they want. I didn't try to change it. The way black people talk is not always respected. But I tried for the first time to discover the poetry and the philosophical ideas that are couched in their minds."

King Hedley II, the show that was opening that night in Pittsburgh, was the eighth of those intensely poetic plays. As he walked around that night, Wilson could look back on *Joe Turner's Come and Gone* (set in 1911 and seen on Broadway in 1988), *Ma Rainey's Black Bottom* (1927 and 1984), *The Piano Lesson* (1936 and 1990), *Seven Guitars* (1948 and 1996), *Fences* (1957 and 1987), *Two Trains Running* (1969 and 1992), and *Jitney* (1977 and 2017, after an initial Off-Broadway run in 2000). In the years thereafter, there would be Broadway revivals of both *Fences* and *Ma Rainey,* and Denzel Washington, a huge fan of Wilson's work, would strive to get as many as Wilson's plays filmed as he possibly could.

Still in Wilson's head that night were the two bookends of the cycle: *Gem of the Ocean* (1904 and 2004) and *Radio Golf*, a play set in 1997 and produced on Broadway in 2007. Once all was said and done, no other playwright—beyond Neil Simon, anyway—would have managed to get so many plays to Broadway in the modern era.

For 20 years, Wilson and his work were constants on Broadway seasons. The entire cycle was an achievement without obvious peer. As John Lahr would later note,[2] Eugene O'Neill, arguably the greatest American-born playwright, had set out to write a nine-play cycle of his own, but in the end had managed to pen only two. Wilson forced his way through all ten.

The Broadway production of *Radio Golf* would turn out to be a posthumous staging. In August of 2005, Wilson, who then was just 60 years old, called a small group of theater critics in the major American cities that had supported his work. He told those critics—who had been startled to hear Wilson's voice on their phones—that that he had been diagnosed the previous June with liver cancer and that doctors had told him that his prognosis was poor. He was announcing his own imminent death. "It's not like poker," he said. "You can't throw your hand in."[3]

During those calls, Wilson also said that his life has been blessed and that he was ready to go. And that he was glad to have finished his cycle of plays—a cycle that had wrought substantial changes in so many aspects of American theatre.

Wilson's plays had built the careers of a substantial number of African American actors—a kind of one-man repertory company—who had been able to appear in not just a single Wilson play but half a dozen or more, thus supporting themselves for years. Virtually single-handedly, he had established both a regional and a Broadway market for poetic, humanistic dramas about the African American experience. And then there was this whole new way of getting plays to Broadway.

Beginning with *Ma Rainey's Black Bottom*, Wilson typically had followed a similar path.

His plays would begin at the Eugene O'Neill Theater Center in Waterford, Connecticut, where his friend, conduit, and mentor, the director Lloyd Richards, ran an incubator for new plays, prior to his death in 2006 at the age of 87. There, these embryonic Wilson works typically would start out being four (or maybe five) hours long, cheerfully rambling banquets of conversation ready for performance in front of a friendly audience. With Wilson in residence, they'd be read two or three times outdoors by a group of dedicated actors, on a rustic stage under an ancient copper-beech tree and among friends. Wilson's first significant play, *Jitney*, had arrived at the O'Neill through the festival's famous open-submission process—without which, it is entirely possible that Wilson's plays never would have seen the light of day—but was rejected. *Ma Rainey,* however, was accepted. Thereafter, new

Wilson works made regularly scheduled appearances at the O'Neill, where he would become a most favored son.

Over time, Wilson and Richards were joined by Benjamin Mordecai, who would become Wilson's producing partner. And from the O'Neill's bucolic setting by the Long Island Sound, the works typically would move to some successive combination of the Huntington Theatre in Boston, the Pittsburgh Public Theatre, the Seattle Repertory Theatre, Yale Repertory Theatre in New Haven, and the Goodman Theatre in Chicago. Wilson would go on the road to all those cities with his plays for up to a year, watching performance after performance, and, over that time, they'd be shaped and honed for Broadway.

Usually, there would be cuts. But on occasion, Wilson would be coaxed into writing additional monologues to please his favorite performers. Long monologues would become one of his signatures; these were tours-de-force for his beloved regular actors.

After this pre–New York tour of as long as a year, the plays would land on Broadway, the commercial producers thus benefiting from a preview period as chronologically extensive as it was geographically varied. This was an uncommonly long gestation period in front of an audience, and it worked time and time again, eventually establishing Wilson as far and away the most prolific Broadway playwright of his generation.

Wilson, though, could often be a harsh critic of those major regional institutions, which he saw as principally committed to the promotion of the culture and values of European-Americans. He was not afraid to say so even while his own works were in production there. "There's nothing wrong with a white theater doing a black play,"[4] he typically would say, "but that does not provide the black community with the cultural institutions that we need to develop our talent and our audience."[5] He fully understood that his own plays needed to be seen at the leading theaters in America, if they were to be made ready for Broadway. Nonetheless, throughout his life, he'd also try to build up theaters dedicated to the African American experience, whether that meant the Crossroads Theatre in New Brunswick, New Jersey, or the Congo Square Theatre in Chicago. He did the same in death: he asked that donations in his memory be made to those theaters, although it would not turn out to be enough to keep all those theaters alive in the long term.

"Black theater is alive ... it is vibrant ... it is vital," Wilson said in an address to the 11th Biennial Conference of Theatre Communications Group. "This is not a complaint. It is an advertisement."[6]

Looked at as a whole, Wilson's ten plays explored myriad themes. But Wilson kept returning time and time again to certain moral truths that he found to be self-evident. His explorations thereof would prove prescient.

One core Wilson truth was that everyone stands on the shoulders of those who have come before—any character in any of his plays who believed that they had done, and could further do, everything on their own was usually in for a come-uppance before the end of Act Two. Wilson's wiser, and more mystical, characters constantly remind their foolish brethren that happiness—salvation, even—was only available to those who paid homage to the ancestors.

A second core Wilsonian truth[7] was that doing the right thing— moral rectitude, you might say—was not always compatible with following the laws of the land. Sometimes, a righteous person had to break the law, which, in each and every one of these decades under his review, usually meant a law designed to favor the white man. At other points in the plays, characters had to learn to be willing to give up their power, their money, or both in order to do what was right.

In fact, most of Wilson's greatest monologues were composed either for characters declaring these truths, or characters, usually intensely self-loathing men, railing against them. Frustration and anger were a huge part of the Wilson oeuvre: characters like Levee in *Ma Rainey's Black Bottom*, Citizen in *Gem of the Ocean*, Troy in *Fences*, King Hedley II in his eponymous play, and Harmond Wilks in *Radio Golf* (to name just a few) would cry out their pain with an eloquence that no writer would soon match.

But if these plays all were the work, fundamentally, of a moralist, they did not lack compassion, and therein, at least in part, lay their appeal for Broadway audiences. Even Wilson's most misguided characters always were smart and fun to be around, and the pulsing dramatic pictures he painted of black life in Pittsburgh felt like vistas into a vibrant world that Broadway had ignored. And such was Wilson's profound and personal understanding of systemic racism, his audiences immediately intuited that he never fully blamed these misguided men. They have been wrong, but it was not their fault. Their main victims were their own selves.

In countless articles, lectures, and debates across the decades, Wilson would say that slavery had ripped apart the black family and unleashed the very demons that these characters would then try to combat in the plays that Wilson so gently and carefully would shepherd to Broadway. He would point out that restitution had not, and could not, ever adequately be made.

But what made his plays so distinctively similar was how Wilson combined that view with the belief that an individual could not serve his community, and certainly not himself, by using those historical truths to dodge personal responsibility. Thus his plays were at once an indictment of white America—whose sins extended throughout the twentieth century—and a moral primer for African Americans. But on Broadway, where Wilson understood the imperative to entertain, his audiences would come for comedy as well as instruction, for verbosity as well as rules and judgements. They'd hope to bathe in poetry and spectacular characterization, and, although some of the plays would prove to be more successful than others both with critics and at the box office, Wilson would rarely let them down. No matter whence they came.

To some degree, this great Broadway Century Cycle was an accident.

The very idea had come to Wilson only when he was already under way with his plays—when he wrote *Jitney*, for example, he had no plans for that work to represent a specific decade. And over the years, he often would express frustration with a stricture that he had, of course, imposed on himself. But it both disciplined the writer—once one decade was finished, he could move on to the next without having to justify his next choice—and branded the plays for Broadway in a way that no other writer had achieved. Neil Simon had used his own biography to structure a small number of comedies and there had, of course, been many Broadway prequels and sequels and thematic linkages. But no other artist had ever either attempted or achieved anything on the level of ten plays, all unspooling one after the other in a great rush of artistic greatness.

Wilson avoided writing about the major historical events of the twentieth century directly, although you can sometimes sense their echoes and consequences in his works. Most of his characters were just ordinary, hard-working, blue-collar Americans with a little time on their hands to talk. They remained on the periphery of major events, and thus they were a window into American lives hitherto unseen by most of the Broadway audience.

Part way through his task, Wilson decided that he would like to add a recurring character, Aunt Ester. She would come to matter greatly to Wilson, functioning within the cycle as an authorial, spiritual rock, and as the conscience of a community. Aunt Ester would become an ancestor who shifts shapes into a mythological presence. The character first is mentioned in *Two Trains Running*, the sixth of Wilson's plays and a work set in the 1960s. Therein she is described as being 349 years old and a spiritual healer. She is a further presence in *King Hedley II*, wherein she is said to have died at the age of 366, a victim of the violence that rages over the entire play. In the preface to the published edition of the work, Wilson referred to Aunt Ester as "the most significant persona of the cycle."[8] He went on to write that, in essence, every other character in every other play of his creation should be thought to be one of her children.

Aunt Ester appears in the flesh only in *Gem of the Ocean*, chronologically the first Wilson play in the cycle, although one of the last he would write. *Radio Golf*, the play set in the 1990s, would be penned later, but, by then, Wilson was dying and unable to complete his tried-and-true process of moving a play to Broadway. *Radio Golf* was rushed and unfinished. *Gem of the Ocean*, then, represents the culmination of what Wilson was trying to achieve at his mature peak. It is, in a way, the equivalent of William Shakespeare's *The Tempest*, although instead of functioning as a last play, it actually laid the groundwork for all that would follow.

Gem is set in Aunt Ester's house, its aged owner still hanging on to the bill of sale that sold her into slavery when she was just 12 years old. For the 1904 setting of the play had allowed Wilson finally to get within a single lifetime of slavery, the original sin of American society.

Aunt Ester may have finally made a physical appearance, but the main protagonist of *Gem* is Citizen Barlow, a young drifter with a past, who, like so many of the Wilson men who would follow him in successive years, seeks the cleansing of his soul. The antagonist is Caesar Wilks, a black police officer with a formidable sense of duty and rectitude but also caught up in the reality of being obliged to enforce racist laws. *Gem* was, at least in part, about the historical relationship of the African American community with the police. It prefigured much that was to come.

So did Aunt Ester, whose house is not just a refuge for the oppressed but a place to learn how to proceed into the future. It is, then, the epicenter of Wilson's overarching point of view: it represents the need for a restorative sanctuary from what slavery had plundered, as well as the need for a school of personal responsibility. Even in *Gem of the Ocean,* Aunt Ester is a mystical figure. She says she was born in 1619, the year that the first shipment of Africans arrived in the State of Virginia. She is a mythic continuance, an amalgam and personification of maternal figures dating back to mother Africa.

Her presence is referenced one last time.

In *Radio Golf*, the final Wilson play staged on Broadway after his death and a probing of the pernicious effects of gentrification on African American urban neighborhoods, Aunt Ester's house finally gets knocked down. Her presence is destroyed by a black developer who is too suffused with self-interest to pay the requisite attention to the ancestors, and who thus is failing not only his community but himself. For anyone who loved Wilson, watching the end of Aunt Ester felt a lot like watching the playwright's own demise, the death of a man who had done everything that anyone reasonably could have asked of him.

What did Broadway learn from Wilson?

The truth that diverse casting did not mean the loss of an audience; the existence of a broad audience for an epic feat of narrative; the crucial role of nonprofit theaters in the shaping and honing of new plays; the value of a storytelling genius and the abiding rarity thereof.

In this case, ten times over.

One day toward the end of his life, Wilson got up from a luncheon in Chicago. He was leaving early and he told a writer in the next seat that he had to fly off to California to try and schmooze a potential investor in *Radio Golf*. Broadway was a tough business, even for Wilson. Even after all these plays, even after such a cumulative achievement, he still could not count on the money being there. The spigots still needed to be loosened; it was lucky that Wilson was a charming man. Otherwise, there was a real possibility that *Radio Golf* would never have opened on Broadway.

At least Wilson lived long enough to find out that he would become the first African American to have a Broadway theater named in his honor—and that the lobby of the August Wilson Theatre would be filled with images and remembrances from all these plays as they journeyed down their long and winding paths to Broadway.

But he did not live long enough to see the first show staged there: *Jersey Boys*.

6
2001: GRIEF, METAMORPHOSES, AND TRANSFORMATION

Jed Bernstein, president of the Broadway League, had heard the mayor's message coming through loud and clear: reopen Broadway as fast as humanly possible.

Tuesday, September 11, 2001, had dawned sunny, clear, and seemingly benign. Until, that is, nineteen al-Qaeda terrorists hijacked four jet aircraft, two belonging to American Airlines and two belonging to United, quickly terrifying and murdering their unsuspecting passengers. One of those planes was then steered and crashed into the Pentagon in Washington, DC; one, following a brave onboard confrontation, would end up diving into the ground near Shanksville, Pennsylvania; and, on this morning no American ever would forget, two would be sent careening into the Twin Towers of the World Trade Center in Manhattan.

Within two hours, the day would become among the most infamous in a nation's history, forever to be known as 9/11, the digits to be dialed in case of a crisis transformed into a shorthand for a day of unspeakable horror.

In New York, the official death toll would reach 2,605 people, most of them people who had been working inside the Twin Towers, toiling above or on the floors where the planes hit, their workplaces soon falling to the earth, taking hundreds of human souls with them as they disappeared in a cloud of toxic dust.

September 11, 2001, almost shattered the spirit of New York, and the country; in the days that immediately followed, when the skies over America's great cities were eerily bereft of planes, it seemed that nothing ever would be the same, that the values of a great liberal democracy had been blown apart forever, that normalcy never would return, that life now involved living the unimaginable. On a national scale.

And aside from such macro concerns, the Broadway community was also faced with the most personal of crises. Almost everyone knew someone who had been impacted by the attack, and many knew someone who had been killed. TKTS, the half-price ticketing service, had maintained an outpost in the Twin Towers, although, given the early hour of the attacks, the counter was mercifully not yet open. But the site of the entire tragedy was just a long, stiff walk down one of New York's majestic avenues from Times Square. It was plenty near enough that, on that Tuesday morning, disheveled human figures covered head-to-toe in gray dust could be seen wandering outside its theaters.

Broadway had gone dark on September 11, just as an entire nation's consciousness had gone dark.

Everything stopped.

But before long, as the pain and confusion raged on, it became clear to Mayor Rudolph Giuliani and Schuyler G. Chapin, his commissioner of cultural affairs, that something had to be done quickly to restore at least some sense of continuance to the city, to avert a potential economic crisis that might cost artists and technicians their jobs and, in doing so, declare that the terrorist attacks had not done permanent damage to what Alexander Hamilton, in a musical made some years later, would call "the greatest city in the world." And so the word went out from city leadership to Bernstein at the League of American Theaters and Producers and then to the theater owners: reopen.

Preferably tonight.

Bernstein, who had seen members of Congress sing together on the steps of the Capitol in wounded Washington, DC, went to work, suggesting to the running shows that they think about maybe ending the night with "God Bless America" or some other soul-stirring song that would acknowledge the extraordinary nature of the moment and the sense of collective accomplishment from both the performers and the audience. The TKTS booth by Times Square was instructed to reopen on September 13, and reopen it did, to the relief of many of the tourists (and air crews) who had found themselves trapped in a city of grieving, unable to fly anywhere and wearied by their television screens playing constant reruns of death and destruction. Many could not have been happier to stand in line and go and see a show for half price.

Remarkably, on Thursday, September 13, just 48 hours after the attacks, all 23 Broadway theaters were up and running. It was—by any historical standards—an extraordinary public and private achievement and a crucial cog in the wheel of the city's recovery. Giuliani quickly expressed his thanks, announcing at a press conference that if anybody wanted to help New York, a really good way to do so would be to go and see a Broadway show.

On that night, all those shows featured a moment of silence prior to the performance. And, as is traditional in times of loss, all of the Broadway marquees dimmed their lights in tribute to the dead, a number that included 14 missing firefighters from the Midtown firehouse on Eighth Avenue and 48th Street, a firehouse so synonymous with Broadway that its denizens boasted of never missing a performance.

But the night really was about the living. Many of whom were finding their job almost impossible to perform.

Many of the problems faced by the shows on Broadway were practical—closed streets, delays in public transportation, restricted access to the bridges and tunnels on which Broadway relies, continued bomb threats in Times Square, increased security everywhere, the sense that another attack might be in the offing at any moment, and that Midtown Manhattan was at a high risk. But they also were psychological. It was no longer easy to trust crowds, nor was it easy to be in one. The attacks had shown that people were vulnerable where they never expected to be; no one knew how to judge their own vulnerability any more.

Many performers found themselves almost incapacitated by sadness, and many more had been hit by a sense of futility to go with their own grieving. All over the Theater District, there were worries that audiences would find these flashy Broadway shows too trivial, unfunny, and wholly out of sync with the new national mood.

The musical *Urinetown*, for example, had all of these problems compounded with the practical issue that the major critics—who see Broadway performances in advance of the official opening night—had mostly been scheduled for September 11. That meant *Urinetown*, which did not have a lot of cash in the bank, had to postpone its September 13 opening; some on Broadway wished that everyone could go home to heal and, in some cases, to try and help put shattered lives of families and friends back together.

But a paycheck required for living required a worker to work, and Broadway was an industry still reliant on last-minute decisions to go to the theater, and it went without saying that tickets sales had virtually stopped on September 11 and 12, compounding Broadway's slowest time of the year. The Metropolitan Opera and other nonprofits were out getting dedicated donations to help them through the tough time, but Broadway was a collection of for-profit businesses. And many shows did not have much of a financial cushion.

That was hardly all. For many of those working on Broadway at the time, that deep-seated truism that the show must go on would become an anchor in a world that suddenly seemed entirely unmoored.

It was that way for much of the audience, too. On the first night they were open after the attacks, the theaters might not have been filled to capacity—for some people, it was just impossible, either practically, psychologically, or both to get there—but actors were hardly facing down row after row of empty seats. On average, Broadway houses that night were between one-half and three-quarters full.

They sang "God Bless America" and read a prayer backstage, at the iconic American musical called *The Music Man*. Everyone joined in on "My Country 'Tis of Thee" at *Proof*, the David Auburn drama about math and intellectual freedom. At *The Allergist's Wife*, Valerie Harper, the star of the show, came out front to thank the audience for being present. So did Michael Cumpsty at *42nd Street*. Bernstein told a reporter he had visited six different shows, watching as many curtain speeches and defiant singalongs as was humanly possible.[1]

The Producers, an adaptation of the famously transgressive 1967 Mel Brooks movie and a hit show at the best of times, was proving especially popular with audiences in those days right after 9/11. Thus the St. James Theatre had become the location of choice for media organizations anxious to be able to report a bit of positive news about American resilience. The act of defiance always had been a current in Brooks' work. After all, he had dared to put a singing Nazi on the stage, swastikas and all, so when it came to laughing through your pain and staring down fundamentalists who would do you violence, Brooks long had been the Chief Rabbi. *The Producers*—which had thrilled audiences in Chicago right from its first tryout preview—was so extraordinarily amusing as to feel empowering. And its success clearly had made Brooks himself infectiously giddy.

One night in Chicago, following a hugely successful opening night there, he had been seen dancing on a table, his beloved wife Anne Bancroft smiling right back at him. Although the show would wane fast after the exit of the original stars Nathan Lane and Matthew Broderick— teaching actual producers to be more aware of the dangers of being overly associated with star performances—this week of all weeks, *The Producers* felt like an act of glorious defiance in the face of those motivated by cowardly terrorist acts.

No rendering of "God Bless America" came with more communal chutzpah. None other, of course, came with Nathan Lane, the consummate resilient New Yorker, capable of landing a gag in the most impossible of circumstances, stepping up to the plate. Both in the audience and on stage in those first couple of nights, people wept.

It would not be true to say that, in the days and weeks of that September, everything was coming up roses. Far from it. A night or two of pulling together soon gave way to the harsher economic realities of box-office losses from missed performances, depressed ticket sales, cost containments, infrastructure problems, and requests for concessions from unions. The demise of any show that had been struggling prior to the terrorist attacks was a foregone conclusion now: actors were losing jobs all over town.

Five Broadway shows—*If You Ever Leave Me … I'm Going With You; Kiss Me, Kate; The Rocky Horror Show; Stones in His Pockets;* and *A Thousand Clowns*—closed at least indirectly due to financial fallout from the attacks in the days that followed them, and, at the time, it felt like many others soon might join them. It still was hard to get into the city for most people, and international tourism had fallen off a cliff—Broadway suddenly had to rely on those who lived nearby and, in many cases, they came through as a matter of civic pride, but that did not mean that long-running shows like *Chicago*, hugely dependent as they were on tourism, were feeling at ease.

Many producers were put in a terrible spot: to close in the face of reduced business after the attacks looked like an unpatriotic admission of defeat, an abandonment of Broadway and its loyal American workers, but these were businesspeople, not cultural institutions. Once the money was gone and a show was running in the red, there would be no more producing left to do. Some producers felt like it was ill-advised to send good money after bad, and far more prudent to live to fight another day, ideally another day when the audience was more in the mood to go to the theater and it was easier to move around New York City.

It was one thing to go to *The Lion King* or *Rent* and pretend that nothing had changed, and many did so proudly, supporting Broadway having become an act of defiance. Indeed, it was remarkable that it was possible to see a show of the human complexity of *The Lion King* less than 72 hours after what had transpired in New York City. Many New Yorkers took their children. They were desperate for something that might make everyone in the family smile.

But everything on Broadway had been there before 9/11, obviously, and most of the fare did not seem to reflect how fast and far the world had changed. The American theater was still searching for a show that would somehow make sense of all that the city had undergone that terrible fall, a show that would feel like a transformative act of healing.

It took a month. And it would not take place on Broadway. But it would get there before long.

* * *

As the planes hit the World Trade Center, a show called *Metamorphoses* was already in rehearsal at New York's Second Stage, an Off-Broadway theater in Midtown. This piece of theater was based on the massive narrative poem of that name by the Roman poet Ovid. Its primary concern was transformation. And—incredibly—it would come to seem to many New Yorkers like a cathartic exploration of the city's contemporary suffering.

Metamorphoses had come from Chicago, where its director and adaptor, Mary Zimmerman, had become well known for her theatrical adaptations of nontheatrical sources. She had already been designated a so-called genius by the MacArthur Foundation and had a theatrical career of some 20 years' standing, beginning with her studies with the adaptor-director Frank Galati at Northwestern University, just outside Chicago.

Zimmerman's previous works had almost all started in Chicago, at either the Lookingglass Theatre Company, where Zimmerman was a founding ensemble member, or the Goodman Theatre, where she was an artistic associate. But as the years had passed, many of them subsequently had traveled to other regional companies like the Berkeley Repertory Theatre or the Mark Taper Forum, although never to Broadway.

Zimmerman wasn't entirely an unknown quantity in New York: she had directed Shakespeare outdoors in Central Park, and Manhattan Theatre Club had staged *The Notebooks of Leonardo da Vinci* in the mid-1990s, but she hardly was a household name, even among the cultural cognoscenti. Of course, that also had been true of Julie Taymor, when Disney had handed her *The Lion King*.

Still, the Zimmerman oeuvre was plenty eclectic compared with the usual ways and habits of commercial producers. In 1992, working in an old Chicago post office, even as the United States was unloading bombs on Iraq, Zimmerman had turned a production of the *Tales from the Arabian Nights* into an emotional reminder of the vulnerability of the show's Arabian-Iranian storytellers and the fragility of Baghdad itself.

In 1993, she'd fashioned *The Notebooks of Leonardo da Vinci* from, well, the notebooks of the famous artist. In 1995, she'd made *Journey to the West* from a sixteenth-century Chinese-Buddhist epic. And in 1999, she'd penned *The Odyssey*, a work that followed the long voyage home of Odysseus, King of Ithaca.

But even with that résumé, *Metamorphoses* was something else: Ovid's narrative, on which the play was based, roamed from the creation of the world through the times of Julius Caesar. The work had influenced everyone from Geoffrey Chaucer to William Shakespeare to John Milton. It comprised 15 books and over 250 separate myths. A far cry, it seemed, from material suitable for a Broadway show, but Zimmerman's *Metamorphoses* was not a usual piece of theatre, and the fall of 2001 was hardly a usual time.

Zimmerman's big idea from the beginning had been to stage the piece around a swimming pool of varied and opaque depth, meaning that actors could, depending on where they stood, either wade in shallow water or dive to the bottom. And there were hidden actor entrances inside the pool.

There was a sensual element to the staging, of course. Ovidian characters could rise up from the depths like a sea monster, or slowly be consumed by its watery mass. The show had opened in Chicago in 1998 (in a space destined to become a liquor store), and it had run for nearly two years, a staggering amount of time for what was, after all, a classical adaptation without any stars beyond the work itself. And before they walked into the theater, very few people knew the source.

In essence, Zimmerman took this great sprawling epic (if that was the right term) and shaped it into a collection of stories about characters who were able to change shape. Its fundamental underpinnings included love and romance, and the water would prove ideal for everything and everyone from copulating couples to sad kings.

As with most of Zimmerman's previous work, *Metamorphoses* homed in on a couple of stories that she quickly found had particular resonance for an audience. One involved the story of a loving couple who find themselves turning into intertwining trees, thus being able to hold each other well beyond the normal human life span. The other involved King Midas, the manifest conscience of the work and a character who, by the end of the show, would finally find himself able to hug his beloved daughter without her turning into burnished gold.

"Bodies I have in mind," said a narrator in the piece, crystallizing its theme, "And how they can change to assume new shapes."

The cumulative effect of all that metamorph-izing was dazzling.

Life is eternal, the show seemed to be saying, we just have to learn to understand that we eventually are going to find ourselves, and those we love, moving from one shape to another. None of that can be changed just by willing it not to be so—we merely vary in how quickly we come to understand that profound truth about our lives on earth.

And there was something else. Whether consciously or not on Zimmerman's part, *Metamorphoses* played out as an ode to the raw power of love, a force not without cruelty and danger, but still our only hope of driving through mortality. The overwhelming emotional impact of the show was the sense that, say, striving for money or pursuing the acquisition of stuff was a pointless. For none of that could be taken along when the change of shape took place. And life was agonizingly short.

Keep looking ahead, not backwards nor sideways, the show seemed to keep saying. Don't worry about money or transient popularity. Fear not self-consciousness. Avoid impatience, especially with those younger and less insightful than yourself.

When the show opened—it was still less than a month after the 9/11 attacks—critics and audience reacted as if the theatre finally had found a way to express the moment. Here, it seemed, was a show that was explicitly designed to help its audience better deal with loss and suffering, which was pervasive. None of this, of course, had been intentionally timed, for loss and suffering are constants at all times and in all locations, but that did not make the confluence any less extraordinary.

The location of her production was indistinct and neither the ages nor the era of her characters were specific. It was as if Zimmerman had found a way to express in the theater what an entire city—an entire nation—felt like they were feeling in their hearts. She had discovered how to let a broad, popular audience into the healing story she wanted to tell. And she had done so in no small measure by explicitly acknowledging the sadness felt in that rehearsal room on September 11.

The ethos of the show—which was, of course, drawn from the ethos of Ovid—was fundamentally comforting. The show was openly acknowledging the pain of loss and the ache of absence, but at the same time it was suggesting that the lost dear one was still present, just manifest in a different form. The show was spiritual, but also inclusive and ecumenical.

If most adaptations of classical works in the American theatre had struggled to re-create the spiritual context of the original performance, *Metamorphoses* embraced it, and at a time when New York needed it most.

"Those who have known the loss of people they love will surely feel echoes of their own pain," wrote Ben Brantley in the *New York Times* the following morning, echoing the general critical reaction to the piece. "But it is what follows them—representations of those metamorphoses that find the solace in sorrow—that opens the emotional floodgates."[2]

Open they did. Audiences on those early nights were intensely moved by the 90-minute production, a truth not lost on the commercial producers who had been following its progress and already were fighting for the rights (a battle won by the producer Roy Gabay, who had, he claimed, been expecting to be seeing "something by Kafka").[3]

The following spring, *Metamorphoses* would move to Broadway, opening at the Circle in the Square. It would run for a year, with most of its original Chicago cast intact. At the theater all those months, as the initial sharp pain of 9/11 gave way to the dull ache of unresolved loss, open displays of emotion in the audience were a common sight. Talking to a reporter some years later, the composer Phillip Glass deftly summed up what Zimmerman had achieved. "What I like about Mary," he said, "is her ability to take abstract ideas and turn them into things that people can feel."

Zimmerman would win that year's Tony Award for best director: an acknowledgment of what her show had achieved with a masterful piece of theatre that provided both distance and context for what had seemed, in that moment, to be something to which there could be no adequate artistic response. Hollywood, of course, could not react as quickly. And although the months that followed would be filled with tributes and fundraisers, political declarations and memorial performances, nothing else seemed to say quite like *Metamorphoses* that those who are gone have not merely disappeared.

Just as had been the case during the AIDS crisis, Broadway had found a way to express spiritual longing without it necessitating either divisive sectarianism or intellectual compromise. It had found a way to be both instructive and inclusive. It had stepped into a breach.

Metamorphoses would hardly be the only play to feel relevant to what had happened on September 11, 2001; as the years went by, the events of that date would recede a little but remain buried in the consciousness of writers who, as the years passed, would often write about that day as something New Yorkers had packed away, so as to be able to go back to work.

In 2016, a play by Stephen Karem called *The Humans* would become a big Broadway hit in part by beautifully articulating the lingering, stress-inducing, and even debilitating anxieties felt by New Yorkers many years after the planes flew into the Twin Towers. Karem's extraordinarily compassionate work would follow on the heels of many other dramatic works anchored by the events of that sunny morning: Neil LaBute's *The Mercy Seat*, Craig Wright's *Recent Tragic Events*, Sam Shepard's *The God of Hell*, Theresa Rebeck and Alexandra

Gersten-Vassilaros's *Omnium Gatherum*, and, on Broadway, Ayad Akhtar's *Disgraced*.

There was, and there would be, many more.

In 2017, a small Canadian musical called *Come From Away* would open on Broadway to a warm reception from audiences: with jaunty music and a proudly geeky spirit, David Hein and Irene Sankoff's populist work would celebrate the people of Gander, Newfoundland, who opened their hearts to marooned travelers from grounded jumbo jets with origins from all over the world. *Come From Away*, a piece that argued for the inherent goodness of humanity in times of great crisis, was set during the very days that the people of Broadway were forcing themselves to go back to work.

As Nathan Lane was leading the singing of "God Bless America," thousands of people were stuck in Gander and reliant on strangers. They had no idea they would end up being the subject of a musical, although many of them came to watch the portrayal of their own ordinary heroism.

Even all these years after 2011, the experience at *Come From Away* would feel cathartic to many.

But none of these works—all of which wrestled with the horrors of an entire city having to live the unimaginable—would have the immediate impact of *Metamorphoses*, the show that brought balm to the people of Broadway and to those who loved them.

7

2002: THE PULL OF LAS VEGAS AND THE RISE OF THE META

On June 5, 2004, the 40th president of the United States, and a former actor, died at home in Los Angeles at the age of 93. Ronald Reagan's death was followed by a state funeral that lasted seven days: he had been the first former U.S. president to die in the twenty-first century. Shortly after his predecessor's death, George W. Bush, the then holder of that office, said that Reagan had "won America's respect with his greatness and its love with his goodness,"[1] while crediting the Gipper with restoring American consequence and banishing its self-doubt. Reagan's funeral was attended by an eclectic array of dignitaries from all over the world, from Lech Walesa to Margaret Thatcher and Mikhail Gorbachev to Tony Blair, as well as friends from Reagan's years in Hollywood.

For a week, the ongoing war in Iraq mostly disappeared from American view.

Since he had been suffering from Alzheimer's disease, Reagan had disappeared from view after the end of his presidency. But Reagan's death brought his legacy back into focus. In the week that followed, Reagan's signature sunniness was much discussed, as was his avuncular, plain-spoken style, his sense of humor, and his formidable abilities when it came to communicating with all manner of American people. Less discussed was his role in widening American inequality, his lack of support (or funding) for artists with whom he did not see eye to eye, his self-evident homophobia, and how his reluctance to say the word "AIDS" for the first seven years of his presidency had been a formidable barrier when it came to garnering sympathy and funding for those suffering from the disease.

Reagan had enjoyed a greater command of narrative, of storytelling, than any president before or after. He was a performer himself—a former artist who had leveraged that training, experience, and understanding to great effect at every stage of his subsequent political career.

Yet few on or around Broadway were admirers of his legacy.

At the Tony Awards on June 6—a scant two days after Reagan's death—great and lengthy tribute was paid during the ceremony to the memory of the actor Tony Randall, who had been outspoken about planned cuts in arts funding during the Reagan administration. Reagan's death did nothing to disrupt the plans for the ceremony. And on the televised broadcast that Sunday night, the name Ronald Reagan was not even mentioned.

Broadway preferred its own heroes. Still, it was a house divided.

The Tonys that year were an epic battle between *Avenue Q* and *Wicked*, two shows that in many ways represented two different ways forward for the Broadway musical, here in the middle of the presidency of George W. Bush.

Penned by two youthful Broadway neophytes, Robert Lopez and Jeff Marx, and performed by live actors carrying puppets, *Avenue Q* was a wry spoof of the popular children's TV show *Sesame Street*, unofficial and unauthorized but performed nonetheless by many puppeteers who had previous experience working on that beloved show.

Avenue Q was also a take-down of liberal educational principles, especially the progressive idea that every kid was special. The show, which had opened the previous summer to great excitement from a mostly Gen X audience and was produced by Jeffrey Seller and Kevin McCollum of *Rent* fame, followed a character named Princeton, a former English major, into the jaws of life's harshest truths. These discoveries forced poor Princeton to discover an unpleasant reality:

when everyone thinks they are special, that means no one really is all that special at all.

Most interesting of all, perhaps, was how the show was the latest of several musicals that appeared to know they were musicals—a self-aware, meta, savvy, self-conscious form of storytelling that thrived on Broadway in the first years of the twenty-first century and had lasting effects.

But that night it had opposition.

Wicked, the loser that Tony night, was a far more traditional musical than *Avenue Q*. Based on Gregory Maguire's prequel to the beloved title *The Wizard of Oz* and directed by Joe Mantello, the $14 million show, which featured a book by Winnie Holzman and a score by Stephen Schwartz, had a laser-like focus on the two young women who functioned as its co-protagonists.

They were former school pals. One was a blonde girl named Glinda, who would, following various vicissitudes and questionable moral decisions, become a good witch. The other was a green-faced girl named Elphaba, whom the travails of childhood duress, anti-green prejudice, and the inequality of Munchkinland would force into a life considered by society to be evil. Although, if you looked at it from a different angle, it merely was a life of principle.

Taking a cue from L. Frank Baum, the show imagined a fanciful alternate universe—where Munchkins and witches were everyday realities—but, unlike *Avenue Q*, which did everything with a nod and a wink, *Wicked* was utterly committed to the truth of its own physical and emotional landscape.

Wicked was primarily interested in the price that always has to be paid for commitment, and in the mitigating power of female friendship. This wasn't a new plotline on Broadway, but *Wicked* would certainly take it to new heights, setting its structure up as something to emulate. When *Disney's Frozen: The Broadway Musical* opened in 2018, bringing to Broadway another work centered on the lifelong bond between two young women, the similarities with the previous blockbuster musical were self-evident.

Years before *Frozen, Wicked* had figured out the power of empathic involvement. Even though its story was about bizarre characters, every audience member felt like they were either the blonde girl (successful, proud, and smiley but secretly insecure) or the green girl (imposter/outsider syndrome writ verdant). Everyone—even if you were, say, a middle-aged man—could identify with at least one of the two leads in *Wicked*, and the show made sure that at least one of them was on the stage pretty much all the time.

"We did enter a lot of blind alleys early on, you know," the composer, Steven Schwartz, would observe many years later. "It took us a long time to realize the girls were the center of the show."[2] Had the creative team behind *Wicked* not arrived at that realization during its tryout in San Francisco, Broadway history might have been very different.

The show also exploited a fascinating truth about most Broadway shows aimed at young audiences—they were based on European fairy tales, such as the works of the Brothers Grimm. *Wicked*, though, was based on the work of a Midwesterner, L. Frank Baum.

The Wizard of Oz was an American story. In 1956, a writer for the *Chicago Tribune*, Russell McFarland, said that Dorothy, the Wizard, and the rest of them had burrowed into the hearts of ordinary Americans because they were "rooted in the soil of the prairie." He was right, and it explains why so many middle Americans came to Broadway to see *Wicked* as well as explaining its formidable success in Chicago and elsewhere out on the road.

Better yet, the book to *Wicked* had a funny, conversational, wry, and moving quality that made the show feel fresh and appealing to the young. Its book writer, Holzman, who came to prominence after writing a TV show called *My So-Called Life*, a show that took teenagers and their emotional woes very seriously, knew how to embody irony in dialogue and characterization. Her show was funny, but the humor never came at the expense of emotional sincerity.

Meanwhile, Schwartz's score, one of the most successful ever to be written for Broadway, was a textbook lesson in how to blend ballads of introspection, odes to love and friendship, and anthems of self-actualization.

It wasn't entirely evident that first season, but *Wicked* had another huge asset: repeat business. Like all satires, *Avenue Q* wasn't anywhere near as funny when you saw it the second (or third) time around, but the audiences at *Wicked* were buying something quite different: emotional engagement. Not only was that attainable on a subsequent visit, but it actually deepened every time you saw the show.

Of course, hit musicals aren't subject to formulas. There is alchemy involved. The creators of *Wicked*, whose royalty checks eventually would reach stratospheric levels, knew that to be true. Schwartz knew that something remarkable was in the air in San Francisco when he watched Elphaba, the green girl, get entrance applause. Some of it might have been for Idina Menzel, but her star had not yet risen. Most of it was for the *character*. "At that moment," Schwartz said, "the hair stood up on my neck, and it has not yet come back down."[3]

One day, years later, Holzman and Schwartz were talking to a reporter about why the show had become such a phenomenon. Holzman came late to the interview. As she walked in to the room, she hugged Schwartz, the man who had offered her the gig of a lifetime, made her rich, and thus changed her life for good.

"You and I gave everything we had to the show," she said, half answering the reporter's question about the secret to her show, and half just saying what she felt at that moment. "There is something wonderful about giving your all to something. Money can't buy that."[4]

* * *

It was unsurprising, then, that at the Tony Awards that year, most of the road presenters were rooting for *Wicked* to be named best musical. History suggests they were right. At the time of those Tonys, no one had any idea what *Wicked* would become. By 2016, *Wicked* would have grossed more than $1 billion on Broadway alone—joining both *The Phantom of the Opera* and *The Lion King* at that auspicious milestone, a figure that did not even reflect grosses from the international productions of *Wicked* and elsewhere, nor its touring incarnations. It would come to seem like a show that never needed to close. And, to date, there have been no signs thereof.

The producers of *Wicked*, Mark L. Platt and David Stone, were as savvy as the show. But they met their match in Seller and McCollum. And in *Avenue Q*.

Unbeknownst to the viewers at home watching the Tonys hoping to soon see *Avenue Q* in their home towns, *Avenue Q* had already made a secret deal with Steve Wynn's new eponymous Las Vegas casino for a sit-down run that would preclude the usual immediate national tour for a Tony Award-winning musical.

Wynn, who prided himself on offering his guests luxurious and unique experiences, was paying well for the privilege, and he'd insisted that his casino be the only place other than Broadway in the United States where *Avenue Q* could be seen.

It always seemed like a weird fit—a verbose and satirical musical by, for, and about urban hipsters on the Las Vegas Strip, where the language-free spectacles of the Cirque du Soleil currently were dominating entertainment. And conventional desert wisdom long had argued that shows had to be short, lest potential gamblers be taken out of the casino.

Ever since Vegas had risen like a mob-fueled Phoenix from the desert, Glitter Gultch's notions of live entertainment basically had meant intermission shows played in theaters without lobbies. Typically, there weren't even any programs to be had. If Frank Sinatra was on the stage, everyone knew who they were watching and nobody needed a biography. Ever since the mobster Meyer Lansky had sent Bugsy Siegel to Las Vegas to develop the Flamingo Hotel with its famous floorshows, there had been no expectation that the shows would be profitable. They were all loss-leaders, tools to keep gamblers (or their nongambling partners) happy. It had been that way from the Flamingo to the Sahara to the Tropicana, from the 1950s through the 1980s. Vegas entertainment often had featured huge stars, of course, but what they had done there had little to do with the entertainment to be found on Broadway, all the way across the country. Vegas meant headliners, comedians, vocalists, and the feathery spectacle of the Folies Bergeres.

But all that had changed.

* * *

Although it would turn out to be a relatively short-lived interest in Broadway entertainment—Scandinavian DJs and pulsing nighteries soon would take their place and the interest in attracting entire families would decrease as Vegas decided to stick to its Sin City branding— the major Las Vegas casinos were, in the first decade of the twenty-first century, pulling out their checkbooks to try and attract Broadway shows. Just as they did with *Avenue Q.*

Facing increased competition from riverboat casinos, and gambling emporia on Native American reservations, the casino owners and city officials desperately needed to diversify the reasons for tourists to come to Las Vegas, since they now could gamble closer to home. They also wanted to decrease the depressingly high average age of the city's visitors. If you could drive for an hour and play the same casino games, the operators thereof feared, you might not have any reason to fly to Vegas. Some of the richest men in America were fearing the most lucrative roulette wheels on the planet might spin to a stop, and sooner rather than later.

So they raced into action. By 2009, even *The Lion King* would end up in Las Vegas, in a custom-built theater at the Mandalay Bay Hotel and Casino (Simba did not travel to Vegas quite as Taymor had first imagined, but he got there just the same, as so many of us do).

Vegas's salivating over the idea of competing directly with Broadway shows actually dated back to 1989, when Wynn's Mirage Resorts had opened the Mirage Hotel, financed mostly with high-risk bonds issued by the future felon, Michael Milken. At the time, the city was seeing a boom in construction, mostly in the sector of luxury hotels, all of which needed to compete with each other for the same pool of high-rollers.

Wynn's Mirage was huge news. It was the most luxurious hotel in the city—it had 3,000 guestrooms, a gas-fueled volcano out in front, a domed tropical garden indoors, and it cost in excess of $610 million. Wynn immediately installed a show featuring the magicians and lion-tamers Siegfried and Roy. There might have been a long history of magic shows in Vegas, but this one was different—it was produced by Kenneth Feld, best known for running the Ringling Bros. and Barnum & Bailey Circus, and it featured the design work of the West End designer John Napier. It was a colossal extravaganza.

From there, Wynn moved on to Treasure Island in 1993—another highly theatrical hotel, this time with a battling pirate show taking place out front. For the entertainment inside, he decided to import the Cirque du Soleil, then an arty, relatively low-budget touring circus based in Montreal and known for touring U.S. cities in its hipster *grand chapiteaux*.

Like *Wicked*, the Cirque du Soleil had a profound understanding of emotional engagement—they had brought it to the old-fashioned discipline of the circus. Instead of the controversial elephants and the sawdust to be found in the three rings of Ringling, which had staked its future on arena-sized shows with animals aimed squarely at families with small children, Cirque had banished animals and instead emphasized boutique adult entertainments that came with a higher ticket price and had demonstrable appeal for urban sophisticates.

They introduced a so-called house company, characterized by performers with artistry, circus chops, and sex appeal. Sure, there were traditional circus acts making use of disciplines that had not changed for centuries, but the presentation and aesthetic unification of those acts represented something entirely new.

Many of Cirque's early productions, such as *Nouvelle Experience*, were described by critics and audiences in terms of dreamscapes. They would have a loose theme—usually something emotional and audience-centered—and they would feature live vocals from a performer who was singing in a language other than English; it was not important to understand the lyrics, in fact it was perhaps better if you did not, since that way there was nothing to interfere with your own interpretation of the experience. There would be clowns, but funny people would never be Cirque's strongest suit. The core of the shows was how the acrobats and trapeze artists were woven into the whole. Before Cirque, individual acts had been structured in a competitive fashion: presented separately, they would compete to offer the biggest thrills to the audience and win the warmest response in return, all under the patriarchal gaze of a referee-like ringmaster. But Cirque understood how that creaking power structure rapidly was on the way out: instead, the savvy Canadians replaced that old nomenclature with a unique kind of awe-inspiring voyeurism.

Yet more significantly, Cirque had a remarkably profound understanding here of what was involved in the act of watching. Look closely at most of the early tent shows and you would find a representative of the audience, often a child and an adult, always working within the show itself. Cirque might have been known for its auteur visions, but it never forgot who was paying its bills.

Cirque, then, was at once hip, sexy, family-friendly, and upscale: it realized that the future of the circus was theatrical and thus it had a prescient understanding of where live entertainment was headed. It would, in the coming years, make a small fortune for its founders, Guy Laliberte and Gilles Ste-Croix. By 2018, Laliberte, the main aesthetic engine in those early years, would have a net worth estimated at $1.3 billion.

Much of that would be earned in Las Vegas.

After Wynn came calling from the Nevada desert, Cirque brought along a Belgian conceptualist named Franco Dragone, whose work on *Mystere* would prove highly influential. *Mystere* was billed as a celebration of play—and indeed it was. Most people who went to see it would later recall a large ball rolling around the theater, but Dragone was fully aware that spectacle was nothing without emotional engagement and thus the show deftly explored the complexity of the interactions between parents and children, without most of the people in the audience understanding that was what it was doing. The work of an avowed avant-gardist with an atypical understanding of what an audience wanted and needed, *Mystere* played to capacity crowds. And it is still in production.

To his surprise, Dragone found that he loved working in Vegas—you got a diverse, global audience and bags of money. "Everyone comes here," he once told a visiting reporter. "The deep person. The scientist. The star. They all come to Vegas."[5]

He was right.

By 1998, Wynn had built the Bellagio Hotel, which cost a stunning $2 billion. He agreed to spend $80 million on Dragone's *O*, an investment that would be repaid many times over in the years that followed. Its brilliant calling card was a pool that could be lowered and raised to create varying depths—which is, of course, precisely the technique that Zimmerman would use in *Metamorphoses*. As with that show on Broadway, Dragone used the ability of the actors to enter above or below the surface of the water to create a series of sensual dreamscapes, albeit on a far larger scale. In the case of *O*, those dreamscapes included the seemingly magical appearance of a watering hole of an African savannah, the kind of thing many audiences would associate with Taymor's *The Lion King*.

As bizarre as it seemed at the time, Vegas was not only on the cutting edge of developments in live performance, it was putting pressure on Broadway. If you wanted to see a really great show, maybe Vegas needed to be your destination.

O did not have a traditional narrative. But Dragone's directorial stamp was so profoundly strong that a global audience found itself entranced by an experience they perhaps felt like they did not fully understand. As was the case with Taymor, an individual vision had caused an immensely powerful imprint and remade the point, which the American theater was slow to understand in the years before *Hamilton*, that audiences were craving profound emotional connections to the entertainment put before their eyes, a consequence, surely, of the increasingly alienating domination of technology in the rest of their lives.

Thereafter, Dragone even put his stamp on Celine Dion, directing (in 2003) a $30 million Dion show in a brand-new venue at the Caesars Palace hotel that would totally change the game for what musical artists were expected to do with their Las Vegas residencies. This was another remarkable directing achievement: Dragone, obviously, had to let a star like Dion be a star like Dion and perform her usual hits for her adoring fans. But in a variety of technological and simple ways, he radically redefined how a diva was able to react to her audience. It was a truly revolutionary fusion of pop concert and theater.

Of course, Dragone's innovations were smoothed by truly massive production budgets, all of a scale of which Broadway could only dream. This was because the economics in Las Vegas were so completely different. The shows were now expected to make money and pull in visitors, but they still were produced by giant corporations and backed by the profits from gambling, which remained an exceptionally popular activity with a far higher rake for the house than Broadway ever had seen.

At the time, the director Robert Lepage, who was collaborating with the Cirque du Soleil on another dazzling show, the operatic *Ka!* at the MGM Hotel and Casino, described Vegas as being exactly like the Italian Renaissance.

"You have a bunch of filthy rich people all wanting to impress each other," he said to a visiting reporter.[6] "And they are all printing money in their basements out here."

Indeed, it seemed that way.

"Vegas Puts Its Chips on Legit," read the headline in weekly *Variety* in March 1999,[7] just prior to the opening of a dedicated Las Vegas production of the musical *Chicago*. Wynn, it was reported, was offering huge sums of money to many of Broadway's top creative professionals in the hopes of coaxing them to work in the desert, rather than Midtown Manhattan. In those early days, the idea was that shows could originate in Las Vegas and then move to New York or London—and that the cultural traffic also could move in the opposite direction, making Las Vegas the most important stop on the Broadway road.

The Cirque shows were making more money than anything on Broadway, due both to the larger capacity of the theaters in which they played and the lack of the eight-shows-a-week structure imposed by the Actors Equity union in New York City. Since the shows (especially *O*) had a reputation for unmatched quality and spectacle, they also could command high ticket prices. Add in a free-spending tourist audience that virtually changed over every few days (typically, people did not come for long to Las Vegas, but they packed their time there with ticketed entertainment), and you had a confluence of cultural factors that seemed to reward commercial entertainment well into the future. When producers felt confident their shows could still find an audience after years in production, they were far more willing to sink in more money in the first place.

The other unique advantage that Vegas seemed to possess was the ability to build performance spaces that were custom designed for the productions, meaning that creatives did not have to limit themselves to the Victorian and early-twentieth-century buildings that made up the vast bulk of Broadway theaters. For some of Broadway's most successful directors, choreographers, and designers, this new creative landscape was very tempting. And so, of course, was the money. As a rule, Las Vegas shows cost up to ten times more than Broadway shows. Indeed, in Las Vegas, it was impossible to separate the production budgets from the build-out of the venues, since both tended to turn over at the same time. No one thought that Las Vegas would want dark or depressing shows, but then such shows were not the main wheelhouse of Broadway in the first place.

All of this competition from Vegas was much discussed in producers' offices, with some bemoaning the unfair competition and others scheming how to get in the boom. Either way, it clearly was dawning on Broadway's brightest minds that their business needed a refreshment.

* * *

Avenue Q had seemed attractive to Wynn, a man who branded himself as collecting unique, premium experiences, because of its atypically youthful demographic. But since presenters of touring Broadway held down a large number of the Tony votes, *Avenue Q* did not make these plans public until after the Tony Award ceremony, lest any resentment from theater owners in Cleveland and Denver scupper their chances at a statuette.

It turned out to be a very smart move. *Avenue Q* won the night, even if history suggests that was not the right choice. And then it went right to Vegas.

It did not work out well. After five months of lackluster sales at the Wynn Hotel, the hotel's namesake pulled the plug on Princeton and his pals in February 2006. It was to be replaced by *Monty Python's Spamalot*, which won the 2005 Tony Award for best musical, and that seemed to everyone to be a better fit for Broadway.

Wynn's subsequent interest in *Spamalot* was not a huge surprise to anyone who had seen the show: one scene of the musical actually took place at the Excalibur Hotel on the Strip. Eric Idle—no fool he— actually had built Las Vegas into his show. If ever you wanted evidence of how much Vegas was on Broadway minds, it was right there in the faux-Arthurian towers of *Spamalot*.

Idle seemed like an unlikely figure to be in the thrall of either Broadway or Las Vegas. He was one of the founding fathers of the British comedy series *Monty Python's Flying Circus*, a group also composed of four then-living men, John Cleese, Terry Gilliam, Michael Palin, and Terry Jones, and one deceased member, Graham Chapman. The Pythons had started gradually in the late 1960s. All but Idle had been from privileged backgrounds. They came to fame in various TV shows, such as *The Frost Report* and *At Last, the 1948 Show*. The BBC had first broadcast *Monty Python's Flying Circus* in 1969.

Unlike some of his old friends, Idle, who lived in California, had displayed a lot of interest in the performance and restoration of what one might call Python-alia. The others merely had been asked to grant their blessing to his idea of a Broadway musical based on one of their most famous films. The interest and enthusiasm of his old colleagues varied, but Idle got his way.

In their famously cultish BBC series, the Pythons had perfected their very particular comedic sensibility, which involved sketch comedy, absurdist animations, a good number of running gags, and, wherever possible, some silly walks. Although they riffed off the popular culture of the day, they hardly were satirists in the twenty-first-century model of Jon Stewart or John Oliver. They were more connected to the historical traditions of farce than to cutting-edge political commentary, and their political ideology actually was difficult to discern. Except you could be sure they liked pricking the balloons of the powerful and the pompous.

Contrary to how some people remember them, the Pythons tended to play things very straight. Unlike many other stars of their era (such as the late Ken Dodd, who was virtually unknown in America), their fame extended to the United States, thanks to their shows being contemporaneously picked up by the Public Broadcasting System. And also unlike many other stars of their era, the Pythons had been smart enough to negotiate the rights of ownership of their own material. So in order to make *Spamalot*, the only permission Idle really needed was from his fellow Pythons.

Monty Python and the Holy Grail, the source of *Spamalot*, was not the only Python movie (there also was *Monty Python's Meaning of Life* and, most controversially, *The Life of Brian*), but it was surely the most beloved. A satire of medieval English tropes, this was the film that cemented the group's American reputation.

Monty Python and the Holy Grail followed King Arthur through various trials and tribulations as he seeks the Knights of the Round Table who might accompany him on his great quest. Its comedic sensibility, of course, had a hand-made quality (clicking coconut shells become horse's hooves) and the film looked cheap (and damp) from both necessity and intention. But it was filled with lines that would become famous: "Your mother was a hamster and your father smelled of elderberries" or "I fart in your general direction." It was, to say the least, very silly.

Idle started working on the musical after attending the 2003 memorial service for his close friend George Hamilton, having, he said shortly afterwards, been reminded that "mortality is a very real thing."[8] After securing the permission of his fellow alums, he arranged to get Mike Nichols hired to direct. Nichols was thrilled with the assignment.

"Eric is a philosopher," Nichols told a reporter at the time. "He writes as low as fart jokes and as high as Heisenberg. He covers the spectrum. He's so highly intelligent, so highly educated and yet also deeply curious. He has enough grasp of the physical universe to be funny about it. Cleese is equally brilliant and equally curious, but he's a little bit in another world. Eric merely is a highly evolved human being."

So this highest evolved human being, working with the composer John Du Prez, came up with a highly self-aware show, which began with an out-of-town tryout in Chicago.

Sir Robin (played by David Hyde-Pierce) now dreamed of taking his song-and-dance act to Broadway, which, of course, he already was doing. The show made hay with other musicals: earnest Broadway shows such as Frank Wildhorn's anthemic *Jekyll and Hyde* were spoofed in the ballad "The Song That Goes Like This."

"Once in every show," went the lyric, "There comes a song this like / It starts off soft and low / And ends up with a kiss." Later in the song, Sir Gallahad and the Lady of the Lake (a character added for the musical, partly to assuage the overwhelming abundance of males therein) point out their own inclination to overact.

"I'll sing it in your face," sang the Lady of the Lake. "While we both embrace / And then we change the key / Now we're into E / Ahem, that's awful high for me."

That hardly was the only *Spamalot* number to hammer home the show's own artifice. In a song called "Diva's Lament," The Lady of the Lake lamented the disappointingly small start of her own part in the show.

"It was exciting at the start," went the lyric. "Now we're half-way through Act Two / And I have nothing left to do."

Analyze the lyrics, and you could see that the characters of *Spamalot* spent so much time talking and singing about being in a musical that there barely was any time left for the musical itself.

Yet all of this worked—in no small part because of Idle's innate cleverness combined with his palpable affection for that which he was spoofing. He might have broken every Broadway rule, and tossed empathic engagement out the window, but he still clearly appreciated the form at whose expense he was having so much fun. Like *Avenue Q, Spamalot* felt like something that was far smarter than the traditional Broadway musical. And a lot of other shows decided to plow the same territory.

Before long, the self-referential phenomenon seemed to be dominating Broadway: *Shrek the Musical*, which followed shortly, did much the same thing as *Spamalot*, with Donkey and the other signature characters making fun of Broadway even, of course, as they themselves appeared on Broadway.

Idle certainly helped to bring all of this into the mainstream, but the self-aware musical was not his own invention. More accurately, this craze of the twenty-first century could logically be said to have begun with *Urinetown* in that awful fall of 2001.

One of the stranger shows ever to hit Broadway, *Urinetown* was a dystopian musical about a powerful corporation that has gained so much power in a drought-plagued city, it had made urination a pay-to-pee activity.

This highly influential show actually had its roots in two small but aesthetically important Chicago theaters.

One was called Cardiff Giant, a left-wing company (it was around from 1987 through 1993) that was rooted in the same University of Chicago sketch comedy that had spawned Second City, the popular Chicago comedy theater with which Nichols once had worked in his youth. Cynical in approach but highly realistic in acting style, Cardiff Giant was known for its original shows attacking corporate greed. Greg Kotis and Mark Hollmann, the creators of *Urinetown,* worked with the company as young artists and first developed their idea for the show there.

But Kotis and Hollmann were also involved in a second company called the Neo-Futurists. This group, which has lasted to the present, its philosophy more intact than its personnel, specialized in self-referential theatre—metatheatre—in which actors constantly broke the fourth wall. At the Neo-Futurists, which produced original works and adaptations in a packed room above a funeral parlor, the performers would always acknowledge they were in a show—that the audience was, in fact, an audience, that the performers were performers and no one was under any illusion otherwise.

The Neo-Futurists would occasionally tour to Europe, and, on one such tour to Romania, Kotis took a side trip to Paris. He found he did not have enough cash for the city's famously luxurious pissoirs. And thus an idea for a musical was born. After the Neo-Futurists turned the idea down—they did not normally produce musicals—Kotis took the show first to the New York fringe and then to Broadway.

Urinetown, then, was a blend of lefty politics, Broadway cash, and Neo-Futurist metadrama. It shamelessly quoted other musicals—especially pompous ones, like *Les Miserables*, mocking its famous flag-waving scene of student revolution. The characters of *Urinetown* kept reminding the audience that they were watching a stupid idea for a musical.

Even the Tony Awards committee was taken in by the metamusical—*Urinetown* would end up winning three Tony Awards.

Without *Urinetown* and its huge success, it seems unlikely that Idle's *Spamalot* would have been so emboldened.

Urinetown had come up with an incredibly imaginative solution to a perennial Broadway problem: how to explain why people suddenly were breaking into song and dance. For decades, Broadway had got around this dilemma by creating musicals involving natural backstage or performative situations: *Kiss Me Kate, 42nd Street, Dreamgirls, Merrily We Roll Along, Follies, A Chorus Line, The Phantom of the Opera* (and any number of others) all were set in environments where performance felt organic to the plot. Even *Rent* drew from this heritage: most of its characters were aspiring performers themselves, so singing their feelings felt inherently logical.

But that time-tested solution obviously was limiting, especially for those who wanted to stay away from those clichés and move down more serious, experimental, or political avenues, as would *Hamilton*. *Urinetown* hit upon the idea of simply acknowledging the absurdity inherent to the musical—just as the Neo-Futurists had been doing for so many years in Chicago—and the show worked so well that Idle could clearly see that here was the way to avoid the obvious criticisms that might flow from his idea of blending show-tunes, the Arthurian, and the Pythonesque. He figured out that he could get away with taking Sir Robin to Las Vegas, if he just made everything a show about a show.

By admitting upfront that it was manipulating artifice, *Urinetown* thus actually opened a whole series of new avenues for musical comedy. And it was brilliantly self-protective. Such shows were difficult for critics to review poorly; the defense was baked into the show. The critical critic was perceived as just not getting the joke.

Toward the end of *Urinetown*, a character called Little Sally (which would become a star-making role for an actress named Spencer Kayden) had a conversation with an Officer Lockstock, both of them functioning as peculiar narrators.

"I don't think too many people are going to come and see this musical," said Little Sally, usually getting a huge laugh from an audience that had, of course, already come to see this musical. Analyze that line and you disappear down a metadramatic rabbit hole.

"Why do you say that, Little Sally?" said Officer Lockstock, a deft hand with the Brechtian shift of focus while the audience had its guard down. "Don't you think people want to be told that their way of life is unsustainable?"

That was the kind of zinger of which Ronald Reagan would have been proud.

Despite its genesis in the 9/11 crisis, from which lesser musicals never would have recovered, *Urinetown* would go on to play for a whopping 965 performances on Broadway, before becoming one of the musicals most frequently performed in colleges and universities.

For a while thereafter, it seemed like every show on Broadway (and a few in Las Vegas) was copying its signature self-awareness. Over time, the trend would dissipate.

When it finally did, no one was happier than that man named Gerard Alessandrini, the producer of *Forbidden Broadway*, the long-running, Off-Broadway franchise that spoofed the new Broadway shows from every season. Alessandrini had been writing parodies for years, but he became disgruntled in this era, and threatened to close down his long-running attraction.

"The shows," he grumbled to a reporter, "are spoofing themselves."

So Alessandrini took a break. He didn't go to Vegas. He just hunkered down and waited for *Hamilton*. The *Forbidden Broadway* boat would rise again.

8

2002: EDWARD ALBEE, THE LOVE OF A GOAT, AND THE DEATH OF OFF-BROADWAY

In February 2005, YouTube was born. And Arthur Miller died.

The loss of the world-famous author of such oft-revived Broadway hits as *Death of a Salesman, The Crucible, All My Sons*, and *After the Fall* caused much hand-wringing that cold winter over the state of the American play.

Miller had been a celebrity playwright, a public intellectual, an essayist, a political standard-bearer for liberal causes, and a household name, the likes of which, many obituary writers said, would never be seen again. Broadway just did not create celebrity writers anymore: Miller was the last of the great triumvirate of Eugene O'Neill, Tennessee Williams, and, well, himself. He also was the last of the so-called issue writers of the fervent years, playwrights who not only believed that Broadway was a place to probe the issues of the day, but had found an audience that was willing to ride a subway train to Times Square, buy a relatively affordable couple of tickets, and engage with them in the stimulating conversation.

Of course, the obituary writers of 2005 had no idea of the impending explosion of user-generated video content nor the coming pushback against patrician figures like Miller, but they still had a sense that a giant of a rapidly disappearing era was gone for good.

Miller had said that writing plays was, for him, like the act of breathing. By any standards his life was one of enormous fame and success. But he had still been put through the reputational wringer by critics he mostly despised: one moment he was described as perhaps the most talented American playwright of the twentieth century, the next as a playwright who could never live up to his own achievements as a younger man.

YouTube, though, and its fellow channels of cultural democratization and amateurization were coming to get the once-comfy theater critics who had stuck up their noses in the face of Miller's later work. Many of them soon would be laid off, victims of the growing popularity of aggregation, commodification, and crowd-sourcing. The newspapers where their essays would appear would become entranced with all of the newly available video content, content that trafficked better than analogue theater reviews.

One singular artist had died; YouTube was about to open the artistic floodgates to everyone. In some ways, this strange confluence of two seemingly disconnected events was apt. Miller had, after all, democratized the classical notions of tragedy, which traditionally had been the province of monarchs and dictators. Miller, by contrast, had seen tragic heroes on every Brooklyn street, their magnitude derived not from their individual greatness but from their ubiquity. Attention, he had said, must be paid to such men (and he usually was speaking of men). Miller's greatest play, *Death of a Salesman*, had been revived on Broadway time and time again. The reason? We'd all known Willy Loman—be it as a father, a co-worker, a grandfather, a friend, ourselves. But it was Miller who had elevated him to the stuff of tragedy.

Much of Miller's fame outside Broadway had come from his relationship with the actress Marilyn Monroe, whom he'd met at a Hollywood party, much to the chagrin of the director Elia Kazan, who had introduced the two of them, despite his own interest in the movie star. Monroe and Miller both became obsessed with each other, although they would not, of course, have anticipated their ultimate trajectory.

Miller's final play, an aptly named work called *Finishing the Picture*, had been seen at the Goodman Theatre in Chicago just the previous fall, a matter of months before Miller's death, but had not made it to Broadway. *Finishing the Picture* was a dark comedy that revolved around the 1961 filming of *The Misfits*, a movie that starred Monroe, toward the end of her marriage to Miller. Throughout the rehearsal process that previous fall, and in interviews with pushy journalists, Miller had insisted the play and its situation were merely fictional invention, with characters no more than archetypes blended with a few vague shadows of memory,

But this was patently absurd. Monroe was in the play; so was Miller. So was the problem that derailed their marriage, over which Miller would obsess for the rest of his life: He had always been in his head. He had lacked an awareness of sensuality. He had misunderstood the world of feelings in which his wife operated with such singular abandon. She had needed him and he had failed her. It was all over the play. In the end, the great chronicler of the human troubles of ordinary Americans had returned to his own regrets regarding one of the most famous Americans who had ever lived.[1]

Miller's death left Edward Albee exposed as the senior American playwright. Although actually only 13 years younger than Miller, Albee generally had been categorized, along with Harold Pinter, as a neo-absurdist from a whole different generation.

Albee's hair was long; Miller had a crew cut. Miller had been scarred by the Depression and was a creation of Brooklyn and a public education: Albee, a son adopted into privilege, had been scarred by suffocating, socialite parents in Westchester County, New York. He had cut his writers' teeth as an openly gay man living in Greenwich Village in the early 1960s. Miller's currency had been straight-up familial realism, writ poetic. Albee's had been life seen from a warped angle, writ poetic just the same.

But both men had been highly successful at a young age: Miller had written *Death of a Salesman* when he was just 34; Albee had written *Who's Afraid of Virginia Woolf?* at the same age.

So in that cold winter of 2005, Broadway was witnessing the passing of a generational baton. On the day of Miller's death, Albee's most famous play, *Who's Afraid of Virginia Woolf?*, was in rehearsal for its second Broadway revival, starring Kathleen Turner and Bill Irwin. There would be another to follow in 2013 from Chicago's Steppenwolf Theatre Company, starring Tracy Letts and Amy Morton.

Albee was at the center of a Broadway renaissance of straight plays. This was partly a consequence of a change in the economics of the theater industry. It had become almost impossible for producers to make a profit Off-Broadway, with or without music.

In 1991, Albee's masterful *Three Tall Women* had been seen Off-Broadway at the Vineyard Theatre, following its premiere at the English Language Theatre in Vienna. This had been a typical facet of the theatrical business in the 1990s: Paula Vogel's *How I Learned to Drive* also had enjoyed a long run at the Vineyard in the late 1990s. Other shows also did well Off-Broadway during this era: *I Love You, You're Perfect, Now Change*, a facile 1996 musical with perhaps the greatest title in the history of the form, would run at the Westside Theatre from 1995 through 2008, for a total of 12 years. Other hits of the era included Alfred Uhry's *Driving Miss Daisy* and Robert Harling's gothic Southern comedy, *Steel Magnolias*, which ran for three years.

But by the 2000s, audiences for such dramas and comedies had become harder to find. And producers were finding that, given the relatively small seating capacity at Off-Broadway theaters (the Vineyard had only 132 seats), it was hard to make money, even when the houses were selling out. And it was becoming ever harder even to find an Off-Broadway theater: gentrification in the lower half of Manhattan, the epicenter of Off-Broadway, had meant that many venues had been demolished to make way for new commercial and residential developments.

The fall of 2001 had been especially tough on the sector; Off-Broadway theater had suffered from collapsing audiences to an even greater extent than their bigger siblings Uptown. But Mayor Rudy Giuliani had not told the world to go and see an Off-Broadway show.

In the late 1990s and early 2000s, depressingly few Off-Broadway shows were recouping any of their initial investments.

Costs also were rising—actor salaries, insurance benefits, and especially marketing expenses. This was also true on Broadway, of course, but the difference on the Main Stem was that the upside there was virtually unlimited. Producers were willing to take bigger risks on the off-chance they might luck their way into a *Wicked*, the kind of show that could make sure a producer then was set for life. Without that carrot offering massive wealth to a lucky few, Off-Broadway started to look much less attractive to investors. And Off-Broadway success, such as it was, did not include the chance to crowd the podium at the Tony Awards and declare yourself a Tony winner.

There were yet more challenges. A lot of the playwrights who traditionally had provided content for these Off-Broadway theaters had, by the early 2000s, been snapped up by TV shows. Cable channels were now competing not just with who had the rights to which Hollywood movie, but through original programming, such as *Six Feet Under*, a brilliant and massively successful existential drama set in a funeral home that had been dreamed up by the playwright Alan Ball and featured such theater writers as Rick Cleveland on its staff of scribes. Many such shows would follow on HBO and Showtime, and eventually Netflix and Amazon, as the amount of original TV production in America exploded, taking talent from the theater and offering playwrights a far more lucrative place to write, not to mention the company of a collaborative writers' room in which a lonely scribe could share and gain ideas.

All in all, by 2005, Off-Broadway had become less of a place to see commercial productions of serious new works by major American writers, and more of a home for a mix of nonprofit shows created by subsidized institutions and long-running, spectacle-driven, event-based attractions like *Stomp* or *Blue Man Group*.

Paradoxically, then, the demise of Off-Broadway actually reopened Broadway to serious writers like Albee. It was a massive change in the American commercial theater business, and a development much underappreciated at the time.

In early 2002, a group of producers led by Elizabeth Ireland McCann had taken an enormous risk on an Albee play called *The Goat, or Who is Sylvia?* If the title of the play, which starred Bill Pullman and Mercedes Ruehl, was bizarre, then the punctuation was even weirder, as if Albee had wanted to erect a smoke screen in front of perhaps the most audacious metaphor ever to be at the center of a Broadway play.

Here was its subject matter: a famous middle-aged architect named Martin found his successful life disrupted due to his unexpectedly and inconveniently falling head-over-heels in love with a goat.

The play started out humorously—at first, the man's wife was incredulous of the turn taken by her spouse—but after she realized his level of dedication to the titular bovid, it ended with a blood bath that felt worthy of Greek tragedy. First bathed with sweet-nothings, Sylvia the goat ultimately was sacrificed to the rage of Stevie, the spouse, who turned before the eyes of the audience into a howling Medea, a clear and present danger to her unexpected four-legged rival.

Believe it or not, this really was a play about the limits and perils of intimacy, one of Albee's most common and devastating themes, and a piece about how cruelty and the violent forces of self-preservation often lurk under the surface of even a seemingly happy marriage. Albee was reinterpreting tragedy just as surely and as radically as Miller had done in *Death of a Salesman*, refocusing the genre away from individual stature. But instead of moving the genre toward how workers all suffer en masse under American capitalism, he was pushing it toward how we all function in relationships; relationships that easily can turn, well, tragic.

The Goat, or Who is Sylvia? was penned in two- and three-person scenes; the action would race from intellectual debate to visceral anguish (and then back again), and characters would tie themselves up in the ropes of self-justification. Just as if they all were creatures of Sophocles.

But that wasn't really what Broadway audiences actually perceived. Here was the thing: *The Goat, or Who is Sylvia?* did not offer the comfort of a metaphoric universe. None of Albee's plays did. Not fully.

Sure, the play seemed to be implanted in a warped reality (as in, who really falls in love with a goat?), but, simultaneously, it was all about an ordinary American family in the throes of the same kind of trust-driven marital crisis that afflicts any number of American families from time to time. As a result, the piece had real shock value—it quickly became known as the Broadway play about a regular old married guy sleeping with a goat—so there was a certain cache and currency to be gained from attendance.

Yes, it offered schadenfreude: Whatever terrible stuff might have happened in your marriage, it could not possibly have been this bad, given that it was unlikely goats were involved. But, like most other effective commercial plays, *The Goat, or Who is Sylvia?* also offered multiple ways for audience members to empathize with its beleaguered central characters.

As you watched, you tended to apply the central questions of the play to your own life.

What would I do if my partner revealed some unspeakably shocking personal predilection? Would I stick around? Or would this undermining of a long personal history send me spiraling off into rage?

Just as Miller had with *Death of a Salesman*, Albee had actually written a very commercial play. He'd just adapted to the times and, in fact, the model set by *The Goat, or Who is Sylvia?* would set the scene for a further redefinition of the dramatic in the years that followed.

The Goat, or Who is Sylvia? lasted on Broadway for, given the subject matter, a very respectable 309 performances. Its success— quite remarkable, when you think about it—handed Broadway producers new confidence that the nature of what constituted an acceptable play for Broadway had changed. If you could sell a play about goat-sex, some reasoned, then the world sure had changed from that of Neil Simon. You now could sell a play about a lot more than you thought you could before.

Especially if they had familiar actors to hang their purchase on (and that was a crucial part of the Broadway renaissance of the straight play), audiences now were more ready to take risks. As long as there were a couple of bold-faced names in the cast-list, audiences were ready to take a leap.

In fact, the huge interest in *The Goat, or Who is Sylvia?* even suggested that the more outré the play, the better its commercial prospects. Shocking content made a play into a must-see event, becoming fodder for opinion pages in newspapers, postings on the newly popular blogosphere, and the kind of engaged and emotional conversation that, merely a decade or so later, once social media had taken over the world, would become live-or-die requirements for any and all Broadway shows, just as they would for the newspapers that covered them.

The Goat, or Who is Sylvia? did all of that first. It might not have been as autobiographically revealing as *Three Tall Women*, a dazzling work based on Albee's own adopted family and a play that would take Broadway by storm with a stunning 2018 revival starring Glenda Jackson, Laurie Metcalf, and Alison Pill, but *The Goat, or Who is Sylvia?* was and remains in many ways the consummate Albee play: audacious, playfully perverse, and in full and dazzling command of the raw power of the theatrical metaphor.

You could not watch it and doubt that Albee was the author. No one else could have pulled it off. No one else that good would have dared.

It's hard to overstate Albee's influence on the twenty-first-century renaissance for serious and experimental work on Broadway. He is more usually thought of as a twentieth-century writer: his career, in fact, spanned seven decades and he won the Pulitzer Prize for drama three times, for *A Delicate Balance* in 1967, *Seascape* in 1974, and *Three Tall Women*, which had opened Off-Broadway in 1994. But he came roaring back to prominence with *The Goat, or Who is Sylvia?*

and his edgy but intellectually rich works brought Broadway along with him. He created a whole new market for high-end commercial drama designed for an affluent, intelligent, and sophisticated audience, willing to pay a premium price for high-quality fare.

Albee had always vexed theater critics. When *A Delicate Balance* opened on Broadway in 1966, the critic Walter Kerr had asked the question, "How do you get hold of hollowness?" implying that the play just was too chilly to work, or maybe just too chilly for him to tolerate. Understandable as this view may have been—Albee's works were hardly warm and cuddly, and neither was their creator—this was nonetheless a misreading of Albee's work.

After all, Kerr and his contemporaries had been more receptive to hollowness—a logical artistic response to our inevitable exit from this life at a time and place not of our choosing, and without regard to deserving—when it had been contained within the explicitly metaphoric work of a Samuel Beckett. They could handle Harold Pinter, another writer who found absurdist horror in mating and familial rituals, because in those classy Pinter plays, the hollowness was mitigated by breathy pauses, glamorous verbosity, and sexy situations. There was a certain remove, and most Pinter plays could be enjoyed as a kind of foreplay that did not spoil your dinner.

But Albee did not so easily let you off the hook.

His major plays managed to be about the unspeakable—getting the guests, killing a child, having a stroke, loving a goat—and yet they also genuinely reflective of the very kinds of upper-middle-class people who still were dominating the audience for any Broadway show that did not happen to be a musical. Whether they were watching *The Goat, or Who is Sylvia?* or *Who's Afraid of Virginia Woolf,* or, especially, *A Delicate Balance*, audiences would look out at these cold, calculating, inebriated, howling characters and have just enough distance to make themselves believe they were not watching themselves and their own despairing marriages. But never enough to make them feel sure.

That was Albee's sweet—or, more accurately, bittersweet—spot. In *Three Tall Women*, revived on Broadway in 2018 with extraordinary success, the autobiographical drama was turned into a treatise on human decay, a mirrored set forcing the audience to confront their own mortality. Albee seemed to be saying that children should be taught about their own coming death, with the same regularity and certitude as if they were being told to wash their hands.

Albee did not have a happy childhood and, like most writers, he wrote from the shadows raised by his demons. Still, that translated into a genuine compassion for young people, especially those raised by far-from-perfect adults in the middle years of the twentieth century. It was never enough for Albee just to point out the absurdity of life, as it was for many of his absurdist predecessors. Albee, who died in 2016, was a unique kind of evangelical absurdist, a writer committed to the idea that the horrors of life could, at least to some degree, be mitigated by love and preparation, especially if we are lucky enough to receive those things while we are young. He cared about the audience, far more than most critics and others realized when he was still alive. And this is what made him a Broadway playwright, with a genre all his own.[2]

Considered as a whole, Albee's work collectively says that the only way to adequately prepare for death, be it your own or that of a loved one, is to actively acknowledge its imminence. Beyond that, there was less certitude. It was as if Albee did not fully know whether or not he believed in love—you could argue that was the main question in anything and everything the man ever wrote. And, of course, it also had been the main question in *Angels in America*. You could argue it had been the main question since Broadway began.

But if you looked closely at all Albee's plays, you also could see people doing everything they could to take care of each other.

Even people in love with goats.

* * *

Many of the plays that succeeded on Broadway in the first decade of the twenty-first century were British or Irish imports—Alan Bennett's *The History Boys*, Michael Frayn's *Democracy*, Tom Stoppard's *The*

Coast of Utopia, Peter Morgan's *Frost/Nixon*, Conor McPherson's *The Shining City*, and Martin McDonagh's *The Lieutenant of Inishmore*. Success also was enjoyed by the intellectually voracious Richard Greenberg, whose hugely enjoyable baseball drama *Take Me Out* was a big hit, as was David Lindsay-Abaire's *Rabbit Hole*, a traditional but nonetheless poignant play about the grief that follows on from the loss of a child and the paradox faced by anyone who has been bereaved.

These were its central questions: Do you try and metaphorically clear out the room of the lost loved one, and, in so doing, erase all that you have left of their existence on the planet? Or do you maintain what little physical connection you have left, intensify the grief you feel, and make it even harder to move on and heal?

Indeed, the difficulty of healing was a potent strand not just in Lindsay-Abaire's work, but generally on Broadway in those post-9/11 years.

You can see it being worried over in John Patrick Shanley's *Doubt*, an inestimably prescient 2005 play, and later a widely acclaimed film, that deftly explored the scandal that was engulfing the Catholic Church as more and more stories emerged about priests abusing the young people in their charge. These events prefigured both the child sex-abuse scandal in the athletics department of Penn State University in 2011 (also a consequence of people, including the famous football coach Joe Paterno, choosing not to see what was, in fact, right in front of their faces), and the #MeToo explosion that still was a dozen years away.

Shanley did not write an overt piece of political theatre, and his play intentionally did not fully answer the central question it raised. But he still homed in on how the church's patriarchal power structure, and its inability to either listen to or empower women, had made everything worse. It understood how many in a position to know had been either silenced or rendered inert by the internal conflict between their sense of duty and their conscience. August Wilson had, in a different community, explored much the same issue, especially in his later plays.

Awareness of the abusive-priests scandal had grown after 2002, when *The Boston Globe* published an investigation of the church's well-documented habit of shuffling offending priests from one parish to another, often resulting in further abuse. Even as the church was signing off on large settlements with victims, the practice was continuing. *The Globe*'s investigation would win the Pulitzer Prize and, in 2015, be turned into a Hollywood movie, *Spotlight*, that would win the Oscar for best picture.

Not all Albee's plays were about abuse, of course. But it would not be inaccurate to say that most of them were about the consequences of abuse, or, at the very least, neglect of someone young and in need. His reputation had risen quickly, expanded once his works came to be produced at the highest levels, and remained until his death.

But a lot of people had missed just how much he cared.

Irascible, uncompromising, and demanding, Albee was in many ways a one-man protest movement against the encroachment of amateurization on American culture. The moment may have been about the exuberant expression of self, but Albee was here to say that you could exuberantly express yourself all you liked, but that would not prevent your own demise, which was coming sooner than you thought.

Better, then, to go and see a play written by someone who knew what they were doing.

9
2007: A RECESSION THWARTED BY AN IRONIC BLAST FROM CHICAGO

The famous Steppenwolf Theatre Company from Chicago had blown onto Broadway before. Gary Sinise, its main mover and shaker, had starred in Frank Galati's hardscrabble adaptation of John Steinbeck's *The Grapes of Wrath* in 1990, and had himself directed *Buried Child* in 1996. But by 2007, Steppenwolf's long-branded identity as a macho ambassador from the wind-swept Midwest who was willing to get right in your face and stay there was beginning to look tired. This was a year when Barack Hussein Obama, who was rebooting the Chicago brand on the national stage, had declared his candidacy for president of the United States of America, promising hope and change, even as the war in Iraq and a debilitating recession continued to grind.

Broadway producers had long been known for biting their nails. But the recession that began in 2007 — and took years to dissipate — represented an especially stressful interlude.

The recession had multiple causes but was rooted in a crisis in the value of property. After years of lax practices when it came to the issuance of mortgages and the provision of cheap credit to those unable to pay back what they had borrowed, a bubble had burst in the housing market. This meant that many Americans were finding that the nation's historic seat of individual wealth-creation — the privately owned home—was, in the parlance of the day, underwater. The ricochet effects were enormous: since many Americans no longer had a nest egg in their homes, if they even still had keys to their homes at all, they cut back on their spending. That sudden change had a major impact on Broadway grosses, since the commercial theaters were the very epitome of discretionary consumer spending.

At a moment when disposable income was drying up fast, very few people felt like they really needed to go and out and see a show. Not when they needed other stuff. And, of course, the industry always had been dependent on tourists. A strong dollar was keeping the number of international visitors to New York relatively buoyant (throughout most of 2007, British visitors could get two dollars for their one pound), but domestic tourism was feeling the pinch. There were fewer people in town to see shows.

That cutback in spending led in turn to job losses in all sectors of the economy, including Broadway. This was an era when it would have been impossible for a show like *Hamilton* to push Broadway ticket prices higher than they ever had been: however much they may have wanted to see a given show, people simply did not have the money or the confidence to spend what the fortunate among them might have socked away in the bank. And although systemic changes eventually were made in the banking and other systems that got America in this situation in the first place, the recovery from the housing crisis, especially in the most hard-hit areas, was agonizingly slow.

One impact on Broadway was a drying up of investment capital. The industry was facing a kind of double-whammy: banks and other formal enterprises didn't want to lend money to risky propositions, and wealthy individuals, upon whom Broadway long had relied, had seen their personal portfolios sink. It no longer felt like it would be as much fun to get involved with that risky new play anymore; there was at least a three out of four chance it would not make back its investment, and, for many people, the potential glamor and excitement began to wane when the cash required was not money the investors felt willing and able to lose.

Of course, the recession also was something convenient to blame when a Broadway show ran into the age-old problem: not enough people wanted to plunk down the money to buy a ticket. Almost every show that went down in 2007 and 2008 was accompanied by someone blaming the recession. But the list of premature closings in those years was still extensive: *The Pirate Queen* (a musical about a semimythic Irish figure that had turned out to be disastrously campy), *Cry-Baby, The Farnsworth Invention*, even August Wilson's *Radio Golf*. Even colossal but aging hits like *Hairspray* had suddenly struggled in the rough economic climate. On September 7, 2008, fans of *Rent* flocked to the Nederlander Theatre to witness the show's final performance. *Rent* had played 5,123 performances. It, too, was a casualty of the economic downturn. Or so it was said.

In the fall of 2007, though, *August: Osage County* had arrived from Chicago, despite having a large cast of actors who hardly were box-office draws on Broadway. It would win both the Tony Award for best new play and the Pulitzer Prize, thus cementing its reputation as the most successful play of its moment, eventually moving both to the National Theatre in London and to Sydney, Australia, and lasting for 648 performances on Broadway. Until *Harry Potter and the Cursed Child* arrived in the spring of 2018, utterly transforming expectations about what kind of impact a nonmusical could have on Broadway, no magnum opus without tunes would have made quite such an impact.

The author of *August: Osage County* was Tracy Letts, a writer who was born in Tulsa, Oklahoma, and grew up in Durant, where his parents both taught at Southeastern Oklahoma State University. Opting to skip college, he moved to Dallas after high school to pursue his ambition to become an actor. By the late 1980s, Letts had landed in Chicago, where he tried to establish himself as an actor. And he started to write plays.

Letts emerged as a hipster playwright in Chicago in the 1990s, during the city's long obsession with what variously was called in-your-face, Chicago-style, or hyperrealistic theater. This was the era of *Reservoir Dogs* and *Pulp Fiction* (an era that would come to be painfully reassessed following the abuse allegations against the Hollywood and Broadway producer Harvey Weinstein) but at the time the nihilism of that genre was all the rage.

In 1993, Letts wrote a shocking little play called *Killer Joe*, a violent, heart-pumping, chaotic, profane, nudity-embracing thriller about a Texan serial killer and a work that intentionally left the audience in doubt as to whether the writer was merely embracing a pulpy, pot-boiling genre or satirizing its assumptions. Michael Shannon, who soon after would become a major Hollywood star, was in the original Chicago cast.

Events in the play revolved around a Texan family, struggling for cash. This was the plot: finding himself in debt to a crowd of local tough guys, the central character, a loser named Chris Smith, comes up with the idea of hiring a moonlighting cop who went by the name of Killer Joe Cooper to kill Chris's estranged mother in order to snag some insurance money. Things deteriorated from there.

Killer Joe, which audiences loved, managed to last for nine months Off-Broadway, and was also a big hit in London, where it was seen as a prairie-style take on the so-called in-yer-face playwrights so popular at the time in Britain. In Chicago, the play was seen as a new take on an aesthetic long associated with writers like Shepard: in essence, Letts had taken the brooding intensity of plays like *The Curse of the Starving Class* and infused them with an arch, pitch-black sense of humor and bucket-loads of irony, all of which were targeted at the Generation X audience who were snapping up all of the available tickets.

Like many other young writers of the moment, Letts eschewed any kind of moralism. It was not expected by an audience that was perfectly willing to wallow in naked sensation.

At the time, Letts told journalists that his work was intended to "get under the skin of a kind of Midwestern puritan ethic."[1] He wanted, he said, to "scrape that away, to get people to wake up a bit." And he succeeded.

His next play, *Bug*, an eerie, menacing play set in a motel room in Oklahoma, was very much in the same mode. It was as if a Shepard play had been mashed-up with a horror film by David Cronenberg. It was, to say the least, a moment of theatrical extremity and, for Letts, it offered a kind of apotheosis. Just as the characters in *Bug* burned themselves to a crisp, Letts largely abandoned that particular style of playwriting, a direct reflection of an unstable portion of his life, and proceeded in an entirely different direction.

His next work was *Man From Nebraska*, the first Letts play to be produced at Steppenwolf, which, by then, had made Letts a member of its famous, if loosely structured, ensemble of actors, writers, and directors. This work, a piece about the meltdown of an ordinary, middle-aged Midwesterner, was a crucial transition between the angrier plays of Letts's youth and his growing interest in the crises of middle-aged characters in the American heartland, for whom options and choices seem to have dissolved into a dull existence pockmarked with obligations to flawed family members.

So by the time he wrote *August: Osage County* (about four years after *The Man From Nebraska*) Letts was attempting something quite different. In the first instance, he'd become infinitely more ambitious: he'd abandoned 90-minute Off-Broadway dramas in favor of a 210-minute epic, a sprawling family drama that was intended to explode the inherent contradictions of trying to live an examined and intellectual life in what the great urban clumps of self-designated sophistication considered flyover country. The work seemed different from that of any recent peer on Broadway: it didn't probe the foibles of the urban intellectual class, as did most of Albee's great plays, and yet it didn't feature the primal writhing of ex-urban sensualists, in all of their glorious dysfunction. *August: Osage County* was a play about an extended family racked not only by drug use but also by their own distance and alienation from the cities that might have actually understood what made them tick.

The play—by the standards of plays—was enormously successful on Broadway, despite its 11-person cast and its relatively modest $2.56 million capitalization. The show was playing at the massive Imperial Theatre, typically the home of major musicals. During many of the weeks of its run, which followed a 19-day strike by Broadway stagehands, *August: Osage County* outgrossed many of the musicals that were playing on the neighboring blocks. And, remarkably, like no other straight play, it turned out to be relatively impervious to the effects of the recession.

Anyone who saw it could not easily forget the intensity of the audience reaction. It wasn't uncommon to hear gasps and such verbalizations as "Oh, my God." You could see people not so much leaning in to hear what the actors were saying as leaning back in their seats, as if they were trying to get out of the path of a tornado.

To what were audiences responding?

For one thing, they were appreciating the quality of the acting: Letts had written *August: Osage County* specifically for a particular group of Steppenwolf actors, many of whom he knew in the most intimate of ways. Clearly, when writing the play with these actors in mind, he was borrowing from his actors' lives as much as from that of his own family in Oklahoma. This personal connection was intensified by the appearance in the original Steppenwolf production of Dennis Letts, a late-in-life actor, who had been cast in the role of the patriarch Beverly Weston. All at once, this felt like a cryptic acknowledgment of the play's autobiographical roots, a simple coincidence, a caustic in-joke, and a son's warm gesture to his beloved father, an intellectual stuck out on the prairie, just like the character he was playing in his son's play.

This latter interpretation came into firmer focus after the Broadway transfer, when it was revealed that the elder Letts was suffering from an advanced form of cancer. Shortly after opening the play on Broadway, he died, making the subsequent success of his son's play bittersweet for all involved.

But the strange personal intensity of this Steppenwolf production was not limited to the relationship between a father and his very complicated son.

Many in the Steppenwolf ensemble had themselves arrived in Chicago if not from the rural Oklahoma setting of *August: Osage*

County, then from comparable small towns in Iowa or downstate Illinois. They understood the landscape that Letts was painting—a landscape, of course, that had been outlined in *Man From Nebraska*. But whereas that earlier play had dealt with the desirability of escape from such places, *August: Osage County* dealt with those who stayed behind. Living, you might say, on land to which they had no right of ownership.

Moreover, Letts had focused his play almost entirely on outspoken, middle-aged (or older) characters, providing a set of impossibly juicy roles for the demographic in which the Steppenwolf acting ensemble then was most generously represented.

There had never been a show at Steppenwolf that fit its actors so much like a glove: the usual gap between performer and material seemed almost to have disappeared. And on Broadway, where Steppenwolf still stood for great acting, this was very much how the show was sold.

Nobody disputed the intensity or the quality of the acting. But Letts had also thrown down a gauntlet by taking on one of the most sacred traditions in the American theater—the really big and long play about the horrors of life in an all-American family racked by substance abuse, alcoholism, failure, adultery, and shame. Before he came along, such plays had been absent from Broadway for at least one generation. They were expensive. They were very difficult to do well, especially with some TV or movie star who was unlikely to be up to their acting challenges. They often would turn out to be boring. Producers worried they were downers, and that the audience would feel like they were going back to school.

But *August: Osage County* had all the traditional goodies: alcoholism, drug use, infidelity, abuse, betrayal, desperation. For good measure, Letts also threw in the idea of an academic family living on what was, after all, stolen land, the former province of Native Americans.

August: Osage County seemed to be at least a semi-conscious attempt to take characters and themes familiar from such semi-autobiographical Eugene O'Neill opuses as *Long Day's Journey into Night* or *Mourning Becomes Electra* and update them for a new theatergoing generation.

How successful it was in that aim remained controversial. But whatever side you were on, there was no question that Letts had, like Miller and Albee, been trying to redefine what serious American drama meant for a new generation.

In both Chicago and New York, almost every critic agreed that *August: Osage County* was a riveting, brilliantly acted piece of theater, and a vicarious good time. But when it came to the question of whether or not this was a truly great American play—an heir to, if not a peer to, the O'Neill model—a fascinating split emerged.

The nuances and verbiage of the arguments varied, but the gist of the debate was easy to discern and understand.

Some critics thought the play was the first great American drama of the twenty-first century, updating the genre for a different generation. Others thought it was an enjoyable but overpraised melodrama in the Lillian Hellman, rather than the O'Neill, tradition.

The side on which one fell seemed to depend on whether or not one saw the characters as sufficiently weighty in metaphor and magnitude, and the narrative in theme and truth.

And it depended on whether or not you thought the great American play could (or even should) be updated for an era when audiences required a little more free-flowing, self-aware juice with their traditional American steak. In other words, the debate ended up being very much about the role of irony in serious writing. This was not full-bloodied realism, for all the shouting and screaming. This was a work that seemed very much aware of its own relationship with excess.

As a result, you could argue with foundation that *August: Osage County* cheapened the form. Or you could argue with even firmer foundation that it revitalized it like no other drama in decades.

Either way, audiences flocked to see the play on Broadway, which had recouped its capitalization by the spring. All in all, *August: Osage County* raked in more than $12.3 million at the box office that season. The must-see play of the season had made serious drama fun to see again, even if fun was not, for most people, exactly the dominant takeaway. Once it crossed the Atlantic (and the London staging was, on balance, its most successful), it was a play that felt like it was trying to define American familial pain. Again.

August: Osage County did not open any floodgates. No similar work was to follow.

Letts's career, though, would achieve a further major boost in 2013 from his playing George in the latest Broadway revival of Albee's *Who's Afraid of Virginia Woolf?* There was something apropos about a playwright assuming that role, especially since Letts and Albee each had admired the other. As different as they were, the two men probably had the most influence on the changing face of American drama on Broadway in this difficult first decade of the twenty-first century, especially as war ended, recession slowly turned into recovery, and hope for some better years returned.

Letts had taken the Broadway play in a completely new direction; a structural change that would, in time, even influence the trajectory of the musical toward *Hamilton*.

How? This was the most ambitious play of its era and, more interestingly yet, a fascinating combination of irony and truth. For better or worse, Letts wanted to turn the traditional American drama of familial dysfunction into a story told with irony and self-awareness. The play was resolutely American—in a way that no other play had been, at least since Shepard's peak years.

In the decade that followed, there would be many other new American plays, but none quite like the recession-busting *August: Osage County*, which broke all of the rules of these hardscrabble times on Broadway, and thus blew apart all manner of assumptions about, well, almost everything that could have been assumed.

10

2010: A BOULEVARD OF BROKEN DREAMS, AWAKENED

"Good evening," said the president of the United States, speaking from the Oval Office on August 31, 2010, interrupting what the television networks still called "prime time." "Tonight, I'd like to talk to you about the end of our combat mission in Iraq, the ongoing security challenges we face, and the need to rebuild our nation here at home."[1]

Barack Obama paused for a moment, switching from commander in chief to counsellor in chief.

"I know this historic moment comes at a time of great uncertainty for many Americans," he said. "We've now been through nearly a decade of war. We've endured a long and painful recession. And sometimes in the midst of these storms, the future that we're trying to build for our nation—a future of lasting peace and long-term prosperity—may seem beyond our reach. But this milestone should serve as a reminder to all Americans that the future is ours to shape if we move forward with confidence and commitment. It should also serve as a message to the world that the United States of America intends to sustain and strengthen our leadership in this young century."[2]

Obama's speech was in fulfillment of a promise he'd made in February 2009, during an address to members of the Marine Corps at Camp Lejeune delivered during his first weeks in office and announcing August 31, 2010, as the end of the war. At one point in the 2010 speech, Obama said he wished now directly to address the people of Iraq.

"We Americans," he said, "have offered our most precious resource—our young men and women—to work with you to rebuild what was destroyed by despotism; to root out our common enemies; and to seek peace and prosperity for our children and grandchildren, and for yours."[3]

In fact, some 50,000 American troops remained in Iraq in an advisory capacity. But Obama, during that summer of 2010, had finally declared an end to a contentious war that had gone on since 2003, when the government of Sadaam Hussein was overthrown by force. The principal justification of the so-called Bush Doctrine was that Hussein's Iraq possessed weapons of mass destruction, was a threat to the national security of the United States, and that proactive preventive action was required from the United States.

The alleged weapons of mass destruction never were found.

While it may have been a slow burn, the war had been smoldering in the consciousness of the country for seven years. More than 4,000 Americans had died during Operation Iraqi Freedom. There was little agreement on the number of deaths in the Iraqi military and among its civilians—it depended on how a war death was to be defined and who was doing the defining—but no credible source had put the number at less than 100,000, and some said the truer number of dead Iraqis was many multiples of that.

Americans at home were watching a war that unfolded in real time on their cable news channels. The scenes of combat found on CNN or Fox might have been broadcast with different ideological imperatives, but neither channel looked so very different from games that now could be played at home on ever more sophisticated PlayStations or XBoxes, systems that were churning out so-called first-person shooter games like *Call of Duty* and *Halo*. Those seven years of the war in Iraq had challenged a number of long-standing assumptions about American competency, efficiency, and openness, given the apparent chaos of the subsequent occupation, if not the shock-and-awe invasion itself.

The war had strained America's relationship with its allies, especially Britain, where it had undermined some of the credibility of its prime minister, Tony Blair, who had supported Bush's decision to invade and had put his own nation's young people in harm's way. And it had ushered in a new era of realpolitik among Americans when it came to international affairs. One of its legacies was an erosion of the once-widespread belief in America's moral obligation to police the world's despots and protect democracy at all costs. At what cost, a lot of Americans now were wondering.

Demonstrably, the nation's initial assumptions about the ease of the war had proven to be faulty. By the time Obama spoke in 2010, a lot of Americans wondered if they just had not been paying enough attention to all that had being going on. Especially if they had been to Broadway and seen *American Idiot*, the most talked-about musical that summer.

American Idiot did not offer a pretty picture of America's youth in these early years of the twenty-first century: the characters around whom the show was built seemed to spend most of their time either in some filthy bed or lying, prone, in a La-Z-Boy, doped up on sugary soda pop they'd chugged in a 7–11 parking lot, munching Ritalin and snorting cocaine they had purloined from someone else.

As these representatives of young America were laid out on the stage like T. S. Eliot's patients etherized on tables—zoned-out, plugged-out, tuned-out—tanks, troops, and the face of President George W. Bush could be seen fizzing on a fleet of flickering television screens that nobody seemed actually to be watching. Were the images on the screens depicting fact or fiction? Where did the video game end and the real war begin? It was almost impossible to tell.

The characters had names—such as St. Jimmy, Johnny, Tunny, Will, Whatsername, and Extraordinary Girl—but while these young people were sufficiently distinctive and human for audiences to recognize their own malaise, their own dread of the danger of amounting to nothing, they were not so explicit that the fluidity of the musical metaphor would be compromised.

There were no cheap strictures, literal vassals, or manufactured scenes. Instead, *American Idiot* seemed to be a recounting of various inuring life choices—find a girl, take drugs, and party all day; or find a girl, get married, and hold the kid all day; or find a cause, get a uniform, and sacrifice your body all day. It broke a lot of the usual rules about character specificity. But by avoiding overly explicit resolutions for overly distinctive individuals, *American Idiot* was able to be about a universal feeling in a specific moment.

And one thing could not have been more clear: when *American Idiot* opened that April at the St. James Theatre, it felt like an indictment of America during the entire duration of the war in Iraq. It did not attack politicians; it attacked the people who had elected them, or who would have done so if only they had been bothered to vote.

American Idiot did not run from the implications of its own title. It was a rage against self-medicated apathy. It was a rant against inertia. It was a condemnation of allowing oneself to be infantilized. It decried America's inability to actually get up, turn off Fox News, take a shower, and get clean. Its narrative was inseparable from how the war in Iraq had been sold to the American people by the administration of George W. Bush; it actually felt like a metaphor for those years of conflict, as if the initial surety of the politicians and the military experts who had predicted that the Iraqi people would welcome the American military with rose petals and smiles had slowly bled out over the years, dripping down into the national psyche, inuring the populace to further political sensation.

It was a repudiation of the famous "Mission Accomplished" banner that had served as a backdrop to Bush's 2003 absurdly premature speech on the USS *Abraham Lincoln*.

The show, which had been developed at the Berkeley Repertory Theatre in California, was based not on a movie or a book, but on a 13-track conceptual album released in 2004 by an American punk band called Green Day, which was fronted by a multitalented singer-songwriter called Billie Joe Armstrong. Like, for example, The Who's *Tommy, American Idiot* was Green Day's attempt to explore the narrative possibilities of an album, to introduce at least some shards of characterization, to maybe tell something approaching a story, rather than just painting one musical soundscape after another in the usual way. Self-described as a punk rock opera, *American Idiot* centered around the dystopian story of a kid known as Jesus of Suburbia, a kid living under a ruler with a "redneck agenda," a kid who is desperate for an anthem the world can hear.

Hence the title song.

Green Day—initially made up of Billie Joe Armstrong, Mike Dirnt, and Al Sobrante—had first emerged in Northern California as part of the underground punk scene. They had been around, in various guises, for more than 15 years before they released *American Idiot*, which would become both the band's best-reviewed album and a major hit all over the world.

Punk, or rather neo-punk, may have been their genre, but Green Day hardly was the Sex Pistols. Their music may have been dominated by thrashing downward guitar strokes but was far more melodic than their more inherently atonal British ancestors, and even seemed open to a certain optimism: Green Day represented, you might say, punk with possibility. There was plenty of nihilistic fury in Green Day compositions, but also aspirational dreams of make-believe. Green Day did not run afeared of major keys. They made more ample use of arpeggios—and keyboards in general—than either their predecessors or their peers.

And for this Broadway show, which was directed by Michael Mayer, the composer and orchestrator Tom Kitt had added a variety of instrumentation to the classic, raw, Green Day sound: the show used both a violin and cello that Mayer spread out across a design that really was more of a video installation than a traditional setting. Musically, the show made much of its ability to fuse lush Broadway-style melody with Green Day's hard-edge punk sound. There wasn't so much choreography as organic movement created by Steven Hoggett. And the songs in the show appeared in the musical in the same order that they were recorded on the album.

In fact, this show probably came closer than any Broadway musical in history to actually replicating how people listened to rock albums:

frequently alone and forging their own highly personal and subjective connections to the music and lyrics. Albums—unlike shows—had long trafficked in isolated, inner feelings, and that was surely the case with *American Idiot*. By avoiding literality, the show both replicated and enhanced what it felt like to play the album: that feeling that whatever you try to do, you still amount to nothing in a world filled with louder and more toxic voices than your own.

Like the album, the show felt young, a vista of a part of our lives when we think our feelings are unique to ourselves—and that our lovers are unique complements to ourselves—even if we later come to see that our feelings and lovers were never any different, really, from those of all of others sitting around and listening to "Boulevard of Broken Dreams" or "Jesus of Suburbia," or whatever happens to be the anthem of the alienation of a particular feeling.

Still. No Broadway show had ever so well captured one simple thing: *American Idiot* was the ultimate musical of the inner feeling.

And it would be back in *Hamilton*.

Which antecedent had come closest? Well, there surely were echoes in *American Idiot* of *Spring Awakening*, an intense, influential, and highly successful 2006 musical with a score by Duncan Sheik, and a book and lyrics by Steven Sater. *Spring Awakening* had already shown that such emotionally charged and hard-edged rock music could work on Broadway. *Spring Awakening*, which was also brilliantly directed by Mayer, had been massively successful. It had run for 669 performances, lasting more than two years (a Broadway revival, by Deaf West Theatre, would come as soon as 2015).

On its face, *Spring Awakening* was just another adaptation of the 1893 Frank Wedekind play lamenting the heart-breaking consequences of scared and conservative adults keeping sexual information away from their hormone-infused adolescents. But this great show, too, had embraced anachronism. The cast initially appeared apple-cheeked and as naïve as their era, but their musical performances pulsed with eroticized angst and longing. When their emotions—or their physical desires—became too much to handle, the cast would pull out hand-held microphones that had been hidden somewhere on their person. And then they would wail their way through Sheik's signature blend of emo-infused rock.

It was as if more than a century suddenly had dropped away. And it was quite something.

For *Spring Awakening*, Sheik had written a beautiful score, the like of which Broadway never had quite seen before: it was introspective, contemplative, and melancholic, but also punkishly driven by the sharp edges of sexual desire. And Sater's poetic lyrics got right to the point in a way a young audience could immediately understand: "The thing that sucks—Okay?—for me? / A thousand bucks, I'm, like, scot-free," being one meticulously punctuated example among a suite of such cleverly titled songs as "My Junk" and "The Song of Purple Summer."

The premise of the show was that the book scenes would feel mostly like they were set in 1893, but that the songs, wherein the characters articulated the agony of young love, would range freely across time and place. It was a radical idea—but there was no question that it worked on Broadway. And its intensity was only multiplied by the choreography of Bill T. Jones, who, in essence, worked up the lithe bodies of the young performers into an expressionistic, choreographic fury, reflecting the tumult of their hormone-fueled emotions, starved by a lack of information coming from the scared, censorious adults who were failing their own children.

Jones had been allowed by the show to do his own thing—even if his referent seemed more to be the world of radically contemporary dance than the traditional vocabulary of Broadway choreography. That resulted in a palpable sense of independence for all the emotionally charged movement, which of course matched the uber-premise of the show, which was to declare that young people should be loved, told the truth, and then guided from afar, even as they are allowed to think and feel for themselves.

The show's risk-taking mostly had originated with Sater, who later would say that he had just wanted to "write this great classical-style play which had a rock concert going on in the middle."[4]

"I didn't want to write lyrics that furthered the plot," Sater said. "I wanted the music to have relevance to the culture at large." The idea, then, had been to create a show where the songs would be what Sater called "time outs."[5] So instead of a traditional show where the songs advanced the narrative, *Spring Awakening* explored the viability of an intentional divorce between story and song.

"When the characters start to sing," Sater said, "the story stops in its tracks and you go inside the hearts and minds of these kids. We drew on what rock does best."[6]

Sater's ideas sat well with Duncan Sheik, because it proffered a way to solve what for him was the most confounding aspect of composing the score to a Broadway musical: the difficulty of handling the transition between narrative and song. In essence, *Spring Awakening* decided to treat these two traditional components of a musical as two entirely separate worlds, even to the point of inhabiting very different chronological periods. This flew in the face of the conventional wisdom of Broadway musicals, which said that the fusion between book scene and musical number ideally should be as seamless as possible.

Or so the lovers of the genre believed.

Sheik, who came from outside the Broadway world, had never really bought into that convention. And he figured out that he spoke for plenty of others who liked rock music a whole more than they thought they liked musicals.

"For a lot of people," Sheik said,[7] "that's the cringe-inducing moment in musical theater. The point where somebody breaks into song. I liked the idea of doing a show that had the rigor, style and aesthetic of straight theater but was also something that the rock culture could get behind." There had been rock musicals before, of course, all the way back to *Hair* and *Jesus Christ Superstar*, but Sheik was talking about rock culture, which he understood to be something different, and cooler.

And that was pretty much exactly what *Spring Awakening* turned out to be.

Add in its sexualized content and *Spring Awakening* thus was able to grab a much younger audience than was typical on Broadway. Such were the formative leaps that the show made, it proved extraordinarily influential: without its success, it is unlikely that Stew's *Passing Strange* ever would have been produced on Broadway, and certainly not *American Idiot*. Its tentacles extended out farther into the future, too. Looking back from 2009,[8] Meyer recalled how much the show had given producers the confidence to do "a different kind of musical," and also how much time a certain Irish rock musician had spent at the theater; because of the level of coolness of *Spring Awakening*, even Bono was becoming interested in Broadway.

When it came to the arrival of *American Idiot* on Broadway, Green Day—and Billie Joe Armstrong in particular—were entranced with the experience. When the show's business started to fail, Armstrong himself would take over the lead role, renewing excitement. On other nights, he'd play unannounced curtain calls, sometimes with the other members of his band, riffing into the night and essentially offering the audience members who were lucky enough to be present two shows for the price of one. There was a real fusion going on: rock concert, collage, album, musical, event.

American Idiot would expand forever the possibility of the American musical, especially its relationship with rock music. It would take advantage of the inherent complexity of its source material: music that may rail hard, loud, and long against the hysteria of a paranoid country compromised and commoditized by a media monolith, but also lament, sweetly, like romantic poems from the days of yore, about the way innocence never seems to last.

It's hard to overstate how clear of a path *American Idiot,* the first political musical on Broadway to be all about individualized inner feelings, built toward *Hamilton*. The Green Day creation lacked defined historical characters, of course, but it still seemed to issue a challenge to the audience to get politicized and get involved, lest the agenda of others be allowed to take over.

American Idiot was a dystopian vision of a bloated, apolitical, sagging, uncaring America—the atrophied flip-side, in many ways, of *Hamilton*, which would be so infused with, and so adept at conveying, the optimism of a young nation. But both shows were attempts at both national definition and, each in their different ways, the promotion of activism. In its earliest incarnation, *Hamilton* was known as *Hamilton: The Mix-Tape*, a reminder, really, of how much Lin-Manuel Miranda initially saw his ground-breaking show in terms of a musical album, a narrative collection of songs, the songs having come first. In that way, among many other such ways, he was greatly indebted to *American Idiot*.

Many of the fervent fans of *American Idiot* would head back to the theater and see it multiple times, finding a show that never quite seemed to be the same whenever you experienced it, a show that might have emulated the feeling of listening to an album, but still was a piece of theatre that lived and breathed in three dimensions. By any Broadway standards, it had been a thrilling experiment.

In 2012, *American Idiot* had a national tour across America. "There is something about shows with 'America' in their name," the actor Van Hughes told a reporter at the time.[9] "There's something really powerful about that. It's like we're an invasion of their hometown." Meanwhile, another actor reported a different experience: "I've been surprised," he said. "The feeling that comes back to me is grief. For addiction. For people who have lost someone or for the someone who was lost. Somehow, the show brings that out."[10]

Indeed it did; it did so because *American Idiot* had the guts to leave more space than any other musical that had come before. It did not have the earnestness of *Rent*, it did not want to flesh everything out for the audience. Instead, it wanted to provide a framework of disruption. That way it could bring out whatever individual audience members were feeling.

American Idiot was a reminder that most Broadway musicals were—and had always been—insecure. They had always been scared to leave gaps. *American Idiot* actually was comfortable in its own political and aesthetic skin.

For all of its formative brilliance and its revolutionary structure, *American Idiot* still was not for all tastes. And when award time came around, there were worries that its touring prospects were limited.

How would Americans outside New York react to its radical reinvention of form? Would they buy what it had to say about media, inertia, and the war in Iraq, still bleeding through these early years of the twenty-first century in America? That seemed to a lot of people like a pretty formidable risk.

As had happened many times before, and would happen again, the forces of conservatism reasserted themselves. Alas for *American Idiot* and innovation, the Tony Award for best musical that year went to a cheery, optimistic, and thoroughly traditional new show named *Memphis*.

11
2010: BLOODY BLOODY WIKI WIKI SELF-AWARENESS

The seventh president of the United States was very familiar to Americans—looking cool, he had stared out from their wallets since 1928.

There always had been some irony in Andrew Jackson's visage adorning the $20 bill, given his fevered opposition to the national central banking system so beloved by Alexander Hamilton. In 1833, the quick-tempered Jackson had attempted to remove the federal deposits from the Second Bank of the United States, arguing that the institution, which had been chartered in 1816 by James Madison, had come to represent only the interests of the wealthy, at the expense of ordinary Americans. That led to a movement in the Senate to censure Jackson. But he had survived the Whigs, just as he had all these years on the greenback.

But by 2010, lots of Americans were looking askance at the Jackson presidency, as at so many other unsavory aspects of the nation's history, especially those pertaining to slavery, its original sin.

Jackson had been a slave owner with holdings of at least 150 enslaved laborers at his 1,000-acre Nashville plantation, The Hermitage, and there was no historical record of him having had any major misgivings about the institution, unlike, say, the more ruminative Thomas Jefferson. Jackson's treatment of Native Americans had been brutal, even by the standards of his day: not only did troops under his management massacre Indians, Jackson presided over a variety of dubious treaties specifically designed to part Native Americans from land that rightly belonged to them.

Most notoriously of all, Jackson had, in 1830, signed the heinous Indian Removal Act, an initiative designed to remove all the southern Native American tribes from their ancestral homelands, in what would later become known as the Confederacy, to federal land west of the Mississippi River. This afflicted such autonomous nations as the Chickasaw, the Seminole, and the Choctaw, but none more horrendously than the Cherokee. In 1838, during the infamous Trail of Tears, at least 13,000 of the Cherokee had been forced on pain of death by the Jackson administration to leave their homeland in the Appalachians and head west through rain, snow, and ice, with many perishing on the way. It was, inarguably, an act of genocide, in practice if not in name.

On the other hand, for those who could get past an act so heinous when it came to historical assessment, Jackson, the first U.S. president who had come from a state other than Massachusetts or Virginia, had been a fervent populist. He was known for his elevation of the lot of the ordinary American—indeed for his definition of the ordinary American—and for his resentment of the educated and well-connected elites.

He had a fervent belief in the populist potential of the union. He paid off the national debt—Jackson was the first and only president ever to do so—and he left the country in the black. He recast the main job of the president as being to exercise the will of the people, and, in so doing, he did more than any other leader when it came to elevating the executive branch to the same level as the Congress. And he was the first self-styled outsider to assume the presidency.

In no way did Jackson put his birth in a log cabin to waste. He was a politician who was highly adept at the manipulation of populist resentment and who knew how to profit from the public's perennial unease with an elite government taking the money of the ordinary American.

"He wanted sincerely to look after the little fellow who had no pull," his devoted fan Harry Truman would write, "and that's what a president is supposed to do."[1]

And with his lush, wavy, well-coiffed hair—on the $20 bill, he is pictured with a lock of hair dangling roguishly over his forehead—Jackson had a demonstrably theatrical flair.

No wonder, then, that before there was *Hamilton*, there was another musical about one of America's first and most colorful leaders: Michael Friedman's *Bloody Bloody Andrew Jackson.*

Friedman, a prodigiously talented young composer and lyricist whose compositional career had blossomed with a downtown theater group known as The Civilians, had started working on the show in 2007. With a book and direction by Alex Timbers, the show had played that summer as a work in progress at the Williamstown Theatre Festival in Massachusetts. Friedman's idea was not necessarily to break new ground about Jackson, and, unlike Lin-Manuel Miranda would do, he did not base his emo-infused musical on a major work of biographical scholarship; rather drawing on the populist identity of Jackson and a great flight of imagination by a gifted young theatre artist, he characterized Jackson as a kind of punky, in-your-face, alt-rockin' president—a frontier populist flying by the seat of his tight-fitting pants.

Bloody Bloody Andrew Jackson was only about a 90-minute show and that was not much time to consider the subject in all of his Jacksonian complexity, but, then again, you could argue the facts and contradictions therein were already well known.

This was, as things turned out, an ideal musical for the Wikipedia age. Actually, it felt like the first such musical.

In 2007, the free, web-based, open-sourced encyclopedia created by Jimmy Wales and Larry Sanger was still only six years old, but, at least according to the Wikipedia page on Wikipedia, it had already become one of the top ten websites in the United States, with 46.4 million visitors, more than either Apple or the *New York Times*. The initial view of the site as a kind of slapdash amateur experience that no major media organization was willing to trust also had begun to dissipate. Even though some 2,000 entries a day were being added— making Wikipedia the biggest encyclopedia in the history of such endeavors—editing protocols and processes had improved to the point where the entries generally were seen as trustworthy. Errors of fact and egregiously partisan points of view were becoming less common.

By 2007, many of the entries therein were being written by experts in the field, even though academics were routinely decrying the influence of so easy and ready a source of nonprimary information on the work of their students. Wikipedia was often cited as a source of the dumbing-down of America, of the blurring of the crucial lines between primary and secondary sourcing and, perhaps most crucially of all, the longstanding academic convention not only of putting your own name on your work but of citing the efforts of those in the same field who had come before. Wikipedia was anonymous. When changes or updates were made, old versions seemed to vanish into the ether, scant record kept of their ever even having existed.

But for all the furious criticism of Wikipedia—and the parodies on late-night television—it fundamentally was changing American society by making even archaic research far more readily available.

It was on its way toward being comprehensive on a dizzying array of subjects, and its central crowd-sourcing philosophy of readers constantly editing the entries of their peers had proven to work remarkably well. In many cases, journalists were turning to Wikipedia as an authoritative source: if, for example, a celebrity were to die, Wikipedia's most enthusiastic users would rush to be the first to update the page with the latest information, often beating the major news organizations whose increasingly archaic protocols required more detailed and comprehensive amounts of confirmation. Wikipedia still was being mocked, but its impact was irrefutable. Everyone was using it; most people just preferred to pretend otherwise.

As a consequence of this stunning rise of open-sourced information curation, the individual revelation of historical fact was becoming de-emphasized—what was the point in doing a lot of individual research in tedious reading rooms, when it was likely that Wikipedia had already got there first?

Especially since the reward system for even doing such research was being upended. Wikipedia, a peer-to-peer service run almost entirely by volunteers, was free and both its contributors and almost all of its editors were unpaid. That meant that legacy pay services such as *Encyclopedia Britannica* and its peers, which long had relied on readers to pay its researchers for their work, found themselves in an increasingly untenable position.

This was emblematic of a massive change in American culture toward the end of this first decade of the twenty-first century.

Most Americans in the culture business were slow to comprehend the change, but Wikipedia was at the center of a great current of amateurization that would soon undermine a whole variety of hitherto stable professional careers, from journalism to researching to driving a taxi. Once the province of the specialist, fact-based information, including critical opinions, quickly was becoming commodified. And, as a result, the economic and cultural power of original factual revelation was being eviscerated.

This would have an enormous effect on, say, the use of history in a literary work or a television program or a movie, or a Broadway musical. For generations, careful research had been prized, and such works could prosper by revealing things that people did not previously know, often the fruit of many laborious hours by entire research staffs spent poring over index cards or microfiche. Writers would disappear inside libraries for months at a time. In plays, novels, and films, such research often had been painstakingly turned into narrative, scenes reconstructed, ideas put into words, all with the overall aim of revealing how things had been. The paying customers traditionally had often been awed by all of the hard work by degreed professionals. It was as if the show had done all the work for them, meaning they did not have to do it for themselves. When somebody paid for a cultural experience, this was what they were choosing to buy.

But by 2007 audiences were beginning to look very differently at all that.

They were realizing that, say, pretty much anybody could research a musical about Andrew Jackson without heading to Tennessee or even the local library. There were no obscure or inaccessible stories anymore. All one had to do was type "Andrew Jackson" and "Wikipedia" into a Google search box. Not everybody grasped the enormity of this change, which occurred over several years. And some have yet to grasp what Wikipedia has wrought when it comes to work based on history. But by 2007, the savvier minds had already started to realize that something would have to take its place, if audiences still were being expected to plonk down large amounts of cash.

And what was that going to be?

Friedman had figured it out far earlier than most of his peers.

His answer? Attitude.

To put that another way: Point of view now had replaced factual revelation.

Actually, point of view now was everything in the cultural discourse. Unless you had a point of view, you were dead in the water. Nobody wanted to buy unvarnished facts anymore; they did not have as much user value. Nobody wanted carefully reasoned, nuanced, unbiased arguments on both sides of something. You had to have a take, and the stronger that take, the better your chances of being heard.

* * *

By 2009, Friedman had several shows on the go, and *Bloody Bloody Andrew Jackson* had, following another developmental production in Los Angeles, landed at the New York Public Theater, where it was billed *Bloody Bloody Andrew Jackson: The Concert Version*. By then the actor Benjamin Walker had become attached to the title role: his was a sexy outside presence in tight black jeans, a kind of walking, brooding, warbling manifestation of Friedman's central idea: American President as Rock Star.

The aesthetic of the show had begun to coalesce: a fundamental conceit was that even though this was a historical piece, the show did not have to stick to its actual period. Rather, it could embrace anachronism and float around as it chose.

And Friedman also had an idea as how to give the piece some emotional oomph: emo.

As a style of music, emo (from "emotive hardcore") had its roots in the post-punk mid-1980s. Its rebellious heart was in punk-rock, you might say, but more the American wing thereof than the British. Emo was much less averse than true punk to the embrace of melody, and its lyrics tended to be infused with emotional angst, a bitter sense of nostalgia for a better time, a poetic desperation. Full of minor chords and lyrics sung by singers who seemed perpetually on the edge of tears, emo was punk without the associated nihilism nor its anarchist gestalt. *Rolling Stone* called emo "punk rock's moody younger sibling," and it was right. This was the music of crisis-outrage-hurt; it represented the scoring overreaction.

In the years that followed, emo's signature combination of hard riffs, sweaty angst, and tender melodies—along with palpable anthemic ambition—proved itself very adept at translation into the theater. Green Day, for example, might not have been an emo band to most minds, but *American Idiot* certainly trafficked in some of these same qualities. For even as musical and aesthetic styles had come and gone, emotionalism had always been the major currency of Broadway musicals, even of tough-nosed rock musicals. Both classic punk and heavy metal had been a tough sell in the theater. Both of them lacked enough vulnerability. Broadway audiences were perfectly willing to engage in ideas, just as long as they were able to feel something at the same time.

Of course, Friedman wasn't writing about sexually ambitious adolescents, as had been the case in *Spring Awakening*, but an American president. But he felt like Andrew Jackson was emo just the same.

And not just Jackson but his entire era.

If there was one explicit thing that *Hamilton* learned from *Bloody Bloody Andrew Jackson,* it was that the leaders of the nascent nation known as the United States of America were young men, as hormonally challenged, sexually compromised, and mistake-prone as young men of any other time and place (it's also worth noting that, especially after its peak was over, the emo genre was often ridiculed for its obsession with the male point of view and its inclination to reduce women to being causers of feelings in men, not people actually having them). Entirely of that vogue, *Bloody Bloody Andrew Jackson* argued that we've stared out too long at portraits of old men on our currency, and thus we have forgotten that truth. And, therefore, it energized and, crucially, sexualized the early years of the history of the United States, in a way that worked for Broadway—and allowed the musical of political substance to continue its great rise. It had now been given much better tools.

Right from the start, it was this emo-esque element of *Bloody Bloody Andrew Jackson* that caused the most excitement.

"It's this angry, pubescent time where things are complicated and frustrating and frightening and dangerous," Walker told the *New York Times* that May.[2] "That's where the emo idea comes into play. As a country, we are young adults. We are these hormonally raging citizens. We are swayed by someone who seems like us. We're excited by an inaugural ball where we feel like we've elected someone like us."

Walker became enthused with his use of first person.

"It's also not a horribly rational time," he went on, assuming the voice of this hormonal America. "We want land. We are expanding. We are like puppies with huge paws. We're clumsily expanding as a nation and as citizens, in the same way that the powers of the Executive branch of government are expanding. We're expanding into the West. And we're rejecting Washington, these overbearing parents who don't seem to have our interests in mind, who are not protecting the westerners on the frontier satisfactorily. Jackson was willing to stand up and do that in the best way he knew how."[3]

The interview proved prescient. *Bloody Bloody Andrew Jackson* clearly was determined not to be your parents' historical musical about the founding fathers.

That would have been *1776*, a musical that would be mentioned often in reference to both *Bloody Bloody Andrew Jackson* and, a few years thereafter, *Hamilton*.

First seen on Broadway in 1969 (and revived at the Roundabout Theatre in 1997), *1776* featured a book by Peter Stone and music and lyrics by a former history teacher (and Broadway neophyte) named Sherman Edwards, who had imbued a few lessons from his teacher, the legendary Broadway figure Frank Loesser. *1776* focused in on the existential decision-making of the titular year, especially the efforts of John Adams, the second president of the United States, to persuade his nervous colleagues to vote for American independence, and the difficulty everyone had in figuring out what should be in the document.

1776 was no emo musical, of course. On the contrary, it was more like a contemporary opera. But *1776* had also been innovative in its own right: it ranged far from the then-traditional structure of the Broadway musical, just as its subject was at variance with most of the romantic, or hippy-dippyish, narratives of its touchy-feely day.

1776 had only one set. The show began with a solid ten minutes of music—complicated music that seemed to belong more in an opera house. Yet long sections of Act One did not feature any music at all, but assorted machinations and political posturing in dialogic form. The climax of the show was not the usual rousing closing number, but a silhouetted vista of men signing the Declaration of Independence, accompanied by the slow tolling of the Liberty Bell. Despite a hefty running time of two hours and twenty minutes, there was no intermission. By Broadway standards, there was also relatively little choreography. And there was no traditional chorus: all 26 of the actors on stage had a principal role, or so it felt. Women were hardly a presence at all (the character of Martha Jefferson got one big number). And some of Edwards's songs were, to say the least, esoteric: the show's musical tribute to Thomas Jefferson was entitled, "He Plays the Violin."

The show's advance was only about $60,000, despite a production cost of $500,000, a substantial amount for the time.

At the time, a lot of critics had expected the show to pay homage to the music of its eighteenth-century era and come up with some kind of pastiche of revolutionary tunes; that was where Broadway heads were at. Very few people could imagine a historical musical with music that belonged to any period other than that of its setting. But Edwards had other ideas, even if this historical musical with "modern" music still was very much a radical idea.

Most of Broadway's leading lights had tagged *1776* as a likely failure, due to their perception that audiences surely would be bored by a musical about the signing of the Declaration of Independence. But they had been wrong: on the contrary, audiences had been both moved and fascinated. And the show had remained popular over the years that followed precisely because it had not been afraid to assert itself as an intellectually substantial show, and to reveal the price paid by early Americans for the nation's nascent, flawed democracy. Over time, parents would bring children to learn about the founding of the nation they called home. And at the point when *1776* opened on Broadway, and for years thereafter, the list of Broadway musicals that had tapped into American history, and taken the nation's origin story seriously, was very small.

Looking back on the initial reaction to the show, the resistance of critics to a musical about the creation of the American democracy, heck, even a musical that dared to be about American history rather than boy meets girl, was strikingly intense. Many of them were simply amazed that anyone would ever attempt such an audacious act. This kind of history was just not what Broadway musicals were thought to do.

"What Broadway needed was a patriotic musical?" asked Martin Gottfried, sarcastically, in *Women's Wear Daily*. "I don't think so."

Gottfried was of course partly referencing how the show seemed to be so out of step with the very different kinds of revolutions taking place beyond the doors of the theater in 1969, but that also blinded him to the show's qualities: *1776* was hardly, as he claimed, "a wooden replica of souvenir-shop patriotism."

No one dared to say that about *Hamilton*. But by then the Broadway musical had moved on from 1969.

1776 did make it to the White House, just like *Hamilton* a generation or two later. On George Washington's birthday in 1970, the entire show was presented in the East Room of the White House. William Safire, an ever-savvy aide to President Richard M. Nixon, asked the show to cut a couple of politically questionable songs for the Nixonites, especially the pacifistic number "Momma Look Sharp," but the producer, Stuart Ostrow, refused. Safire stood down. And Nixon sat down and watched the whole thing. At the end, he stood up and cheered.

So did plenty of people when *Bloody Bloody Andrew Jackson: The Concert Version* opened up at the Public. To say that the show embraced anachronism was an understatement: its song titles included "Populism Yea Yea" and "Illness as Metaphor." As Ben Brantley pointed out in the *New York Times*, the first lyric to the first song was "Why wouldn't you ever go out with me in school?" And there was much fascination at this radical characterization of a maverick, populist president, the like of which America had not (yet) seen again.

For it was far too early for anyone to anticipate the rise of Donald J. Trump.

* * *

By the spring of 2010, the show had received a full production at the Public Theater. And by that October, *Bloody Bloody Andrew Jackson* was on Broadway.

Its marketing tagline? "History just got all sexypants."

In Friedman and Timbers's work you could see the meta influence of *Urinetown*, the bifurcated worlds of *Spring Awakening*, and the political collage of *American Idiot*. But *Bloody Bloody Andrew Jackson* had more attitude than all of those other shows put together. And Walker, the star actor, fully understood as he winked his eyelined eye in the first moments of the show, that both he and the audience had to be in on the same joke, to display the same level of self-awareness. Attitude was the name of the game now.

There were narrative events taken from Jackson's life, both personal and professional, but they were snapshots. They never were allowed to exist on their own terms, but were constantly contextualized in terms of point of view. Anachronisms were not only abundant but audacious. Characters would claim to know things because they had read about them in history books that had not yet been written: tour groups would parade through Jackson's White House in the modern-day vogue of such groups, parading past White House "staffers" dressed in cheerleader costumes, all part of the rogue president's rock-star entourage.

Musically, this was something quite different from *American Idiot*. This was not a conceptual album. Friedman's score was written by and for the theater: it had a kind of restless quality. And it felt like it was being sampled as much as played. To experience it being performed in the theater was not unlike watching a video clip online. There was that kind of remove.

On the other hand, *Bloody Bloody Andrew Jackson* homed in on some of the paradoxes inherent to this presidency and, indeed, to the nascent American identity, all of which were themes that *Hamilton* later would explore. Here was a president who did a lot for personal freedom, the American footprint, and even the preservation of democracy, but who also embraced slavery and forcibly removed Native Americans from their lands.

So, was he a key instigator and defender of the American way of life or "an American Hitler"?

Was Jackson an aberrant, amoral, American anomaly or a savvy, self-aware guy who did what he had to do to move a young, precarious country forward—and thus was little more than an embodiment of America itself?

Those were the heavy questions of the evening. But they didn't stop the show from enjoying itself. Celebrity culture, it seemed to say, had always been part of the American identity, so there was no reason not to both critique and celebrate it at the same time. And it was OK to party with a dead president.

Bloody Bloody Andrew Jackson did not even try to reveal anything new about its subject: how could a 90-minute musical possibly do that anyway? Instead, it put all of its creative energy into presenting his story in the freshest and most opinionated way possible, and in making its title character live as much as possible in what felt like the present.

The show lasted only for a while. This president had limited appeal with Broadway audiences who hardly were being asked to pay populist prices. Within three-and-half months, the show had closed. People wondered why—especially given the generally favorable reviews. The answer would be better understood after *Hamilton*, which borrowed some of the *Bloody Bloody Andrew Jackson* theatrical vocabulary, but was telling the story of a much more empathetic historical American figure, a political leader with strong opinions like Jackson but who had explicitly known the pain of personal loss himself.

And in doing so, it added two of the crucial Broadway criteria that had eluded Friedman and Timbers: Miranda's Alexander Hamilton had vulnerability where Friedman's Jackson had sass and eye-shadow. And whereas Jackson felt like a cautionary tale of celebrity excess and populist megalomania, Hamilton reminded us of ourselves. That was the difference between the two shows. That was why one closed relatively quickly while the other would turn into the biggest Broadway phenomenon in years.

* * *

On September 9, 2017, Friedman died, apparently from complications due to HIV/AIDS, an unsettling reminder that, for all the advances in healthcare and containment, the plague was not yet finished with the American theatre. He was 41, and his death caused a great outpouring of grief. He had been in the middle of a new musical. Among the projects he left unfinished was a potential sequel to *A Chorus Line*, set a decade after the original, when dancers were dealing with their ranks being depleted by AIDS; and an adaptation of the film *All the President's Men*, the movie about the investigation of the Watergate break-in, as authorized by President Nixon and investigated by *The Washington Post*. Friedman, clearly, had his finger on precisely where the Broadway musical was heading; he just did not get the chance to accompany it yet further on its way. Friedman would not live to write any more emo musicals, or explore any musical ideas at all.

Bloody Bloody Andrew Jackson, though, had started something. The loss was staggering. Few of Friedman's friends knew of his health crisis: it appeared that his HIV-positive status had only recently been diagnosed. Many of his friends and past collaborators were devastated by the death of a theater artist with, it seemed, a personality every bit as big as that of Andrew Jackson.

But the Broadway beat went on, as it has always done, now hardly afeared of the Founding Fathers of the United States.

There can be no doubt that the massive popularity of *Hamilton*, especially among current and former employees of the Department of the Treasury, helped preserve its subject's place on the $10 bill, after a push to diversify the portraits on American currency threatened also to snare the first Secretary of the Treasury, a guy who had, at least, believed in the stabilizing possibility of a central bank that would issue such notes.

But what of Jackson? Did Friedman's musical do the same for him?

At first, it seemed not. In April 2016, during the last days of the Obama administration, the Treasury Department announced that Jackson's coveted place on the $20 bill would be taken by Harriet Tubman, a former slave who not only had escaped to freedom but had, through her subsequent work with the Underground Railroad, prepared a pathway for others to do the same. Jackson, who had of course owned slaves like Tubman, was to be bumped to the back of the bill, where he would share his spot with an image of the White House. At the time, it was noted that the Treasury Secretary, then Jacob J. Lew, appeared to be walking back his previous commitment to make a woman the face of the $10 bill. Hamilton had survived, it was widely reported, due to a certain Broadway musical amplifying both his profile and popularity. His removal would have sparked an outcry.

But *Bloody Bloody Andrew Jackson* not only had closed much faster and made much less of an impact on the national consciousness, it had not even tried to make its subject more likeable. On the contrary, it had reveled in his bad-boy identity. If *Hamilton* was Apollonian in its ambition, *Bloody Bloody Andrew Jackson* had been cheerfully and unapologetically Dionysian.

Unsavory political figures of the past—slave-owners and Confederate heroes especially—were being removed from plinths all across the country. So, it then seemed, Jackson was surely condemned to make his exit. And for the first time in American history, an African American woman would appear on one of the most important denominations of the nation's currency.

It was pointed out by the Fed that any such change likely would take a while, being as the world of currency redesign moves slowly. The suggested target date was 2020. And some of Tubman's supporters worried that the victory would by then turn out mostly to be pyrrhic, given the inexorable progress toward a cashless society.

At the announcement, it was pointed out by reporters that Lew and Obama had only a few months left in their offices. They expressed confidence that their changes would surely stand with any future administration. Who could possibly disagree with such an idea?

Of course, neither man had anticipated an administration led by Donald J. Trump.

In September 2017, Trump's new Secretary of the Treasury, Steven Mnuchin, declined to endorse the currency redesign plans passed along by the Obama administration, suggesting that the administration had more important things about which to be concerned.

But it was lost on no one that Mnuchin's boss had, as part of a victorious presidential campaign built on the back of a new kind of populist uprising that had risen in the shadows but bitten down hard on America's liberal elite, in the past spoken very warmly about a certain populist president in whom he clearly saw the first shadows of himself. That summer, Politifact had called Trump's affectionate veneration of Jackson "a bromance across the centuries."[4] Trump, Politico pointed out, had put Jackson's portrait in the Oval Office, and made a pilgrimage to his tomb shortly after taking office. Clearly, Trump greatly admired Jackson's reputation as a decisive president generally untroubled by any political consequences of impetuous action.

The smart money now was on Jackson staying on the money. At least while Trump was in the Oval Office. Perhaps *Bloody Bloody Andrew Jackson* had made one mistake above all else: it had showed up too soon.

12

2011: UNLUCKY: SPIDER-MAN AND THE GREAT BROADWAY OVERREACH

In February of 2011, Broadway's typically mild-mannered critics were in furious collective revolt.

From its earlier moments of gestation, the musical called *Spider-Man: Turn Off the Dark* had declared its intent to be one of the biggest and most important shows Broadway ever had seen: a singular marriage of the super-auteur, the supergroup, and the superhero. Few shows in the history of Broadway had ever had such populist bonafides, and none of those ever had come with the budget to match its ambition.

The director, Julie Taymor, had created *The Lion King*, one of the most successful Broadway shows ever, cementing her reputation as Broadway's leading auteur. Not only was the new musical to be her first major Broadway project since that hugely profitable phenomenon, but, by the time the dust settled, she was in charge of an eye-popping budget of $75 million: *Spider-Man: Turn Off the Dark* would end up being the most expensive show in Broadway history.

And, it would turn out, among the most disastrous.

When Glen Berger, the original book writer for the show, published a 2013 book looking back on the entire experience from his own perspective, he called it *Song of Spider-Man: the Inside Story of the Most Controversial Musical in History*.

That was not much of an exaggeration, given the eye-popping series of events that were about to unfold. But it's easy to forget how much this show at first seemed to promise.

For starters, there was to be a score by Bono and The Edge, leading members of the anthemic, post-punk Irish rock band U2, not only one of the best-selling musical groups of all time, but a mega-band known for its spectacular and innovative live performances. Much more famous globally than either Green Day or Duncan Sheik, they were a huge coup for Broadway, which was hungry for a new international brand.

Unlike most rock bands, U2, and Bono in particular, had branded themselves as artists dedicated to global issues: they had worked with LiveAid, Greenpeace, Amnesty International, and Nelson Mandela, and they'd tried for years to fuse their musical careers with campaigning for social justice.

They had done all this at the very highest levels. In April 2010, Bono had met with President Barack Obama, apparently to discuss the administration's development strategy heading into the upcoming G-8 and G-20 meetings in Canada and September's United Nations Summit on the Millennium Development Goals, or so Bono's advocacy group, ONE, had claimed in one of the more pompous statements a rock star ever put out.

And then there was Spidey himself: the most famous and lucrative Marvel super-hero of all time.

Stan Lee and Steve Ditko had created a comic-book character who would become not only well known but beloved, even to people who had barely ever picked up a comic book. Bigger than Batman or Superman, Spider-Man had long been Marvel's flagship character, company mascot, and its most valuable property; his likeness had grossed in excess of $1 billion, even before any Broadway musical including his name. Everybody understood what the altruistic Spider-Man did, and his exquisite sense of mission. His appeal to teenagers seemed to transcend the changing generations, only intensifying over time.

But despite the most formidable pedigree imaginable, *Spider-Man: Turn Off the Dark* turned out to be a scandal- and catastrophe-plagued enterprise. Its title may have implied a willingness to stand in the light, but *Spider-Man: Turn Off the Dark* had been subject to endless delays, countless injuries, cast members coming and going, many of them by way of the hospital, and, as a consequence, enough spinning of stories on the World Wide Web to tie Peter Parker up in knots. And critics had been strung along.

The production history of the show dated back to a workshop performance in the summer of 2007, when it already was rumored to be one of the most expensive Broadway musicals in history, although the number being shot around at that time was only about $30 million. The show had been conceived by a producer named Tony Adams, but he died from a heart attack in 2005, leaving his former Chicago lawyer, David Garfinkel, a relative neophyte, to pick up the pieces, alongside Sony and Spider-Man's rights holders at Marvel Entertainment, who could, of course, have authorized the appearance of various other superheroes and super villains in the show, whatever the creative team so chose. Garfinkel had formed a company, optimistically naming it Hello Entertainment.

But things did not go well.

Right from the start, the show had posited making major physical changes to what then was called the Hilton Theatre to accommodate the show. In the spring of 2018, another much more stable Broadway show, *Harry Potter and the Cursed Child*, would also redo the roughly 1,700-seat theater, turning it into a virtual Harry Potter theme park at a reported cost of $68 million,[1] more than any other play in the history of Broadway. But that was for *Harry Potter*, a proven hit from London. *Spider-Man: Turn Off the Dark* had proved nothing.

As the planned, then delayed, then replanned opening of *Spider-Man: Turn Off the Dark* neared, the size of the budget kept increasing: first it was reported as $30 million, then $40 million, then $50 million, then $65 million, and finally $75 million, a progressive and costly march toward one of the biggest overreaches in Broadway history.

Given the advent of the 2008 recession, so expensive a production was less than admirable timing. Moreover, it was immediately clear to most potential investors that the show's massive projected running costs—the weekly expenses a show spends on salaries and marketing—would be so high as to swallow a high percentage of the potential gross, making *Spider-Man: Turn Off the Dark*, in essence, a lousy investment. Even if it managed to sell every seat. As a result of all of the creative and fiscal troubles, the production did not open during that 2007–8 season, as first had been expected. Nor did it open during the 2008–9 season.

As the summer of 2009 rolled around, the show was still looking for money, its creative process constantly being put on hold; the show's budget was now reportedly stretching to $50 million or more. Broadway investors and reporters generally found all of the money being spent on the theater, as distinct from the show, to be weird. Despite all that had gone on in Las Vegas, where space reconfigurations were routine, Broadway still was not used to theaters being changed drastically for every show. It just was not the way Broadway previously had done business, despite Taymor's insistence that her show would not only be no ordinary musical, and not even so much a musical as a giant, thoroughly immersive, rock'n'roll extravaganza.

Producers did the shows; the theater owners, historically the adults in the room, took care of the theaters, which did not change their front of house areas at the whims of a show that might well be closing on Sunday. *Spider-Man: Turn Off the Dark* was upending all of that. And it was doing so at great expense. Broadway was, to say the least, unnerved.

Whatever else eventually could be said about this bizarre Broadway show—and enough was said to fill several books—immersion was one of the few promises the show actually delivered. The show was immersive, all right.

But for a while, nearly nine years after Bono and The Edge first had signed on the dotted line, it looked like the show would not deliver anything at all. Opening dates were put back again: it was to be the fall of 2009, then the winter of 2010. As delays had multiplied, actors like Alan Cumming and Evan Rachel Wood had come and gone, moving on to more certain projects. Corporate sponsorships shifted, too: the Hilton Theatre had become the Foxwoods Theatre. Another producer, Michael Cohl, was added. The show became a staple of the theatrical gossip columns, with the *New York Post* and the *New York Times* competing furiously for scoops about injuries to cast members (there were several during rehearsal, a couple of which had involved broken bones), budget overruns, and a veritable plethora of directorial meltdowns. The first preview performance kept getting postponed, which sucked up more millions of dollars. And the show's injury-prone flying stunts (performed in harnesses but without safety nets) were attracting attention from Actors' Equity and from health and safety officials. Taymor had not confined her production either to the proscenium or to the floor of the auditorium. Actors were flying all around the theater.

The show finally began performances on November 28, 2010, albeit in a state of some chaos: those who were there reported the show ran almost three-and-a-half hours, including five stoppages for technical glitches and a 40-minute intermission. Act One had ended, more quickly than planned, with the title character, played by a young actor named Reeve Carney, left dangling over the audience.

During Act Two, the *New York Times* reported, an audience member had shouted out the phrase, "I don't know how everyone else feels, but I feel like a guinea pig today—I feel like it's a dress rehearsal." She'd been met with boos, the paper said, but it was still an extraordinary Broadway occurrence, on many different levels. It suggested that audiences were losing patience with the whole enterprise.

And there were plenty of people there with access to a megaphone to report all of these annoying snafus, including Patrick Healy, that reporter from the *New York Times*, and Michael Riedel from the *Post*, who had been following and amplifying the many travails of the show on an almost-daily basis. Such was the interest in the show that no first preview in the history of Broadway previews had ever been reported in such detail; such catastrophic detail, it turned out.

It quickly became clear that the show was a victim of its own hype and its most disastrous of creative processes. Not only had its scale and complexity precluded the customary Off-Broadway or out-of-town tryout (even *Spider-Man: Turn Off the Dark* could hardly ask investors to pay for the renovation of two different theaters in two different cities), a show that probably needed previews more than any other show in the history of Broadway musicals was forced to undergo its preview process under the klieg lights of the media, which meant that they were not really previews at all. Predictably, the results were terrible. And, of course, the show had never been set up properly to be profitable.

Things only got worse.

At the December 20 preview performance—one of so many preview performances that it still seemed like the opening never would actually arrive, that *Spider-Man: Turn Off the Dark* would never dare to stand in the light—one of the show's aerialists, a longtime dancer named Christopher Tierney, took a serious fall about seven minutes prior to the end of the show. Even in 2010, there were people surreptitiously taping all the preview performances—especially since curiosity was running so high—and Tierney could be seen in the shocking bootleg videos tumbling to the ground, apparently as a consequence of a harness not being properly attached to his body by a stagehand. Although he would recover and rejoin the show a few weeks later—and, remarkably, he'd pointedly refuse to join the chorus of negativity—he'd initially landed in serious condition at Bellevue Hospital, with CNN reporting he had broken ribs and internal bleeding.

By then it was clear that the show had lost control of its own narrative.

The 31-year-old Tierney was the fourth injured actor (another had suffered broken wrists), and, by now, there was widespread concern that the show was just not a safe environment in which to work. Actors' Equity, the federal Occupational Safety and Health Administration,

New York's Department of Labor, and even the Fire Department of New York—all of which shared responsibility for workplace safety for actors—were being urged to take more proactive roles, but although the producers cancelled the following Wednesday matinee, they claimed they would be back up and running that Wednesday night. It actually took another day, but the show went on. For preview after preview after preview.[2]

Until the word went around on the critics' transom that enough was enough.

There was no organized rebellion, but it was clear to insiders that the major American newspapers were not going to honor the request to delay the opening night until some time in March, as the show was requesting, despite, of course, continuing to sell tickets to the public. And so, a few days before one of several previously scheduled opening nights, this one being February 6, critics began quietly buying their own tickets. On February 7, reviews magically appeared in, among other outlets, the *New York Times, Los Angeles Times,* the *Washington Post*, and *Chicago Tribune*.

The show the critics had paid good money to see had been pretty terrible, not least due to its incoherent story, surely a self-inflicted problem given the usual narrative clarity of the melodramatic comic-book genre. But there were no clear rules, nor were there any characters to invite an audience member's emotional investment. You would have expected the show to engender a feeling of empowerment, the kind that comes from sitting in a room where everyone is cheering a guy who walks up the sides of buildings to save lives. But although the show was trying to be a kind of Spider-Man backstory, or prequel, it engendered no such feeling.

In what had seemed like an attempt to connect the piece to grander mythic themes, *Spider-Man: Turn Off the Dark* had borrowed a character from Graeco-Roman mythology, a weaver-spider named Arachne. In the piece, Arachne had become a kind of siren of desire for Peter Parker, Spider-Man's alter ego. Arachne—who felt a lot like a metaphor for Taymor herself—had swallowed the show.

The show also was using a confusing outer frame of comic-book lovers; this motley crew of adolescents were there to comment on the show everyone else was watching, but their meta-theatrical presence served mainly to make the inner show even less involving and believable. By Act Two, the brooding Spider-Man, played by the truly fortitudinous Carney, seemed to be battling his own inner demons, not so much the Green Goblin.

All in all, that night revealed a fundamental discomfort, and thus disconnect, between the material, the artists engaged in its interpretation, and the typically melodramatic form of the Broadway musical, especially one that had so much action. Everyone had over-reached. No one had been comfortable with what genre-based entertainment demanded, even though the self-styled artistes were, paradoxically, all being paid massive fees because it was assumed that such heavily branded, genre-based entertainment would bring in revenue to match.

Not so much, it turned out.

Here was a populist show that defiantly refused to be populist; a brand extension that seemed to actively hate the brand; a work that had no demonstrable interest in romance or the eventual defeat of villainy. Here was the work of a deconstructionist who had forgotten that the material she had been handed required a moral center: it was no good peeling back the onion—a relativistic and hubristic onion at that—when there was no center to be found. This was a cautionary tale in how not to make a musical.

Lesson one? Do not let a deconstructionist run riot with a comic-book.

For many producers, this was a lesson in what could happen when talent is allowed too much free reign, especially when that talent was headed toward the defiantly quixotic, otherwise known as "off the edge of a cliff." But what was on stage that night also was a repudiation of one of the most important requirements of any Broadway show of any era: to start with, end with, and always care for the experience of the audience.

Instead, the show had delivered a fractured mythic fantasy— dangerous to perform to boot—when audiences instead clearly wanted their fantasies to be protected with one of the safety nets that the show had been having such trouble employing with any success for its own employees

Spider-Man: Turn Off the Dark also was a cautionary tale when it came to the marriage of avant-garde artists like Taymor and Berger with a mega-brand. Such artists were, of course, interested in such brands, for they were the easiest path within live entertainment to major financial reward as well as colossal international attention. And the urge to undermine—or at least critique—entertainment franchises based on melodramatic heroes is a perfectly valid artistic impulse. But there was nonetheless a current of dishonesty in a show that deconstructed Spider-Man without at least proving that it also could do Spider-Man, given what such a hero had represented over the years in popular culture. And the audience—who mostly had shown up and put down their hard-earned money because they loved Spider-Man—clearly smelled the deception.

In the years that led up to *Hamilton*, no show would ever be allowed to get so out of control, to so forget its core audience, to treat a beloved property with such woeful disregard. Rights holders would start to assert themselves more, to ensure that what happened in the theater would be in keeping with the brand. Many movie studios were developing their own units to exploit previous movie hits as Broadway musicals— and thus they were picking their own creative artists and guiding the subsequent process. And producers were not producing shows with such epic running costs: even *Hamilton*, a relatively low-cost musical by Broadway standards, would figure out how to keep costs down.

The absurdly excessive structure of *Spider-Man: Turn Off the Dark* had made it virtually impossible to tour; it could never have had a roll-out to rival *Hamilton*, even if it had been a huge success. It had made even its own potential success unscalable. There would be plenty of Broadway flops to come, but no musical would make the same mistakes again on such a colossal level.

In his self-reflexive book about the experience, Berger would praise Taymor and cast himself as doing everything he could to please his idol, even though the adulation hardy would be returned. "Julie Taymor," Berger wrote in a book that often seemed to have been written on a plane of high emotional complexity, "despises me with photograph-shredding rage."[3]

Berger, though, seemed to despise with his own rage the character of Arachne, which in some ways meant he was hating Taymor, or, at least, an aspect of the director that had proved so challenging. He did not praise the Marvel executives who had meddled with the show (even though this was a character for whom they had responsibility) and he had no love for the show's other producers. He also pointed to the bizarre experience of being an essentially ordinary playwright—one who still had to worry about where the money was coming from each month—stuck in a world of pretentious creative billionaires. Bono, he implied, had meant well but ultimately had been too busy trying to save the planet to fix the show. He had been far removed from the traditional image of the Broadway composer in the hotel room, hurriedly writing a new opening number. It was rare, Berger said, that Bono even was in town. And the more the show had fallen apart, the less Bono had cared to be around. Berger, his entire book seemed to scream, had been betrayed.

From then on, Broadway producers would take more care when it came to collaborating with busy rock stars. Sting, who penned the 2015 musical *The Last Ship*, would be found often at the back of the rehearsal room. Bryan Adams, who penned the 2018 musical *Pretty Woman*, was seen rewriting songs in his Chicago hotel room, for *Pretty Woman* had first gone out of town. That had been the idea for *Spider-Man: Turn Off the Dark* but, well, events had overtaken intent. It was too big to move.

For fans of Taymor, fans who understood that her artistry had been born in a determination never to take the obvious road and matured in a belief of the purity of a director's vision, it was perplexing that her involvement in *The Lion King* had gone so right and her next project had been such a disaster. But then again, everything on Broadway tends only to work on a case-by-case basis. Very little can be fully predicted. If it was easy to make a hit, every show would be a hit.

In this fascinating case, Taymor had tried to turn the Spider-Man brand into an art piece in a bubble inside her own head—in trying to elevate comic books to cosmic dimensions, she had designed a high-end meditation probing the mythic roots of our cultural heroes. But she had encountered an audience that was more interested in the old-fashioned belief therein. And since it was the audience that was being expected to pay some of the most massive bills in the history of Broadway, never before had an auteur been given such leeway with such financially disastrous results. On a deeper level, you could see the *Spider-Man: Turn Off the Dark* debacle as a metaphor for the two Americas that soon would emerge: there would be progressive relativists, most in big cities, and they'd constantly be butting heads with exurban or small-town centrists. As a Broadway show, *Spider-Man: Turn Off the Dark* had needed to speak to both groups, but had ended up pleasing neither. It was the worst of all possible endings.

But the "Spidey" story was not over that night.

Critics returned to the show in June, after a major retooling following those disastrous February reviews, and found a very different Broadway musical—jokingly referred to as "Spidey 2.0."

A new writer, Roberto Aguirre-Sacasa, had been added to the Broadway team (Berger sucked up the embarrassment and the implied betrayal and accepted a credit of co-writer), and a new "creative consultant," which really meant "director," Philip William McKinley, was installed. Taymor's name remained on the show, but she had in essence been fired in March 2011. Given the fame of Bono and The Edge and their public silence regarding Taymor's ouster, it was difficult to believe they had not been part of the decision.

That led Taymor to pursue a variety of legal challenges to the producers, in an attempt to get back pay she said she had been owed, as well as future royalties. So there was that. Taymor could not be extricated—and, over time, she would get much of what she wanted legally, even if her creative impulses had been thwarted. As she exited the building, figuratively speaking, she lamented how her version of the show had, she said, been reviewed by critics before it had been ready. The show she had wanted to create, she said, had never been fairly judged. And a reasonable person would have allowed that she had a point.

Still, the two new men in charge of "Spidey 2.0" were practiced hands in epic live-entertainment events. The show's retooling meant it had to close for three weeks—this was yet another unprecedented event in the tortured history of the show. It was not that unusual to fire a director during the creative process (mostly early on therein), but it was bizarre indeed to keep a director through opening and many performances, only then to fire her and pretty much dismantle her contributions to the show. But *Spider-Man: Turn Off the Dark* was not only trying to save face, it was trying to stay afloat and claw back at least a portion of its epic production budget.

So it was unsurprising, then, that the difference between the two versions of the show was drastic. Spider-Man no longer was a Chekhovian malcontent. The comic-book nerds, the so-called Geek Chorus, had been banished. Peter Parker was interested once again in Mary Jane, not Arachne, whose presence had been reduced and diminished, as had that of her creator and alter ego. Even the more dangerous stunts had been nixed, suggesting they never were really necessary at all. And there were no more highly public injuries to cast members.

Instead, you met Peter Parker, saw him get bullied, watched him fall for Mary Jane, and saw him acquire his special powers from an escaped mutant spider. (Ah! The backstory!) Then you watched him fight the Green Goblin as he made his decision to be on the side of the good. And then you saw him try to resolve the competing attractions of (a) love and (b) saving the world.

And finally—without sitting through any absurdly long intermissions or pauses—you cheered as he figured out that (unlike most of us ordinary suckers), he was so great that he did not have to choose.

As the actors flew around the theater, stagehands still were visible, watching for any further problems. But by now, the past problems of the show were so well known that the reporting on the show had become welded to the show's aesthetic—or, by June, more accurately, its aesthetics.

Had this been the show that critics first saw, it is likely that the show would at least have received respectful reviews, if not outright raves. And no audience member would have been vocalizing her disappointment. There was even a good shot that *Spider-Man: Turn Off the Dark* would still be playing. But by that June, this already was a tainted brand.

For some who had been at both openings, there was some wistfulness to be had at "Spidey 2.0", shorn as it was of all Taymor's epic risk-taking, and reduced as it was to a serviceable, self-deprecating, and entertaining comic-book spectacle, a family-friendly, arena-style entertainment in a Broadway theater. It was impossible not to mourn the vanquishing of ambition; the abandonment of an epic creative odyssey; a great risk unrewarded. There were a few fleeting moments of beauty, when you could see the Taymor vision that might have been. But these were mere shards. And that first show was now ancient history, although ancient history from which it was impossible for the present to recover.

Spider-Man: Turn Off the Dark closed on January 5, 2014. It had run for 1,268 performances but had made barely a dent in its production costs. The *New York Times* dutifully reminded its readers of the $75 million budget and the show's status as the most expensive theatrical production in the history of the art form. The producers said they were intending to move the show directly to Las Vegas, where they thought it would be more at home. But although there were some negotiations with Steve Wynn, the planned move never happened. Wynn may have booked a lot of live entertainment, but he liked to associate himself with the most exclusive and prestigious properties. He was not fond of being associated with a loss-making enterprise known for landing actors in the hospital.

The investors, the paper said, were out at least $60 million, despite the length of the run. Patrick Healy showed up on the final night and reported that, although the mood overall had been festive and supportive, there had been a technical snafu. Even in its very last gasp, *Spider-Man: Turn Off the Dark* had not been able to go according to plan.

By the time the Foxwoods Theatre, now renamed the Lyric Theatre, perhaps in attempt to banish any demons, was anticipating *Harry Potter and the Cursed Child*, hardly anyone still talked about *Spider-Man: Turn Off the Dark*. If lessons had been learned, they had quietly been imbued.

Except those few who had seen both versions. At least one of them wished that there could have been only one version, a show that would have married the two branches of American theatrical entertainment, rather than set them against each other in an explosively expensive war, ultimately serving neither, and certainly not the poor audience, who were there out of their love of a superhero.

But then that's showbiz. Things can go very wrong.

13
2014: A DREAM, NO LONGER DEFERRED

It was date night in Manhattan for Barack and Michelle Obama. The president, the Associated Press reported, was wearing a suit and the First Lady was clad in a "sparkly black top and a chic black leather jacket."[1] They were out on the town.

Their Friday night-off this April 11 began at Maialino, a swanky Italian trattoria in the Gramercy Park Hotel. From there, the presidential motorcade headed to a cordoned-off 47th Street and to the Ethel Barrymore Theatre, where the Obamas' friend Denzel Washington was headlining a revival of Lorraine Hansberry's poetic drama about a struggling black Chicago family with dreams of leaving their cramped, roach-filled apartment and moving to a new house, dreams so forceful and determined that they might just overcome the resistance of a white neighborhood that did not want them. In 1959, when the famous Supreme Court case known as *Brown v. Board of Education* still was less than five years old, *A Raisin in the Sun* had become the first play by an African American woman ever to appear on Broadway.

With Sidney Poitier playing the role now played by Washington, *A Raisin in the Sun* would try out at the Blackstone Theatre in Hansberry's home town of Chicago, where it struggled to attract an audience for its early performances, with most of the tickets being given away. But just a few days later, it would be so buoyed by a critic named Claudia Cassidy at the conservative *Chicago Tribune*, a critic whom Hansberry had feared to the point where she had written a fake review in Cassidy's acidic style decrying her own play, box office receipts would lend courage to the lead producer, Philip Rose, who had been struggling to raise enough money for a Broadway run.

Cassidy had said the play suggested "something urgent was on its way," and that she admired the talent of its writer. "This is theater with reverberations," Cassidy had written, "echoes and a tug at the remembering heart."[2]

Cassidy would prove more correct than she could possibly have realized when it came to reverberations.

Hansberry's most interesting character was Walter Lee Younger, a chauffeur who was too smart for his job and whose frustration with doors being slammed in his face boiled over into the kind of raging dysfunction that would spark many an August Wilson monologue. He would become a prototype of all kinds of rebellion, much of it to follow a decade or so after the Broadway success of a play that was far ahead of its time.

That night in 2014, Washington was (and seemed on stage) at least two decades older than Hansberry had intended Walter to be, but Walter Lee Younger was the iconic role Washington had wanted to play, and that desire, coupled with Washington's formidable star-power and clout at the box office, is what had made the revival viable. Everyone knew that without Washington, none of this would have been happening, including the visit of the Obamas.

Projected on the pre-show curtain that April evening was a quote from the poem by Langston Hughes from which Hansberry, a child of the Depression, a daughter of Chicago's highly segregated South Side, a woman who said she had often seen examples of man's inhumanity to man, had borrowed the title of her revolutionary play: "What happens to a dream deferred?/Does it dry up/like a raisin in the sun?"

To many in the theater before the show that remarkable night, both out front and backstage, it seemed like the dream deferred was about to walk through the door.

* * *

To anyone who had read Hansberry's writing, there could be no doubt that Obama was a president she would have loved.

Although her various radical memberships, associations, and proclamations had put her on the radar of the notorious FBI director J. Edgar Hoover when she was just 22 years old, Hansberry was a humanist who consistently and constantly articulated her conviction that a racist society dehumanizes everybody, whites as well as blacks. She often repeated her belief that small changes eventually topple old prejudices, and she thought that to write about the pain of racism did not mean that you could not also write about the inexorable march of progress. Plus she understood people in a notable nonjudgmental way—especially married men. In one of the most moving lines of the play, Ruth says to her husband, Walter Lee, "How did we get to a place where we are scared to talk softly to each other?" It was a line that would be greeted by murmurs of recognition from the audience in 2014, just as it had been in 1959.

Prior to the 1959 opening of A Raisin in the Sun on Broadway, Hansberry had written a letter to her mother: "Mama," she had written, "it is a play that tells the truth about people, Negroes and life and I think it will help a lot of people to understand how we are just as complicated as they are—and just as mixed up—but above all, that we have among our miserable and downtrodden ranks—people who are the very essence of human dignity."[3]

The necessity of empathy, of furthering the American promise of for human dignity for all, would be a constant theme of the presidency of Barack Obama, who would be called upon, among many such duties, to explain to the rest of the mostly oblivious country the pain felt by African Americans after the 2012 Florida shooting of the unarmed Trayvon Martin, shot by a neighborhood-watch volunteer. He did so. Nonetheless, Obama's firm conviction was that he was the president of all Americans and must be seen as such, and thus it did not behoove him to use any kind of exclusionary language that might encourage Americans to pit themselves against each other.

Throughout his presidency, Obama rarely used the language of identity politics. He did not need to do so.

The cast of *A Raisin in the Sun*—working alongside Washington were the high-powered actresses LaTanya Richardson Jackson, Sophie Okonedo, and Anika Noni Rose—had been hearing rumors all week about a VIP guest that Friday night. The lead producer, Scott Rudin, had been told who was coming, but had also been sworn to secrecy.

But by the middle of the day itself, word had gotten around the Broadway community that the guest was to be the president of the United States and the First Lady. Kenny Leon, the director of the production, hurriedly flew back from his vacation, so he could sit by the Obamas. Rudin, who put the revival together in consultation with Washington, and who had hired Leon, headed early to the theater, where he was destined to spend much of the night in tears.

Those lucky enough to have bought ordinary tickets that night realized something was up when they found a temporary white tent in front of the theater, containing obligatory metal detectors. A few minutes after the advertised curtain time, everyone was asked to put away their cellphones and told to take their seats.

A door flew open. And the Obamas could be seen coming through from the street, rapidly taking their seats in the orchestra section, just off the center-right aisle. There was thunderous entrance applause. And despite the admonitions, many could not resist pulling out an illicit cell-phone camera in a determination to document the presence on Broadway of the president of the United States.

Obama then was halfway through his second term, with just two years to go before a subsequent administration would march in a very different direction. At his State of the Union address earlier that year, Obama had declared 2014 to be a "year of action" on such issues as immigration reform (which never happened), job creation, and environmental protection, all policy areas that sparked a significant amount of Republican opposition. Much of that opposition was especially fervent when it came to an Obama proposal very much in the air that spring: the Patient Protection and Affordable Care Act, soon to be branded by the opposition as Obamacare and a healthcare initiative that most Republicans loathed. Just a few months away was Obama's controversial announcement of his plans to use his executive-action authority to enact some immigration reforms, the cause of further backlash from Republicans who viewed the move as Obama bypassing the legislative process. Still, the political sea-change that was to come could not possibly have been anticipated.

The show did not start for the next several minutes, during which a piercing alarm sound could be heard throughout the theater (*The New Yorker* later reported that an emergency alarm had been accidentally tripped by a member of the Secret Service) and a cast of nervous actors was obliged to cool their heels backstage.

At intermission, the first couple went backstage to meet the cast—a surreal experience, several of them reported later, and an encounter that made the second act of the play very difficult to perform. One of the actors, Stephen Henderson, told the Associated Press that it was immediately clear to him that Michelle Obama, who had herself grown up in Chicago not far from Hansberry's old neighborhood of Washington Park, was intimately acquainted with the details of this play. Which was not, all things considered, at all surprising. Like Michelle Obama, it was very much rooted in Chicago's South Side; Hansberry was, of course, a child of a different era from the First Lady, but there was similarity in their backgrounds in the African American middle-class.

Somehow, the actors managed to focus on the job in hand and they managed to get through the most important Act Two of their careers. During the curtain call, Washington could be seen pointing and tipping his cap in the direction of the presidential couple, who had remained in their seats longer than the Secret Service had planned. The Obamas joined in the standing ovation. And then they headed away, walking quickly up the aisle, shaking hands as they went.

The exhausted but elated actors—many now convinced they just had experienced the greatest experience of their professional lives— headed to the bar. The night was not entirely untypical then—except, of course, it was an extraordinary Broadway microcosm of just how much America had changed.

Highly influenced by Sean O'Casey's *Juno and the Paycock*, a political play she much admired, Hansberry had found her raw material for *A Raisin in the Sun* in her own father's battles against the racist covenants that propagated segregation. Carl A. Hansberry had figured out that the regulation of real-estate transactions—Chicago's tacit equivalent of Jim Crow—was at the root of both segregation and systemic racism: and he attacked those covenants all the way up to the highest courts of the land, eventually opening up more Chicago neighborhoods for African American residents, including his own family. But not without cost to himself.

His daughter's play could never have been written without the elder Hansberry's efforts, and his determination to ensure that African Americans were guaranteed the right to life, liberty, and the pursuit of happiness in any neighborhood where they could afford to buy a house. Some of the older people in the audience that night were wondering if this Obama presidency, born on the same Chicago streets as the play the president was watching this very night, could even have happened without this play. In all likelihood, given all the poignant lines in Hansberry's story of the Younger family about hopes, expectations, and faith, of dreams deferred but also righteous struggles passed on to subsequent generations, the Obamas were wondering the same thing.

This hardly was the first time the theatre-loving Obamas had been to Broadway. Michelle had seen the musical *Fela!* She had also taken the couple's daughters, Sasha and Malia, to see *Spider-Man: Turn Off the Dark, Motown the Musical, Memphis, Sister Act, The Trip to Bountiful*, and *The Addams Family*. Five years previously, in 2009, just a year into the Obama presidency, the first couple had left the White House and flown to New York to take in August Wilson's *Joe Turner's Come and Gone*. Their love of the theater dated back to their days in Chicago, when they'd often be seen having date nights, starting with dinner on Michigan Avenue and continuing to Goodman Theatre, the Northlight Theatre, or Second City.

And it was not just a question of visiting Broadway. For the previous six years, Broadway had often visited the Obamas, since the administration had welcomed artists to the White House with more focus and regularity at least since the administration of John F. Kennedy, a half-century earlier. Kennedy had famously said that "the arts incarnate the creativity of a free people," and the administration's interest in glamorous, artistic people earned it the sobriquet "Camelot," as co-opted from the 1960 Broadway musical, even if it had often seemed that Kennedy himself would have preferred to be out on the golf course. Although celebrities were frequent visitors to the Reagan White House, and the Bush administrations had been reasonably friendly to the more conservative branch of the cultural professionals, no administration between Kennedy and Obama had been as vocally or visually supportive of the performing arts.

And the interest of the Obamas was hardly limited to music. Broadway was a significant beneficiary.

The musical *Hamilton* would, of course, especially have reason to appreciate Obama's personal interest in the theater, as nurtured in Chicago. Indeed, without the help of the Obamas, maybe the *Hamilton* phenomenon would not have happened at all. You could, then, construct an argument that just as *A Raisin in the Sun* had helped beget the Obamas, so the Obamas had helped beget *Hamilton*, or, at least, shot *Hamilton* out of a canon.

At the White House in 2009, as part of "An Evening of Poetry, Music and Spoken Word" hosted by the Obamas, Lin-Manuel Miranda had performed an embryonic version of what would become the opening song from *Hamilton*, winning Obama's interest and support. No other Broadway show ever had so clear a developmental line to the White House—heck, no other Broadway show had any kind of developmental line at all to the White House. And certainly not to a very particular president and First Lady of the United States.

None of this is to say that they did not spread their artistic largesse around, or that their interest did not have a component of self-interest, given that Broadway had been a significant source of fundraising during Obama's first presidential campaign in 2008. The Obamas and the theatre industry had some powerful connectors, to the benefit of both parties.

Still, whatever their motivations, during their eight years in office, the Obamas had welcomed a broad array of artists to 1600 Pennsylvania Avenue but they had seemed to be especially energized by African American artists: Al Green, Bill T. Jones, Smokey Robinson, Stevie Wonder, Berry Gordon, Beyoncé. Their private parties, often featuring live music and a diverse array of musical guests, had become highly sought-after soirees. To be granted entry was to be cool with the hottest celebrity couple in the world. Over time, this significantly buoyed the celebrity of artists of color.

By 2014, the Obama family had themselves been in the center of the globe's gaze for six years. They had become an enormous source of pride to most African Americans: dignified, highly intelligent, and scandal-free, they were clearly a loving, unpretentious, and warm-centered family, the kind of family about which Wilson rarely had written in his plays, an aspirational family for all Americans. They were at once presidential and refreshingly rooted and ordinary; they were smart and down to earth. The First Lady, being a daughter of the South Side, was widely seen as the kind of woman that African Americans hoped such a man as Obama, whose talents were clear and formidable but whose peripatetic background was less securely rooted in a strong black family, would choose to marry.

As a bonus to feminists, Michelle Obama previously had been Barack Obama's boss at a Chicago law firm. And the couple's daughters, it seemed, were living as normal a life as it was possible to live under such a microscope. Some older African Americans had to pinch themselves that all of this had happened since their own childhoods in a much bleaker America.

So for those who were at the Ethel Barrymore as the Obamas walked through the door with their entourage, it was impossible not to marvel at how the world had changed from when Hansberry wrote this play. It was similarly impossible not to think about how much this writer would have been delighted by these changes—and, of course, by the ongoing centrality of her play, increasingly recognized as one of the masterworks of the twentieth century.

It was similarly impossible not to wonder how she would have reacted to her play being revived, 50 years later, starring the biggest black movie star of his generation, and attended by his friend, a former community organizer in the very same South Side Chicago neighborhood where Hansberry was raised, and now the first African American president of the United States.

In the Obama White House, there would even be a highly influential grandmother, not so far removed from Lena Younger, the matriarchal character at the center of Hansberry's play. Marian Shields Robinson, a Chicagoan herself, was the mother of the First Lady, and would be often described in the press as utterly dedicated to her granddaughters, both of whom frequently were placed in her charge, linking the Obamas to the matriarchal family at the center of *A Raisin in the Sun*.

For all the troubles of the era of her birth, Hansberry had baked hoped-for change into her play.

You can see this most in Asagai, an outsider to Chicago and the African boyfriend of the Younger daughter Beneatha. Like many playwrights, Hansberry essentially had split herself in two. There were echoes of her warm and engaging personality in the highly empathetic Ruth, the wife of Walter Lee Younger, the man desperately trying to grow into his own potential. And Hansberry also could be seen in Ruth's sister-in-law, a woman trying to figure out where to put her own anger, being convinced that she is trapped inside a vicious circle designed to keep her in her place.

Asagai, who comes from Nigeria and thus has not been so imbued with the legacy of racism in the United States, urges Beneatha to realize that progress takes time. "It isn't a circle—it is simply a long line—as in geometry, you know, one that reaches into infinity," he tells her, "and because we cannot see the end—we also cannot see how it changes."

This is especially true when we die at 35 years old.

* * *

By rights, Hansberry should have been alive to see the Obamas attend her play; she would only have been 78 years old in 2014. But that was not how her life worked out. Less than six years after first making it to Broadway, and in the midst of previews for a production of her much underrated second major play, *The Sign in Sidney Brustein's Window*, Hansberry had died from pancreatic cancer.

The success of *A Raisin in the Sun* had made her a major celebrity: Sammy Davis, Jr. and Malcolm X were both at her funeral, and Nina Simone sang in tribute to a woman who had become such a successful writer at a very young age. Yet although Hansberry was known for writing plays, essays, articles, and speeches at a furious pace, she had not been given enough time on the planet to form a body of work like August Wilson. It is impossible to imagine what might have gone unwritten, but, given the evidence of both *A Raisin in the Sun* and *The Sign in Sidney Brustein's Window* (two works of such diversity that critics were perplexed), it is not unreasonable to assume that it would have been spectacular.

Anyone who had seen the show along with the Obamas—or at a different performance—could not have doubted that *A Raisin in the Sun* had stood the test of time and was fully comparable with anything by Tennessee Williams, Eugene O'Neill, or Arthur Miller. The play would prove enormously influential, even sparking sequels like Bruce Norris's Pulitzer Prize–winning drama, *Clybourne Park*.

That play—which took its cue from Hansberry's interest in neighborhoods and the racist history of housing, and that even used as its title the neighborhood into which the Youngers aspire to move—had won the Tony Award for best play during the 2010–11 season. It was another example of the renaissance of *A Raisin in the Sun* during the Obama administration.

Yet Hansberry was not just a writer who broke down racial barriers, a writer of political influence. She was a formidable poet; in the theater that night, her lines rang out with aching beauty. Nonetheless, her poetry was placed in service of her dreams of change, ambitions that must have seemed undoable in the 1950s, ambitions that since had been realized. Or so, at least, it felt on this one historic night on Broadway. Even as oppositional forces quietly were gathering momentum.

* * *

In 2015, in the waning years of the second Obama administration, the Obama Foundation would announce their intention to locate their presidential library in Chicago. Their preferred site was Washington Park, the heart of the very neighborhood into which Carl Hansberry had wanted to move his family, flying in the face of the covenants designed to prohibit African Americans from buying homes in that neighborhood and thus giving his daughter the raw material for what would become one of the most famous and influential plays ever written.

Hansberry had, of course, used a fictional neighborhood in the play, if only to avoid legal trouble: Clybourne Park bore some resemblance to Lincoln Park on Chicago's North Side, an affluent district bisected by a street called Clybourne Avenue. But the neighborhood that Hansberry knew personally as unwelcoming to her own people was Washington Park. Her father had bought his family a house there in 1938, only to encounter new neighbors trying to prevent his family from moving there, just as the representative of the white resident's association, played in Leon's revival by David Cromer, tries to do in the play.

On that night in April, the Obamas sat in a Broadway theater and watched that replay of their home city's ugly racial history. Years before, Hansberry had watched her own father slowly become disillusioned with the country of his birth, which he eventually would leave for a new life in Mexico.

"One cannot live with sighted eyes and feeling heart and not know and react to the miseries that afflict this world," Hansberry had written,[4] as if describing the feelings expressed in *A Raisin in the Sun* instead of those belonging to her own father.

There would be controversies surrounding the library: some residents had not forgotten that the University of Chicago, where Obama had taught law prior to his fast-tracked political career, had financially supported those racist real-estate covenants in the 1930s. The coming of the library would mean giving up open access to at least a portion of a verdant park of enormous historical and personal importance to those who grew up on Chicago's South Side.

But this was Obama's presidential library. No one else's. It was inconceivable that a library that was designed to memorialize the work of the first African American president of the United States, a man whose political career had begun on the South Side of Chicago, be located anyplace else. It had to be here, even if there was a price to be paid.

In ways that no one possibly could have anticipated when the Hansberry family first took their stand, both Broadway and Washington Park had ended up at the cultural heart of American racial progress— ever painful, ever complex, but, at least in this remarkable coming together, suggesting that at least one dream deferred had been realized.

And, finally, could come home.

14

2016: LOVE IS LOVE IS LOVE IS LOVE IS LOVE IS LOVE IS LOVE IS LOVE

Sitting close, President Barack Obama and his wife, Michelle, looked into the camera. The optics, clearly, had been set up so the two seemed to be speaking on an equal footing. They seemed to be enjoying themselves.

"Good evening," said President Obama.[1] "Seven years ago, a young man came to a poetry jam we held at the White House."

"He took the mike," continued the First Lady, "and said that he was gonna perform a song from something he was working on, about the life of somebody who embodies hip-hop … America's first Treasury secretary."

The tag-teaming Obamas shared an ironic, quizzical glance.

"I confess we all laughed," said the president. "But who's laughing now? Seven years later, *Hamilton* has become not only a smash hit but a civics lesson our kids can't get enough of. One with fierce, youthful energy. One where rap is the language of revolution and hip-hop its urgent soundtrack."

"It's a musical about the miracle that is America," said the First Lady, "a place of citizenship, where we debate ideas with passion and conviction."

"A place of inclusiveness," said her husband, "where we value our boisterous diversity, as a great gift."

"A place of opportunity," said the First Lady, "where no matter how humble our origins, we can make it if we try."

"That's the story of America," said the president. "A project that is not yet finished. A project that belongs to all of us."

"America is what we the people make of it," said the First Lady. "As long as we stay, just like our country, young, scrappy, and hungry."

"That's the story of *Hamilton*," said the president of the United States, sounding more and more like a network pitchman, "and you get to see it. Coming up."

* * *

At the time, that little video at the Tony Awards from the White House was not fully appreciated for the utterly unprecedented nature of its very existence.

Never before in the 69-year history of the Tony Awards—never before at the Oscars, the Emmys, or the Grammys—had a sitting president of the United States introduced a performance on a televised awards show.

Sure, Broadway shows had performed extracts at the White House, and presidents occasionally had found a way to get a night off and take in a Broadway show. Political leaders had, from time to time, shown up on these broadcasts in service of some cause or other, some worthy program or entity. But this was something different. This was—incredibly—an endorsement of a Broadway show that was, after all, a private business. In its fiscal and corporate structure, it was no different, really, from any other business, none of which the Obamas would even have considered endorsing using the full dignity of their elected office. Had they done so, the pushback would have been colossal.

But the video was proof: the Obamas and their administration did not think of *Hamilton* as they would any other business, or even as they would any other artwork. You only had to listen to what they had been saying. It wasn't exactly vague or understated. This show, they were telling their Sunday night audience in this cozy fireside chat, was America at its best, America in fulfillment of its greatest promise, the America that the leader of the free world, and his partner in chief, dearly wanted it to be. *Hamilton*, they were saying, embodied values at the very core of American idealism. The Obamas even were saying that this was a show that was teaching teachers how to teach the young about their own country.

It was remarkable, when you thought about it, that a sitting president was taking the time to endorse any musical at all. Before *Hamilton,* that had always been an inconceivable kind of notion. Musicals did not have that much gravitas. Much to the ongoing chagrin of successive generations of those that loved them, they were marginalized, like most artistic endeavors, by those in political power. Especially in America.

Politicians, let alone presidents, usually stayed away from the theater, which they feared would either trivialize them or bring them into uncontrollable contact with dangerous, radical artists. Even though some Democratic politicians had supported the so-called "NEA Four"—the performance artists Karen Finley, Tim Miller, John Fleck, and Holly Hughes—when Republicans like Senator Jesse Helms had, in 1990, pressured the National Endowment for the Arts to withhold its federal grants on the basis of their allegedly distasteful subject matter, that did not mean that you found such politicians attending their performances. Many of their political supporters did not even know what the artists did.

For anybody who remembered all of that—or the decades of the federal government's official disinterest in, and lack of support for, the arts—the presence of and verbiage being used by the Obamas were more remarkable yet.

The Obamas were using some extraordinary language. Going to this show, the president basically was saying, means you are going to the White House–approved story of the United States of America. If you loved the Obamas and all they stood for, he was implying, like a theater critic making her most enthusiastic endorsement, then you must love this show, as do we.

Even rival producers had to be impressed. Here was prima facie evidence that *Hamilton* had not just branded itself as the most successful musical of its generation, it had branded itself as America.

And the president and the First Lady had anointed themselves as its spokespeople.

How—on God's green earth—had a musical, just a musical that surely was not so very different from any other musical, pulled that off?

* * *

The answer, of course, begins with Lin-Manuel Miranda, the show's writer, composer, and star.

Miranda was born in 1980 in New York City, of mostly Puerto Rican descent, and he was born into a political family. His mother, Luz Towns-Miranda, was a psychologist. His Puerto Rican–born father, Luis A. Miranda, Jr., was a well-known operative within the Democratic Party who, for much of the 1980s, served as special advisor of Hispanic Affairs to the New York mayor Ed Koch, a position that morphed into director of the Mayor's Office of Hispanic Affairs from 1987 through 1989. In 1990, Luis Miranda became president of the Hispanic Federation, a New York–based membership organization with a mission to empower and advance the Hispanic community—which included fortifying Latinx nonprofit organizations and building up new political leaders from the Latinx community, which is, of course, precisely what Luis Miranda's own son would become, as did his older sister, Luz, albeit in a less public way.

From there, the elder Miranda started consulting on national political campaigns for the likes of Charles Schumer, Kirsten Gillibrand, and Hillary Rodham Clinton, when the former First Lady was running for the United States Senate. In the minds of these, and many other, powerful national politicians, Miranda had positioned himself as a leading liaison to Latinx voters. And in return, the politicians courted his attention.

As the success of *Hamilton* grew exponentially, first in Chicago, then on the West Coast, then across the Atlantic, the elder Miranda worked to include the show in these nonprofit endeavors, brokering his son's celebrity to create the kind of educational programs that had historically been associated with nonprofit theaters, not commercial Broadway productions, which traditionally had no educational programs whatsoever. The elder Miranda's involvement, and his moral authority, would prove crucial to a show that was in such massive demand that it could, and would, charge unprecedented amounts of money for tickets; to a great extent, he added its mission-based component. This was never more apparent than following the devastating Hurricane Maria in Puerto Rico in September 2017, when *Hamilton*, and both Mirandas, led fundraising efforts for the devastated island.

The younger Miranda, then, was born into a political family in which activism was second nature, but the two men also developed a powerful personal bond. In any crowded room, the younger Miranda typically would listen first to his father.

One night in Chicago, backstage prior to a public event attended by some 4,000 cheering Chicagoans, the elder Miranda first checked his son's clothes and then advised him to go to the bathroom, and off the younger Miranda went without a moment's hesitation, leaving the stage crew, and the audience, hanging. Luis Miranda was not only his son's most enthusiastic cheerleader and advisor, but also his political conscience and conduit.

He also was, early in his son's career, a provider of work: Miranda would write jingles for campaign ads for political candidates who were working with his father. All in all, this was an unusually politicized background for a Broadway composer and lyricist, most of whom grew up either in arts-oriented families or far from the rough sport of New York politics.

Miranda was raised in Inwood, a Manhattan neighborhood located at the northern tip of the island, just below the Harlem

River. For much of the twentieth century, the neighborhood was the province of Irish immigrants, although there also were a significant number of Jewish residents, spilling south from the mostly Jewish neighborhood of Washington Heights, nearby. But by the time Miranda was born, the demographics had shifted. Many of the Irish immigrants had moved out to the suburbs and they had been replaced by a wave of immigrants from the Dominican Republic, who were especially likely to settle in the section of the neighborhood that was located east of Broadway. That demographic shift would form the basis of Miranda's first major musical, *In the Heights*, which would, in essence, tell the story of three days in the life of the people of Washington Heights through the eyes of a narrator, supporter, activist, poet, and confidante who looked and sounded very much like Lin-Manuel Miranda himself.

Miranda first wrote a draft of *In the Heights* in 1999 while he was an undergraduate at Wesleyan University in Middletown, Connecticut, where he would meet many of his future colleagues, including the director Thomas Kail, both a close friend and a professional collaborator who would prove so vital to Miranda's later career. An early version of *In the Heights* was first performed there. And after Miranda graduated, development on this piece rapidly propelled him to Broadway; Kail, who would go on to direct *Hamilton*, was a crucial force in the forward trajectory of this earlier piece.

In 2005, *In the Heights* was accepted into the Eugene O'Neill Theater Center's National Music Theater Conference, a summer program focused on the development of new musicals, and thus Miranda's early career was nurtured in the same location as that of August Wilson, one generation prior. That summer, Miranda could be seen carrying his own portable keyboard down the dirt track to one of the old farm buildings that had been repurposed as studios where promising creative teams could work on developing their material—far enough away from the pressures of Broadway that they could get some work done but also close enough that such Broadway producers as Jeffrey Seller could hop on a train and come up and see what was transpiring.

Unlike some other development programs for new musicals—such as the Sundance Institute founded by Robert Redford—the O'Neill program had always included a handful of public performances. These were staged readings with the actors on book, but, unlike standard practice for invited workshops in New York City, they were open to everyone. Some celebrity writers didn't care for the imminent visibility—especially at an institution that also was training critics—but the atmosphere nonetheless was warm and supportive. Part of the philosophy of the workshop was that creative teams would try a constant stream of changes based on audience feedback and that of a team of mentors: it was expected that no performance would be the same as the one before, and that mild pressure of needing to be ready for a performance that was maybe just hours away often sparked vast quantities of highly creative work. This was a workshop process with the useful pressure of a deadline.

Everyone involved would live in dorm-style accommodations, and, at night, they would gather in the Blue Gene's Pub, the epicenter of the O'Neill, an institution dedicated to artists who were prepared to live and breathe the project under development. This was the same development process that *Avenue Q*, another nascent Broadway hit, had undergone just three years before. In precisely the same spaces.

With a creative team that now included the writer Quiara Alegría Hudes, a playwright making her first serious foray into musicals, and the musical director Alex Lacamoire, a gifted American musician of Cuban descent whose role in *Hamilton* would be crucial, *In the Heights* had its first major public performance at the O'Neill that summer. From there, it moved Off-Broadway to the 37 Arts Theatre in 2007 (the choreography was by Andy Blankenbuehler, who would go on to choreograph *Hamilton*), and then, in 2008, to Broadway.

In the Heights was unlike any show Broadway had seen before. Its main character was not a person on an emotional journey, but a neighborhood to which Broadway had never previously paid much attention. That was a political statement in and of itself, but *In the Heights* was a joyous show that put its focus firmly on the youth of that neighborhood, most of whom were trying to reconcile their love for their familial community with their own ambition to take on the world. That was where the conflict in the show resided: the question was not so much *could* you get away from a neighborhood with more than its share of poverty as *should* you?

But for anyone first experiencing *In the Heights* on Broadway, what leapt most readily from the stage was the exuberant vitality of the entire neighborhood, a vista hidden away, as one of Miranda's lyrics put it, at the tip top of Manhattan, the final stop of the A train, which made the children of that neighborhood feel like they were living at the top of the world itself. Yet the unbridled optimism of the show meant that it also felt inclusive: the feeling that spring night at the Richard Rodgers Theatre was that sunny days were here, and that wherever you happened to live yourself was nowhere near as nice or as supportive as Washington Heights.

Miranda's lyrics were atypically stocked with wit: and there were a whole lot of those witty lyrics, since his music for the show mostly was a blend of salsa, rap, and what you might call traditional Broadway. He'd found a mode for a musical that simply was more stimulating than most of what Broadway had seen before—his words came faster and with more palpable joy at their very expression and, even if the book had a mostly predictable trajectory as musicals go, the lyrics were as sophisticated as they were engaging. The central character, Usnavi de la Vega, whom Miranda had based on himself, was an engaging ambassador, unwavering in his advocacy for his community, but also open and accessible to anyone who had no understanding whatsoever of what it was like to be Latinx, or living at the top of an island called Manhattan.

Anyone could enjoy the harmonies, the tempos, the rhythms, the musicalized emotion, the love of life itself, the snapshot of a community coming to life before your eyes. It did not matter whence you came. As at a lot of ground-breaking musicals, it seemed that night like Broadway just had changed in an instant. This time, though, it wasn't just what the show was saying or doing, or even what the characters represented, it was just as much about *who* was performing. In one night, you could see how limited and exclusionary Broadway had been, what stories it had told, and who had been chosen to tell them. *In the Heights* would start to change that reality, but it would do so while genuinely welcoming everybody to Washington Heights.

Miranda was, of course, its star, eight times a week. He rarely missed a show. But then everybody needs a vacation.

And on one such holiday, in Mexico, he happened to pick up a best-selling work of historical biography from 2004, a book scholarly and authoritative enough to be of interest to him (it was written by a winner of the Pulitzer Prize), but also sufficiently populist to make for good vacation reading. The book[2] was an unusual and distinctive fusion of traditional biography and what you might call "narrative history": the writer, Ron Chernow, did not just describe the life of his subject, as did most dry biographers, but he made continuous reference to the social, political, economic, and cultural contexts within which this man operated. Chernow didn't just recount of the life of a man; he analyzed his motivations from a psychological point of view, as if he were a contemporary figure. The book thus was far closer to a Dickensian novel—or a play—than most works of historical biography, yet it made all of its narrative leaps while remaining thoroughly grounded in research and scholarship. The book's title was *Alexander Hamilton*.

The Brooklyn-born Chernow was a man whom Miranda was destined to make one of the happiest—and most wealthy—presidential historians in the world. And after *Hamilton*, Miranda would say at every opportunity that anyone who hoped to have big creative ideas needed to take a vacation, it being on vacation that such ideas tend to flow.

After the success of *In the Heights*, Miranda did not have a lot of vacation time for years to come.

Almost immediately, he was hired to work on Spanish translations of the lyrics to *West Side Story*, a beloved musical that was returning to Broadway after a 29-year absence. The conception behind this revival—which was to be staged by the 91-year-old book-writer Arthur

Laurents—was that the Sharks would speak and sing in Spanish, as distinct from the blend of English and Spanglish that had been used in the original 1959 production. There was logic in that idea, of course: Why would Anita, Maria, and the show's other characters speak or sing in English when they were alone together and would logically have been speaking Spanish?

But by its opening night in 2009, the producers had gotten cold feet over their own radical idea, and much of the Spanish was removed from the show during the rehearsal process, mostly due to worries that audience members who did not speak Spanish would miss something important in the narrative, or that they would resent not hearing one of the famous lines within either Laurents' book or Stephen Sondheim's famous lyrics. This was a shame: the change could have meant that the show could offer greater insight into what it was like to be a Puerto Rican immigrant in the New York of the late-1950s, also making clearer how those linguistic differences served both to alienate and terrify the Jets. On a metaphoric level, of course, the two gangs always had been fighting about issues far larger than themselves. But the idea never was fully expressed and thus Miranda's new lyrics did not bring the attention they deserved.

Miranda's next Broadway project was another new musical, *Bring It On*, a piece about cheerleading that would seem like a million miles from *Hamilton*, but was, as Miranda later would frequently acknowledge, a crucial if underappreciated part of its genesis. The show was based on the 2000 movie of the same name, which had starred Kirsten Dunst. The arena was competitive cheerleading and the plot of the show revolved around the cheerleading squad that had been chagrined to discover that its showcase routine had, in fact, been stolen from another school, and thus was forced to come up with something new. The piece was first produced at the Alliance Theatre in Atlanta in 2011 and then went on a pre-Broadway tour.

There were a few crucial things in *Bring It On* that related to *Hamilton*. One was that Blankenbuehler's choreography was a combination of traditional Broadway choreography and the athletic routines from the world of cheerleading. Another was that the music—co-written by Miranda and Tom Kitt—was an exciting, high-energy composition. And a third was that the show, in essence, pit a mostly white school against a more diverse rival.

The score hardly was hip-hop, but the creative team was actually engaged in quite a similar process as the one they would face in *Hamilton*, namely, how to compose for, and physicalize, a highly competitive world that was moving rapidly through time and space. Blankenbuehler (who was serving as both choreographer and director) was figuring out how to adapt to Miranda's rapid-fire style of composition, while Miranda was trying to figure out how to compose around the moves and beats expected of cheerleaders, which helped both men develop the singularly unified physicality—the robust musical athleticism, you might say—that became *Hamilton*. The cheerleading setting meant particular demands for rhythms and rhymes. With his partner, Kitt, Miranda had to work out how to create a musical language of self-actualization, for a world well beyond his own experience.

The book to the show was by Jeff Whitty of *Avenue Q*. Miranda shared the lyrics credit with Amanda Green: the two came up with some rich ideas; they even worked both Bristol Palin and Genghis Khan into the same line, arguing that the daughter of the former vice-presidential candidate and the notorious Mongol invader each were examples of opportunism run amuck.

Bring It On officially arrived on Broadway in August 2012 and was a modest success, running through the end of the year, but likely remembered in the future mostly as a show that further developed Miranda's chops.

* * *

Meanwhile, Miranda already was at work on *Hamilton*.

In the early years after Chernow's book sparked his interest, he was seeing the material in the terms of a concept album. As the Obamas later referenced, Miranda had indeed been invited to the White House for the White House Poetry Jam in 2009 (being the scion of a political family paid some dividends), and, when he showed up there, he had indeed told the assembled audience, including the newly elected Barack Obama, that he was working on a "concept album" about Alexander Hamilton—someone, he said, who "embodies hip-hop."

"You laugh," Miranda said, in his introduction that night, "but it's true. He was born a penniless orphan in St. Croix."[3]

Right at the start of the show's gestation, then, Miranda had revealed (to the president!) that the thing that fascinated him the most about his subject was the disparity between where Hamilton had started out and where he eventually ended up as one of the Founding Fathers of a great nation. He had done so as an immigrant—which, at the time, was hardly an unusual thing to be—but Miranda clearly saw the potential echoes of the immigrant experience at a much later time in American history.

Miranda—who was accompanied that night by Lacamoire— then said he was going to do the first song from the album. "I'll be playing Vice President Aaron Burr," Miranda said, to the White House audience, "and snap along if you like."

From there, Miranda launched into the lyric that would become famous: "How does a bastard, orphan, son of a whore and a Scotsman … "

It was a dazzling performance, accompanied only by Lacamoire on the piano. At the end, Obama led the standing ovation. It would not be the only time Obama stood up for *Hamilton*. The show would return to the White House; and most of the White House would find its way to the show. Including Obama himself.

That 2009 event was live-streamed from the White House: it had taken place on the same day that the longtime Broadway producer Rocco Landesman, the producer of the first Broadway production of *Angels in America*, had been named chairman of the National Endowment for the Arts, and it clearly had been designed to signal a new, closer relationship between the White House and the cultural professions, with a new focus on youth and diversity. At the beginning of the live-stream, which had been technically unimpressive but revolutionary nonetheless, the First Lady had talked about her desire to hear the spoken word at the White House and also about how she hoped that the artists who came to 1600 Pennsylvania Avenue might be capable of getting people outside of their comfort zones, something that had not previously been a part of White House policy on the arts.

Miranda kept working on *Hamilton*, which he still was calling *The Hamilton Mix-Tape* and which was usually being described in the media as a song-cycle, or something along those lines. In January 2012, he performed an extract as part of the American Songbook series at Lincoln Center; audiences paid as little as $35 a ticket to see the man who still was best known as the star of *In the Heights* (he had returned to the show in the weeks before its closing). One of the performers that night was the actress Karen Olivo, whom Miranda knew from *In the Heights* and who, following a hiatus from the business, would end up in the Chicago cast of *Hamilton*.

But on that night at Lincoln Center, which happened to coincide with the (likely) 212th anniversary of the birthday of the subject, Miranda was still only 31 years old.

That January, Miranda told the *New York Times* that he still didn't see *Hamilton* as a show but as a "rap concept album."[4] But he clearly had figured out a dramatic arc.

"Alexander Hamilton," Miranda told the newspaper, "was someone who on the strength of his words and ideas pulled himself from unbelievably humble circumstances to the top of the nation. Then he sort of destroyed that good will as he continued to fight and continued to believe he was the smartest guy in the room. He was so earnest and so honest that games of political tact that his contemporaries played better, like Jefferson and Burr, he couldn't play them."[5]

That would become a key component of the musical: but what Miranda did not say was that the show also would revolve around Hamilton's loss of his own child, in circumstances that led him to blame himself for the loss, and that he there would find the way to emotionally engage with his audience. He was still focusing on the parallel between the hubristic Founding Fathers, who battled each other with eloquent verbosity, and who often did not know when to stand down, and the similar wars between rap stars, who did much the same thing both with words and, alas, on occasion also with guns. In other words, he had part of the allegorical structure with *Hamilton*, but not yet its epic quality, nor its transcendent ability to align the emotional trajectory of one man with that of a young nation itself.

That night, Miranda, a small group of performers, and six musicians (under Lacamoire's direction, of course) would stage 12 numbers from … nobody knew quite what, least of all Miranda himself. An album? A cabaret act for himself? Some kind of rock-theater, multimedia thing? A Broadway musical of the future? But there was a cabaret critic there from the *New York Times*, and he described Miranda's performance as "sensational."

"Its language is a seamless marriage of hip-hop argot and raw American history made startlingly alive,"[6] Stephen Holden wrote, in a widely read piece that ensured that every producer on Broadway would want this show if, in fact, it actually turned out to be a show. "The music," Holden wrote, "is flexible, undigitized hip-hop rock fusion."

Undigitized would prove less than fully accurate (the final version of *Hamilton* would make ample use of electronic music), but fusion and flexible were pretty decent descriptors, even if at least one song in *Hamilton*, "You'll Be Back," wherein an English king lamented the loss of a former colony in the language of a Beatles-like break-up song, would turn out to be pure pop.

In 2013, *The Hamilton Mixtape* was part of the summer season at the Powerhouse Theater at Vassar College, another new musical incubator. By this point, Kail was attached as director. In 2014, it was announced that *The Hamilton Mixtape*, now just called *Hamilton*, would head to the Public Theater. It was further announced that a group of Broadway producers, led by Jeffrey Seller, previously responsible for *Rent* with his then-partner Kevin McCollum, was to provide enhancement money, signaling their intent subsequently to produce the play on Broadway.

The engagement at the Public Theater allowed Miranda to amp up the development work on the project. At the same time, his personal celebrity was quickly growing.

Meanwhile, in the summer of 2014, Broadway finally had dipped its toe into the world of hip-hop with a new musical, *Holler If Ya Hear Me*, about the music of Tupac Shakur, as directed by Kenny Leon, the same director who had directed the revival of *A Raisin in the Sun* with Denzel Washington. Shakur had been a huge star when he was gunned down in a drive-by shooting in Las Vegas in 1996. He was just 25 years old when he died.

The show, which featured a book by Todd Kreidler, a writer who often had collaborated with the playwright August Wilson, did not go well. Business proved to be terrible, and the show, which received less than favorable reviews, announced its closure after just 17 previews and 39 regular performances, losing its entire $8 million capitalization. The show's failure seemed to suggest that Broadway and hip-hop were not meant for each other and that, despite the 75 million records that Shakur had sold and his self-evident celebrity, Broadway audiences were not interested in the genre, just as hip-hop fans seemingly were not interested in Broadway. In the various post-mortems for the show, much was made of the challenges provoked by the lyrical density of rap music—how the sheer number of lyrics per second in the typical Shakur song meant that they were difficult to track or follow in a theatrical setting, where they also had the burden of a narrative. And there were similar concerns about the profanity inherent in the material, which was as raw as its anger.

Holler If Ya Hear Me, which probably arrived on Broadway two or three years too early for its own good, also wanted to impart a moral message, which it drew in the broadest of sermonizing strokes, thereby deviating from the sophistication of Shakur's actual material, which was ill-served by being stuck in a Broadway box that felt uncomfortably like everything Shakur had been rebelling against. Unlike

American Idiot, which had drawn from a world foreign to Broadway and accommodated that material by being willing to reinvent itself, *Holler If Ya Hear Me* did not feel like it had adapted itself to the world of hip-hop, nor found a way to be true to its soul.

So as *Hamilton* moved forward, *Holler If Ya Hear Me* was out there as a cautionary tale. On the other hand, for anyone who had seen the show, the Shakur show also was a reminder that the musical form had been stuck in the same grooves for a long time, not only failing to embrace the hip-hop revolution in music, but failing the audience invested therein. The show's demise did not mean it had not signaled the kind of change that ought to be embraced.

By that fall, *Hamilton* had announced that it would be employing a multiracial cast to play the role of the all-white crew that were the Founding Fathers of the United States, thus sending the message that so American a story should be told by a group of performers who actually looked like modern-day America. It's hard to overestimate the impact of this decision on the future success of the show: aside from being the right thing to do, that casting also proved to be a kind of brand, something for writers covering the show to put in their headlines. The diversity of the casting quickly became utterly inextricable from the show itself. Had it been otherwise, it's inconceivable that *Hamilton* would have broken out as it did.

That casting included the role of George Washington, the first president of the United States, who was to be played by Christopher Jackson, the very actor whose job in *Holler If Ya Hear Me* had come to a premature end. Leslie Odom, Jr., with whom Miranda had worked before, was to play Aaron Burr; Philippa Soo, who had been noticed in the musical called *Natasha, Pierre and the Great Comet of 1812* was to play Hamilton's wife, Eliza. And the actor Daveed Diggs was to play Thomas Jefferson. Jackson and Diggs both had been part of a rap improv group that Miranda and Kail had founded together. Indeed, many in that original ensemble already were close to the two men.

By the time the show opened at the Public, Miranda's wife, Vanessa Nadal, had given birth to their first child, Sebastian. In the weeks up to the show, Miranda gave many interviews about his thinking for the show, which was gathering all kinds of promotional steam, even as Miranda was himself working with the literary office at the Public and his longtime friend, Jeremy McCarter, to arrive at a final form for the material. He'd already dropped the mixtape idea, of course, having figured out that his expertise actually lay in the creation of musicals.

The production, which opened on February 17, received rapturous reviews. "*Hamilton*, Lin-Manuel Miranda's independent-minded new musical for the masses at the Public Theater," wrote Ben Brantley in the *New York Times*, weighing in on the show for the first time, "shot open like a streamlined cannon ball on Tuesday night. When one of the young rebels who populate this vibrant work says, 'History is happening in Manhattan,' you can only nod in happy agreement."[7]

The Public was successful in getting a lot of influential columnists and other media people to its theater—especially media influencers like the *New York Times* columnist David Brooks, who typically did not write about theater, and thus, as had been the case with *Rent*, momentum began to build for the show well beyond the usual show-business sphere of influence. Celebrities appeared in singularly large numbers for an Off-Broadway production—from Paul McCartney to Jon Bon Jovi. Politicians showed up at the Public, too: including a former president, Bill Clinton (who saw the show with his wife, Hillary, and daughter, Chelsea), and a former vice president, Dick Cheney, who was spotted in the audience with his wife, Lynn, herself a presidential biographer. A senator or two was spotted. So was a former Treasury secretary.

Given all this brouhaha, the question became how quickly to open the show on Broadway. Seller, who was now in producing control, made the decision, vindicated by the subsequent trajectory of the show, not to rush things in order to make the April deadline for Tony eligibility, even though the show would have been a sure winner, but instead to let that deadline pass. On the other hand, he could not wait so long that momentum for the show would dissipate and the actors might head off to other projects, especially as nobody in the original cast yet had made any substantial amount of money, having worked under the standard Off-Broadway contract at the Public Theater.

Seller decided that the summer would be his sweet spot and so the first Broadway performance of *Hamilton* was announced for July 13, 2015, with opening night scheduled for August 6. Advance sales were brisk; even before the first preview, the show already had a $27.6 million advance and had sold nearly a quarter of a million tickets. Meanwhile, articles about the show were numerous and frequent, with many wondering just how big this show might prove to be. There were examples that suggested caution (*Bloody Bloody Andrew Jackson* and *Holler If Ya Hear Me* being two), but there also were hard facts, many millions of which were being sent directly to the box office: *Hamilton* had not only sold pretty much every seat at the Public Theater, it had entered the American zeitgeist in a way no other show had managed. Ever.

And all of this was going on even before the Broadway opening.

Also before the Broadway opening: President Barack Obama came to see the show at a Saturday matinee during the preview period. Miranda was not even performing. Javier Munoz was scheduled to play the leading role at the matinee, and the show kept to the schedule. That allowed Miranda (who had, after all, already performed for Obama) to sit in the theater, next to the president of the United States, who had been anxious to see the show he first had seen at the only White House workshop performance in the history of Broadway musicals.

A sitting president had been so anxious to see a Broadway show, he had not even wanted to wait for the show to open officially. This was the alternate universe inhabited by *Hamilton.*

On Broadway, the reviews only got better. The main performance for critics had been a sensational success. That unforgettable night, it felt as if you were at a show determined to remind everyone that the vista of the old white men on the banknotes had just been shoved to the side: the American Revolution, *Hamilton* was declaring anew, actually was fought and won by the young, the energetic, and the profoundly radical. These were forceful men with complicated personal lives and intramural rivalries, and there was no preexisting blueprint for their nation-building. Yet these men also were determined to forge a new country in their own brazen and messy image. Alexander Hamilton himself had been cast here as the real intellectual of the bunch, a man with a mind superior to the minds of those who actually landed in the White House or who generally get more credit for parenting American democracy. And he was a recent immigrant, with all that implies.

Immigrants, the show said, in a line that would progressively become more and more famous as the months and years unspooled, were the ones getting the job done in America. Right from the start.

This was a truly stunning achievement for a musical—to reinvigorate the way in which a nation viewed its own history and to help it realize that, if the cobwebs of time were swept away, the founding of the United States of America would be revealed as a truly radical act, the creative province of risk takers and public-sector entrepreneurs. The audacity was exceeded only by the sheer scale of the achievement that followed.

Various truths were apparent that night. One was that Miranda had, in *Hamilton*, found and forged a figure whose story was of tragic proportion—a man who achieved greatness in the public sphere but at the expense of the people he loved the most. He had found a revolutionary who flew too close to the sun and did not know the right moment to leave the stage. He had found a man who had suffered unspeakable grief, who had lived through what Miranda called "the unimaginable," who had gained so much only to discover that he would willingly have thrown it all away if only he could have prevented the death of his only begotten son, a death caused by that son trying to emulate his own father.

And this great subject was not a fictional character, but a real founding father. An emblem of a whole country.

Musically, Miranda had managed to be true to the greats of hip-hop, to honor his initial impulse: there were parallels in the life of Alexander Hamilton to that of Jay-Z or Eminem in Detroit. He also had written a score that was not just hip-hop, but rather paid homage to a slew of Broadway predecessors, explicitly shouting back to the likes of *Les Miserables* and *Rent*. He had figured out that the best approach to diversity was to go all-in, and that America was ready, in what many people thought was the beginning of a post-racial America, to embrace a cast with a level of diversity that Broadway rarely had seen. And, of course, he had allied himself with the young administration of the first black president of the United States, a man who looked out at *Hamilton* and immediately grasped what message Miranda was trying to impart, it hardly being much different from the one he was trying to impart himself.

But Broadway also was in the business of art, and *Hamilton* had somehow managed to also be a beautiful show, its many gorgeous ballads speaking of love, fear, hope, pain, and determination. And, of course, the show seemed to understand one of the most painful occurrences in human life: the loss of a child. It was a musical about one man's extraordinary rise and political achievement, but also a work that understood how such a loss could draw a curtain of sadness over the most remarkable of lives, even a life that had fully participated in the writing of one of the greatest documents ever written in the history of human democracy. *Spring Awakening* and *American Idiot* were both intense and beautiful, but only *Hamilton* could claim to be the story of America itself.

It hardly was a whitewash of the less savory early aspects of that story. Aaron Burr, the narrator of the show, was both the moral conscience of the piece and, at the same time, a self-aware participant in early democracy who foreshadowed both the American governmental interest in pragmatism (at best) or corruption (at worse). And then there was Miranda's fascinating conception of Thomas Jefferson, an improviser of expedient sensibility who well knew that you always have to pay attention to how they might tell your story when you are gone. The typologies would remain in the American political system, just as *Hamilton* seemed set to remain in the theatrical system for a very long time.

After the opening night, the demand for tickets became unprecedented in its intensity. By December, the show had announced a second production, in Chicago, with an opening set for the fall of 2016.

During that fall, Miranda sat down in a bar in New York with a reporter who asked him, in a long-winded kind of way, how all of this felt.

"You know what?" he said. "My answer to you on all of this is actually embedded in the show. I cannot worry about how the world perceives the show. I can worry about the quality of the production, the words being spoken and sung. But I have written a show where everybody is grappling with their legacy. Look at [Alexander] Hamilton's legacy. A guy who did an enormous amount in his short lifetime. But you also saw it get buried. His enemies all succeeded him. There was a period when he was the bastard of American history. He falls in and out of favor. Jefferson falls in and out of favor. All I can control is the work itself. There will be times when *Hamilton* is hailed. There will be times when *Hamilton* is pilloried."[8]

Those will have to be different, unfamiliar times, suggested the reporter.

"The wind will do with it as it does," said Miranda. "All you can do is throw the kite in the air."

The reporter pushed some more. Miranda must have some insight into how the show became such a phenomenon. Sure, any artist might demur when asked that question, might claim not to know what moved people, or what gave him such prowess. But great artists actually sometimes do know, if you can get them to articulate those feelings. The reporter suggested that *Hamilton* had been uniquely successful because Miranda was perhaps the only person in America to be steeped in the traditions of musical theatre, but also capable of writing in an entirely new language, with unimpeachable hip-hop bona fides. And he'd written an inclusive show with palpable appeal for everyone, a show that was serious, not a parody, and a show about America, not some love affair, parent issue, or voyage through a fantastical realm. And incredible as it may seem, no one had actually managed to write anything even remotely like it before.

Miranda laughed.

"Interesting ideas. Truly. But I am at a loss as much as anyone else. I do think that Hamilton's life is a hell of a story. And what I tend to get from people who have seen it, when the friend sends me that dark night of the soul email at 3 a.m., is that they tend to say, 'This made me think about what I am doing with my life. Hamilton was a guy who hit the ground running when he got here.'"[9]

Miranda did not have to say this also applied to himself. The reporter had already grasped that point.

Several other things of note happened before the Tony Awards.

One was that the original cast got together and, in essence, agitated for a share of the profits from the show, arguing with considerable foundation that at least some of the lines (such as Jefferson's "Wassup?") therein had flowed from the workshop process at the Public Theater. Although they were met with initial resistance, they were successful in their endeavor, not only ensuring that those actors would have an income stream from *Hamilton* for the rest of their lives, but also setting a crucial precedent for the blockbuster shows that followed. Even though the economics of Broadway had long revolved around union actors being paid scale-based salaries that were earned without regard to the financial well-being (or lack thereof) of the production in question, the *Hamilton* actors still made a moral case for profit-sharing, at least in the face of massive success. When *Frozen* opened on Broadway in the spring of 2018, Disney already had agreed that the original cast would receive a small share of what were likely to be massive profits.

Hamilton would further revolutionize how tickets to hit shows were sold on Broadway. As the success of the show increased, Seller became more and more outspoken about what he saw as the pernicious effects of ticket reselling and brokering, arguing that such actions hurt the industry and the creative artists therein who were creating its products. In essence, *Hamilton* began to increase the price of its tickets to meet what it predicted would be the demand. There was a downside for the public: the data may have been anecdotal, but one *Hamilton* effect was that tickets to all Broadway shows became more expensive, this one hit show having shattered so much resistance to price. But Seller generally answered that charge with a kind of Robin Hood philosophy: by selling the premium weekend tickets at the highest possible price, it thus became possible for the show to sponsor Luis Miranda's educational programs, not to mention its famous lottery that helped some people get into the hottest show going for very little money.

The lives of everyone involved in the show would change forever. Just weeks before *Hamilton* opened, Blankenbuehler still had been sending out envelopes with DVDs of his work, hoping that some producer might watch one. He would not have to worry about that any more. Kail would be able to direct most any show he wanted. Lacamoire would become the most sought-after arranger and musical director in his industry.

Seller had a lot of time to think about his own hit.

"For the first three years I worked on it, I just kept saying I think it is just a good show," Seller said to a reporter in the fall of 2016.[10] "But I now have come to see its power as a beautiful reflection on the values of our country. It is saying something positive and potent about our history. About what is possible in America."

The most successful producer in recent Broadway history paused for a moment. He acknowledged the fame of such shows as *Rent* and *A Chorus Line*, and the debt owed by *Hamilton* to all of them. And then he paused again, for a longer moment.

"I am 51 years old," Seller said. "We all felt tremendous patriotism after 9/11, but that was in sorrow. This might sound pretentious, but I really think this show revives the appreciation that we all have for our living in this great country that provides us with so many unique opportunities to flourish as human beings. And I think the show is a most beautiful reflection of that ever to be written for the musical theater. There has never before been a Broadway show that captured the spirit of a country."[11]

By then, there was a lot of evidence to suggest that he was right.

For the first time in history, a Broadway show had been elevated to the Apollonian. It had been described—often, with soaring rhetoric—by politicians at the very highest levels of American democratic governance; this show served up sweet revenge for every theater-loving child whose parents had told them that to enter the theater was the harbinger of an unstable life of triviality. *Hamilton* seemed fully capable of banishing, all on its own, the anti-theatrical prejudice that had existed, and applied with particular brutality toward performers, ever since the very earliest days of the commercial theater industry.

It even seemed to have elevated the institutions of elected office, to have provided a way forward for those who maybe wanted to serve the American people, but who could not feel their way out of the partisan swamp of the mediatized politics of the moment; even if its portrait of its subject inarguably was painted in a rosier hue than the political reality (there would be many stories suggesting that the real Alexander Hamilton was considerably less progressive than the one appearing eight times a week on Broadway), then so what? *Hamilton* was declaring that leadership could and should be about far more than expediency and ambition. And if they dug deep into their own hearts, no one could really disagree.

Hamilton certainly had precedents and precursors—a whole book full of them, you could argue. And it had at least one American angel in its corner. But none of them detracted from the singularity of its achievement.

Here was a musical wherein Americans of all stripes, played by Americans of all stripes, could be seen wrestling with fiscal policy, pondering what constituted democratic representation, musing on the benefits of a meritocracy versus equality, wondering just how monarchical the American president should or should not be, wondering just what America should be.

Here was a musical that embraced complexity and relativistic thinking, that wondered aloud about whether personal success could assuage personal misery and concluded that it could not. It is better to love and be loved, it said, than to achieve.

Here was a musical that seemed to understand that however successful we might be in life, we would eventually overreach, or suffer a decline, and that we would not then be able to predict or control the agenda of those who would decide to go ahead and tell our story from their own point of view, even if they hardly knew us at all.

And—above everything—here was a musical that declared that America's benefits are fully open to and achievable by all, all being created equal and all being fully entitled to try to have their shot. No exceptions.

* * *

There was not much drama leading into the Tony Awards in June of 2016; everyone knew which show was going to win the major awards. The only question was how many it actually would win.

But on Saturday, June 12, 2016, a man named Omar Mateen walked into a gay nightclub called Pulse in Orlando, Florida, and opened fire.

The club had been holding a "Latin night," which meant that most of the victims were gay Latino men. In the minutes before Mateen was shot by the Orlando police, he managed to kill 49 people and wound 58 others. This was hardly the first American mass shooting and it certainly would not be the last; many were yet to come as the plague continued. But the news hit the Broadway community especially hard. Some of the people at Pulse that night had managed to survive the AIDS epidemic, only to be gunned down just when they were having the most fun. The incident was the deadliest hate crime targeting LGBT people in the history of the United States, and the deadliest terrorist event since the attacks on September 11, 2001. It was yet another reminder of the omnipresence of deadly gun violence in America, and it all took place on the eve of the Tony Awards that were supposed to be the coronation of the greatest American musical in a generation.

On Sunday morning, there was discussion about whether or not the Tony Awards should even take place.

But the ceremony went ahead anyway. It was decided, though, that the cast of *Hamilton* would perform without their usual props, their muskets and rifles.

And as was expected, Miranda was soon at the podium. As he ascended the podium, his hand was shaking.

"I'm not freestyling," he said, looking far more nervous than was typical for him. "I'm too old. I've written you a sonnet."

He started in on what he had prepared—a tribute to his wife of six years, Vanessa Nadal, who was sitting in the seats at the Radio City Music Hall, a camera trained on the tears flowing down her cheeks. It was a sweet composition about how the two chased melodies together, how his partner nudged him "toward promise," how their newborn son was the couple's "most beautiful reprise."

But Miranda had quickly realized that on this day and with this show, it would not be enough just to talk about his own family. So he expanded the speech he had planned.

"We live through times when hate and fear seem stronger," went his sonnet to his wife, now addressed, as well, to all of America. "We rise and fall and light from dying embers/Remembrances that hope and love last longer."[12]

And then he unleashed the line that would be remembered and quoted and tweeted and Facebooked and generally used as the best defense against another miserable weekend of suffering: "And love is love is love is love is love is love is love is love."

All at once, all in one perfectly chosen line, there was balm for people in mourning, a declaration of independence, a defiant assertion of what Broadway was supposed to mean. On this Sunday night in the summer of 2016, it felt like Broadway had learned to assert itself and its role in American society. It stood for love in the face of violence and it could not, would not, be swept aside.

As all those "love is" repetitions unspooled, it seemed for a moment that the Broadway theatre had never been more central in the United States of America.

It had stared down hate with unity.
It had brought America hope.

* * *

That fall, there was an election.

In a surprise victory, the American presidency was assumed by Donald J. Trump, and, in what felt like a matter of days, any semblance of a united, evolved, post-racial America evaporated.

In its place emerged two very separate Americas, each half so furious at the other, its very existence was almost intolerable. Social media channels were consumed with anger. What some saw as news, others declared to be fake. Considered and gentle official words were replaced by the profane and the divisive. Everything completely changed.

One night following the election, and like many politicians before him, Mike Pence, the vice president elect, found his way to Broadway and to *Hamilton,* as was his right as a free American.

But the times had changed. By then, even Broadway, even *Hamilton*, had been forced to pick a side.

NOTES

Prologue

1 Christopher Mele and Patrick Healy, "*Hamilton* Had Some Unscripted Lines For Pence. Trump Wasn't Happy," *New York Times*, November 19, 2016.
2 Chris Jones, "Performance of *Hamilton* Disrupted in Chicago," *Chicago Tribune*, November 21, 2016, p. 4.

Chapter 1

1 This description is derived from the 1992 published edition of *Angels in America*, a joint project of the Royal National Theatre and Nick Hern Books.
2 John Lahr, *New Yorker*, December 13, 1993, p. 133.
3 Tony Kushner, *Angels in America, Part One: Millennium Approaches* (New York: Theatre Communications Group, 2003), p. 118.
4 This and some other details of the history of the show are dependent upon *Angels in America: A Complete Oral History* by Isaac Butler and Dan Kois, *Slate*, June 29, 2016.
5 Kushner did not, of course, then know that Cohn would pop up again, deep in the biography of one Donald J. Trump.
6 Randy Shilts, *And the Band Played On* (London: St. Martin's Press, 1987).
7 Ibid., p. xxi.
8 Ibid., p. xxii.
9 Larry Kramer, "1,112 and Counting," *New York Native*, March 14–27, 1983.
10 Shilts, *And the Band Played On*, p. 557.
11 As told to Butler and Kois.
12 Frank Rich, *New York Times*, March 5, 1992.
13 Ibid.
14 Frank Rich, *New York Times*, May 5, 1993.

15 As quoted in Chris Jones, "Angels in a Strange New World," *Chicago Tribune*, November 30, 2003.

16 Ibid.

17 Interview with the author, November 2003.

18 Ibid.

19 Ibid.

20 Interview with the author, October 2009.

Chapter 2

1 Cornel West, Forward to Anna Deavere Smith's *Fires in the Mirror* (New York: Doubleday, 1981).

2 Frank Rich, "Whoopi Goldberg," *New York Times*, October 25, 1984, p. C17.

3 Interview with the author, September 1, 1999.

4 Ibid.

5 Ibid.

6 Ibid.

7 "Spalding Gray's New Reality," *Chicago Tribune*, March 12, 2002, Chicago Tribune Arts and Entertainment, p. 3.

8 This revelation appears in an interview Smith gave to Richard Stayton for the July–August 1993 issue of *American Theatre*.

9 See Smith's introduction to *Fires in the Mirror*, ibid.

10 Ibid.

11 Richard Stayton, "A Fire in a Crowded Theatre," *American Theatre*, July/August, 1993, pp. 20–22 and 72–75.

12 See Smith's introduction to *Fires in the Mirror*, ibid.

13 "Anna Deavere Smith Wields Words to Reach Out Across Racial Divides," *Chicago Tribune*, February 4, 1998, p. 2.

14 Ibid.

15 Stayton, "A Fire in a Crowded Theatre."

Chapter 3

1 *New York Times*, March 17, 1996, Section 2, p. 1.

2 Ibid.

3 Ibid.

4 Jack Kroll, "Rent Strikes," *Newsweek*, May 13, 1996, p. 54ff.

5 John Guare, "Smash!" *Vogue*, May 1996, pp. 305, 347.

6 See Chris Jones, "Big," *Variety*, February 26, 1996, p. 179.

7 Frank Rich, "Journal: East Village Story," *New York Times*, March 2, 1996, p. 19.

8 Kroll, "Rent Strikes."

9 David Lipsky, "Impossible Dream," *US Magazine*, November 1996, p. 103.

10 Kroll, "Rent Strikes," p. 54.

11 Lipsky, "Impossible Dream," p. 3.

12 Guare, "Smash!," p. 305.

13 Chris Jones, "Hamilton in the Heartland," *Chicago Tribune*, September 25, 2016, Arts + Entertainment section, p. 1.

14 John Sullivan, "Bohemians of the Moment," *American Theatre*, July/August 1996, p. 3.

15 *Plays International*, Vol. 13, 1997, p. 10.

16 John Istel, "Did the Author's Hyper-romantic Vision Get Lost in the Uproar?" *American Theatre*, July 1996, pp. 13–17.

17 Chris Jones, "Inside Chicago's 'Hamilton' and How Lin-Manuel Miranda Changed Musicals," *Chicago Tribune*, September 22, 2016.

Chapter 4

1 Eileen Blumenthal, *Playing with Fire* (New York: Harry M. Abrams, 1995).

2 Interview with the author at Menken's home, March 15, 2017.

3 Ibid.

4 Frank Rich, *New York Times*, December 29, 1991, Section 2, p. 5.

5 See the introduction to *The Lion King: Pride Rock on Broadway*, by Julie Taymor (Disney Editions, 1997).

6 As quoted in Michael Lassell, *The Lion King: Twenty Years on Broadway and Around the World* (Disney Editions, 2017), p. 85.

7 Taymor, *The Lion King: Pride Rock on Broadway*, p. 190.

8 As she said in an interview with the author in 2003.

9 Thomas Schumacher, "A Word From the Producer," in *The Lion King: Twenty Years on Broadway and Around the World* by Michael Lassell (Disney Editions, 1997), p. 9.

Chapter 5

1 Interview with the author.

2 John Lahr, Introduction to *Fences* by August Wilson (New York: Theatre Communications Group, 2007).

3 As quoted in Christopher Rawson, "Playwright Says He's Dying," *Pittsburgh Post-Gazette*, August 26, 2005, p. 1.

4 Interview with the author, June 11, 1999.

5 Ibid.

6 The full text of this speech, "The Ground on Which I Stand," can be read at http://aas.princeton.edu/publication/thegroundonwhichistand/.

7 These ideas are discussed more fully in Chris Jones, "His Vision: Get Right with the Past and Do Right: Wilson Mattered More Than Flourish," *Chicago Tribune*, October 3, 2005, p. 14.

8 See Wilson's introduction to *King Hedley II* (New York: Theatre Communications Group, 2007).

Chapter 6

1 For an account of the days after the attacks, see "Lights On, Broadway Dispels the Dark" by Jesse McKinley, *New York Times*, September 15, 2001, Section 8, p. 9.

2 Ben Brantley, "How Ovid Helps Deal with Loss and Suffering," *New York Times*, October, 10, 2001, Section E, p. 1.

3 Interview with the author, February 26, 2002.

Chapter 7

1 George W. Bush's full remarks can be read at https://georgewbush-whitehouse.archives.gov/news/releases/2004/06/20040605-7.html.

2 Interview with the author, September 1, 2013.

3 Chris Jones, "Asking Once Again Why *Wicked* is a Hit," *Chicago Tribune*, September 6, 2013, Section C, p. 5.

4 Ibid.

5 Interview with the author.

6 Interview with the author, February 15, 2008.

7 Chris Jones, "Vegas Puts Chips on Legit," *Variety*, March 15–21, 1999, p. 1.

8 Interview with the author, November 5, 2004.

Chapter 8

1 The play is discussed at more length in Chris Jones, "Finishing the Picture," *Variety*, October 11, 2014, p. 66; and in Chris Jones, "Arthur Miller, 1915–2015, Why Miller Matters," *Chicago Tribune*, February 13, 2005, Arts + Entertainment, p. 1.

2   These ideas are discussed at greater length in Chris Jones, "Edward's Albee's Absurdity Was Never Pointless," *Chicago Tribune*, September 18, 2016, p. 15.

Chapter 9

1   Anne Taubeneck, *Chicago Tribune*, April 2, 2000, Arts + Entertainment section, p. 1.

Chapter 10

1   The full speech can be accessed at https://obamawhitehouse.archives.gov/the-press-office/2010/08/31/remarks-president-address-nation-end-combat-operations-iraq.
2   Ibid.
3   Ibid.
4   Interview with the author, July 24, 2009.
5   Ibid.
6   Ibid.
7   Ibid.
8   Ibid.
9   Interview with the author, February 27, 2012.
10 Ibid.

Chapter 11

1   As cited in Jon Meacham, *American Lion: Andrew Jackson in the White House* (New York: Random House, 2008).
2   Eric Piepenberg, ArtsBeat blog, *New York Times*, May 15, 2009.
3   Ibid.
4   Louis Jacobson and Sarah Waychoff, "What's Up with Donald Trump and Andrew Jackson?" PolitiFact. Posted May 2, 2017 at https://www.politifact.com/truth-o-meter/article/2017/may/02/whats-up-with-donald-trump-andrew-jackson/.

Chapter 12

1   As referenced in Michael Paulson, "Harry Potter Feathers His Nest for $68 Million Broadway Drama" *New York Times*, April 15, 2018, Section A, p. 1.

2   See in particular Michael Riedel's extensive reporting on these traumas in the *New York Post*.

3   Glen Berger, *Song of Spider-Man: The Inside Story of the Most Controversial Musical in Broadway History* (New York: Simon & Schuster, 2013).

Chapter 13

1   Associated Press, April 11, 2014.

2   Claudia Cassidy, "A Raisin in the Sun," *Chicago Daily Tribune*, February 11, 1959. B1.

3   This letter is referenced in a *New York Times* article on November 1, 1983.

4   Lorraine Hansberry, *To Be Young Gifted and Black: Lorraine Hansberry in Her Own Words,* adapted by Robert Nemiroff (New York: New American Library, 1970), p. 11.

Chapter 14

1   The full video can be seen at www.tonyawards.com.

2   Ron Chernow, *Alexander Hamilton* (New York: Penguin Books, 2005).

3   The full official video can be seen at https://www.youtube.com/watch?v=WNFf7nMlGnE.

4   Eric Piepenburg, "He's Taking the Hood to the 1700s," *New York Times*, January 8, 2012, Section AR, p. 4.

5   Ibid.

6   Stephen Holden, "Putting the History in Founding Father's Rap," *New York Times*, January 13, 2012, Section C, p. 4.

7   Ben Brantley, "Founding Fathers as a Bunch of Chill Dudes," *New York Times*, February 18, 2015. Section C, p. 1.

8   This interview first appeared in the author's "*Hamilton's* Lin-Manuel Miranda and the Terrifying Urgency of Fame," *Chicago Tribune*, September 7, 2016, Arts and Entertainment, p. 2.

9   Ibid.

10 This interview first appeared in the author's "Inside *Hamilton* and How Lin-Manuel Miranda Changed Musicals," *Chicago Tribune*, September 25, 2016, Arts and Entertainment, p. 1 ff.

11 Ibid.

12 The full speech can be seen at www.tonyawards.com.

INDEX

A Chorus Line 2, 45, 47, 109, 159
Adams, Bryan 172
Adams, John (President) 155
Aguirre-Sacasa, Roberto 173
Albee, Edward 115–24, 132
All the President's Men 160
American Idiot 137–45, 153, 208
American Theatre 34, 51, 52
And the Band Played On 10
Angels in America 7–21, 52, 68, 122
A Raisin in the Sun 177–88
Aronson, Billy 41–2
Armstrong, Billie Joe 138–43
Ashman, Howard 58–60
As Is 12–13
August: Osage County 127–33
Avenue Q 94, 98, 99, 105, 199

Beauty and the Beast 58–61
Berger, Glen 163, 171–2
Berkeley Repertory Theatre 138
Bernstein, Jed 81–3
Big 46–7
Blair, Tony 137
Blankenbuehler, Andy 195, 198–9, 211
Bloody Bloody Andrew Jackson 149–62, 206
Blumenthal, Eileen 57–8

Bono 164, 166
Boston Globe 124
Brantley, Ben 90, 205
Bratton, Bill 38–40
Bring It On 198–9
Bug 129
Burr, Aaron 70–1, 200, 208
Bush, George W. (President) 138

Cameron, James 55
Cassidy, Claudia 177–8
Chernow, Ron 197, 199
Chicago 103
Chicago Tribune 5
Cirque du Soleil 62, 98, 100–1, 104
Clinton, Hillary Rodham 2, 192, 205
Clinton, William Jefferson 18–19, 56, 205
Cohl, Michael 167
Cohn, Roy 7, 21
Come From Away 92

Death of a Salesman 119
Diana, Princess of Wales 55–6
DiCaprio, Leonardo 55
Diggs, Daveed 204
Dion, Celine 103
Disney's Frozen: The Broadway Musical 95–6, 210
Disney Theatricals 56, 58, 67

Dixon, Brandon Victor 1–5
Doubt 123–4
Dragone, Franco 101–3

Edwards, Sherman 155
Eisner, Michael 60, 66
Eugene O'Neill Theatre Center
74–5, 194–5
Eureka Theatre 9
Eustis, Oskar 9, 14, 16

Finishing the Picture 115
Fires in the Mirror 25, 33–6
Forbidden Broadway 65, 111
Friedman, Michael 149, 152–60

Gabay, Roy 90
Garfield, Andrew 20
Garfinkel, David 165
Garner, Eric 35
Giuliani, Rudolph 38–40, 50, 82, 116
Glover, Savion 36
Goldberg, Whoopi 4, 28
Goodman Theatre 72, 75, 87, 182
Gottfried, Martin 156
Gray, Spalding 29–33, 35
Green Day 138–43, 153
Greif, Michael 43–4, 49
Guare, John 46

Hair 47
Hamilton
    Broadway production 2,
        189–92, 193, 197–215
    dispute with original cast 42
    issue of $10 bill 160–1
    relationship to *Spider-Man: Turn
        Off the Dark* 171
    vice-presidential protest at 1–5
Hamilton, Alexander 70–1, 147,
    200, 207, 209

Hansberry, Lorraine 177–88
Harry Potter and the Cursed Child
    165, 176
Healy, Patrick 167, 176
Hispanic Federation 192
Holbrook, Hal 25–7
Holden, Stephen 202
Holler if Ya Hear Me 203–4, 206
Holzman, Winnie 95–7
Hughes, Van 144

Idle, Eric 105–8
Indian Removal Act 148
In the Heights 194–7
Iraq War 135–7

Jackson, Andrew (President) 147–9,
    153, 160, 162
Jackson, Christopher 204
Jersey Boys 80
Jitney 72–3, 77
John, Elton 63–5
John F. Kennedy Center 72
Jones, Bill T. 141

Kail, Thomas 3, 194, 211
Karem, Stephen 91
Kerr, Walter 121
Killer Joe 128
King Hedley II 69–73
King, Rodney G. 23–4
Kitt, Tom 139, 199
Kotis, Greg 108–9
Kramer, Larry 11–14, 45
Kreidler, Todd 203
Kroll, Jack 45, 47, 51
Kushner, Tony 8–21

Lacamoire, Alex 195, 202, 211
Lahr, John 7, 73
Landesman, Rocco 16, 200

Lane, Nathan 20, 92
Larson, Allan 42
Larson, Jonathan 38–53, 59
Las Vegas 98–105
Leon, Kenny 180, 203
Lepage, Robert 103
Les Miserables 109, 208
Letts, Tracy 127–33
Lew, Jacob J. 161
Lincoln Center 201
Loesser, Frank 155

McCarter, Jeremy 205
McCarthy, Joseph (Senator) 7
McCollum, Kevin 44, 48–9, 94
McKinley, Philip William 173
Mackintosh, Cameron 58
Man From Nebraska 129, 131
Mann, Emily 33
Mantello, Joe 13
Ma Rainey's Black Bottom 73–4, 76
Mark Twain Tonight 25–7
Martin, Trayvon 179
Marvel Entertainment 164, 165
Mateen, Omar 213
Mayer, Michael 139, 140, 143
Memphis 145, 182
Menken, Alan 58–60
Metamorphoses 87–92
Miller, Arthur 113–15, 119, 132
Miranda, Lin-Manuel
    appearance at White House
        (2009) 183
    Hamilton 2, 189–92, 193,
        197–215
    influence of Anna Deavere Smith
        36
    Tony Awards speech 44
Miranda, Luis A., Jr. 192–3, 211
Miranda, Sebastian 204

Mnuchin, Steven 161–2
Monty Python's Flying Circus 105–6
Monty Python's Spamalot 105–8
Munoz, Javier 206
My So-Called Life 96

Nadal, Vanessa 204, 214
*Natasha, Pierre and the Great
    Comet of 1812* 204
National Endowment for the Arts
    16, 200
Newsweek 45
New York Post 167
New York Public Theater 9, 152,
    203, 210
New York Theatre Workshop 43, 52
New York Times 3, 42–3, 154, 167

O 102
Obama, Barack (President)
    attendance at *A Raisin in the
        Sun* 177, 180–3
    declaration of candidacy for U.S.
        presidency 125
    meeting with Bono 164
    National Endowment for the
        Arts 16
    speech about Trayvon Martin
        179
    speech ending war in Iraq 135–7
    Tony Awards introduction
        189–90
    transition to President Donald J.
        Trump 2
    White House poetry jam (2009)
        199–200
Obama Foundation 187
Obama, Michelle 177, 180–3,
    189–90
Odom, Leslie, Jr. 1, 204

Off-Broadway, decline of 116–18
Oken, Stuart 62
Olivo, Karen 201

Palmer, John 5
Pence, Michael Richard (Vice
        President) 1–5, 215
Pittsburgh Public Theater 69–72, 75
Platt, Mark L. 98
Poitier, Sidney 177
Politico 162
Pretty Woman 172
Pulse nightclub massacre 213

Radner, Gilda 27
Rapp, Adam 52
Reagan, Ronald (President) 93–4
Rent
    comparison with *The Lion King*
        57, 68, 87
    development of 37–53
    influence on *Hamilton* 208
    musical theater heritage of 109
Rice, Tim 63, 65
Richards, Lloyd 74
Rich, Frank 15, 28, 47, 50, 61
Riedel, Michael 16, 167
Roth, Robert Lee 61
Roundabout Theatre 155
Rudin, Scott 180

Sater, Steven 140–3
Schneider, Peter 62, 66
Schumacher, Thomas 61–2, 66, 68
Schwartz, Steven 96–7
Seller, Jeffrey
    comparison of *Rent* and
        Hamilton 53
    pricing philosophy 211
    producing decisions for *Avenue
        Q* 94

producing decisions for *Hamilton*
        205
producing decisions for *In the
        Heights* 194
producing decisions for *Rent*
        48–9
protest speech about Vice
        President Michael Pence 3, 4
1776 155–7
Shakur, Tupac 203–4
Shanley, Patrick 123–4
Sheik, Duncan 140–3
Shilts, Randy 10
Simon, Neil 78, 120
Sinise, Gary 125
Six Feet Under 117
Smith, Anna Deavere 24–5, 27,
        33–6
Sondheim, Stephen 48, 50, 67,
        198
Soo, Phillipa 204
Spider-Man: Turn Off the Dark 66,
        163–76, 182
Spring Awakening 140–3, 153,
        208
Steppenwolf Theatre Company 125
Stew 143
Sting 172
Stone, David 98
Stone, Peter 155

Taymor, Julie 57–68, 87, 163,
        169–75
The Edge 164, 166
The Goat, or Who is Sylvia? 118–22
The Humans 91
The Lion King
    arrival in Las Vegas 99
    Broadway gross 97
    impact of September 11 on 86

Julie Taymor's reputation 87
process compared to *Spider-Man: Turn Off the Dark* 172
production and influence of 56–68
The Neo-Futurists 109–10
The New Yorker 7
The Normal Heart 12–14, 45, 52–3
The Notebooks of Leonardo da Vinci 87–8
The Phantom of the Opera 97
The Producers 85
The View 4
The Wizard of Oz 96
Thomson, Lynn 42
Three Tall Women 116, 120–2
Tierney, Christopher 168
Tomlin, Lily 27
Tony Awards 44, 189–91
Truman, Harry (President) 149
Trump, Donald J. (President) 2, 161, 215

Tubman, Harriet 160–1
Twilight: Los Angeles 25

University of Chicago 188
Urinetown 84, 108–10
U2 164

Walker, Benjamin 152, 154
Washington, Denzel 177–8
West, Cornel 25
West Side Story 197–8
Who's Afraid of Virginia Woolf? 115–16, 133
Wicked 94–8, 100
Wikipedia 149–52
Wilson, August 69–80, 123, 182, 194
Winslet, Kate 55
Wolfe, George C. 16, 25, 36
Wooster Group 29
Wynn, Steve 98–101, 103, 175

Zimmerman, Mary 87–92